Ellis Robert

The Armenian Origin of the Etruscans

Ellis Robert

The Armenian Origin of the Etruscans

ISBN/EAN: 9783337291013

Printed in Europe, USA, Canada, Australia, Japan

Cover: Foto ©ninafisch / pixelio.de

More available books at **www.hansebooks.com**

THE
ARMENIAN ORIGIN

OF THE

ETRUSCANS.

BY

ROBERT ELLIS, B.D.,

FELLOW OF ST. JOHN'S COLLEGE, CAMBRIDGE;
AND AUTHOR OF 'A TREATISE ON HANNIBAL'S PASSAGE OF THE ALPS.'

"LANGUAGES ARE THE PEDIGREE OF NATIONS."—JOHNSON.

LONDON:
PARKER, SON, AND BOURN, WEST STRAND.
M DCCC LXI.

LONDON:
SAVILL AND EDWARDS, PRINTERS, CHANDOS STREET,
COVENT GARDEN.

CONTENTS.

	PAGE
THE ARYAN RACE, AND ITS DIVISIONS	1
THE ETRUSCANS A BRANCH OF THE THRACIAN RACE—HISTORICAL EVIDENCE OF THE EXTENSION OF THE THRACIAN RACE FROM ARMENIA TO ETRURIA	3
LINGUISTIC EVIDENCE OF THE EXTENSION OF THE THRACIAN RACE FROM ARMENIA TO ETRURIA	9
CAPPADOCIAN WORDS	11
PHRYGIAN WORDS	13
PHRYGIAN INSCRIPTIONS	20
LYDIAN WORDS	38
CARIAN WORDS	45
THE LYCIANS AND THE CAUCASIAN NATIONS	46
LYCIAN INSCRIPTIONS	49
LYCIAN WORDS	58
THRACIAN WORDS	62
SCYTHIAN WORDS	66
DACIAN NAMES OF PLANTS	70
ALBANIAN WORDS ALLIED TO THE ARMENIAN	81
RHÆTO-ROMANSCH WORDS ALLIED TO THE ARMENIAN	90
ETRUSCAN WORDS	97
ETRUSCAN INSCRIPTIONS	101
SEPULCHRAL INSCRIPTIONS	103
VOTIVE INSCRIPTIONS	118
VOCABULARY OF VOTIVE WORDS	130

CONTENTS.

	PAGE
THE INSCRIPTION OF CERVETRI	135
THE PERUGIAN INSCRIPTION	151
GEOGRAPHICAL NAMES IN ETRURIA AND OTHER COUNTRIES	161
THE PELASGIANS	175
POSSIBLE EXTENSION OF THE THRACIANS TO THE WEST OF ETRURIA	179
NAMES OF GLACIERS	180
THE BEBRYCES OF THE EASTERN PYRENEES	182
CONCLUSION	183
APPENDIX	189
INDEX OF ETRUSCAN WORDS	198

The Armenian letters are represented by the following equivalents:—

1. *a.*
2. *b.*
3. *g.*
4. *d.*
5. *e* (Eng. *e* or *ye*).
6. *z.*
7. *é*
8. *ĕ* (neutral vowel: Germ. *ö*, Sansk. *a*).
9. *th.*
10. *t* (Fr. *j*, Eng. *s* in *measure*).
11. *i.*
12. *l.*
13. *kh.*
14. *ç* (Eng. *ds*).
15. *k.*
16. *h.*
17. *ṡ* (Eng. *ts*).
18. *ḷ* (Welsh *ll*, Polish thick *l*).
19. *ǵ* (Eng. *j*).
20. *m.*
21. *y* (partakes of the sounds of *h* and *y*: as a final commonly mute).
22. *n.*
23. *š* (Eng. *sh*).
24. *o.*
25. *ć* (Eng. *ch*).
26. *p.*
27. *ǰ* (between Eng. *j* and *sh*).
28. *ṛ* (strong *r*).
29. *s.*
30. *w* (as *v* when beginning a syllable).
31. *t.*
32. *r.*
33. *ṡ* (Eng. *tz*).
34. *v* (*u*, *v*: never a vowel when alone).
35. *ph.*
36. *ch.*
37. *ó* (broad *o*, like Fr. *au*).
38. *f.*

The effect of the (.) is to strengthen, of the (') to soften, the consonant which it qualifies. The letters, 37 and 38, are of late introduction: 37 was formerly written *av*: 38 is only used in some foreign words. The following are regularly diphthongs, when followed by a consonant:—

ev, Eng. *u* or *you*.
iv, Germ. *ü*, Fr. *u*, occasionally Eng. *u*.
ov, Eug. *oo*, Germ. *u*.
ow, long *o*, Germ. *oo*, Gr. ω.

Some make 2, 3, 4, tenues, and 26, 15, 31, medials.

The Albanian is written in Latin characters, and the following equivalents are adopted for the alphabet of Dr. Hahn:—

1.	*a.*	18.	*ly.*
2.	*v.*	19.	*m.*
3.	*b.*	20.	*n.*
4.	*y.*	21.	*ny.*
5.	*ǵ.*	21a.	*ñ.*
6.	*g.*	22.	*x.*
7.	*gy.*	23.	*o.*
8.	*dh.*	24.	*p.*
9.	*d.*	25.	*r.*
10.	*e.*	26.	*s.*
11.	*ë.*	27.	*ś.*
12.	*z.*	28.	*š.*
13.	*th.*	29.	*t.*
14.	*i.*	30.	*u.*
15.	*k.*	31.	*ph.*
16.	*ky.*	32.	*ch.*
17.	*l.*	33.	*kh.*

Y is always a consonant, even at the end of words: thus *kaly*, 'a horse,' is pronounced nearly like Fr. *caille*, as *ly* = Ital. *gl*. *Ny* = Ital. or Fr. *gn*. The sound of *ñ* is as in the Fr. *on*.

The following abbreviations have been employed—

Abas. = Abasian: Alb. = Albanian: Ang.-Sax. = Anglo-Saxon: Arab. = Arabic: Arm. = Armenian: Bret. = Breton: Cappad. = Cappadocian: Circas. = Circassian: Eng. = English: Esth. = Esthonian: Etrusc. = Etruscan: Fr. = French: Gael. = (Scotch) Gaelic: Georg. = Georgian: Germ. = German: Goth. = (Mæso-) Gothic: Gr. = Greek: Heb. = Hebrew: Hung. = Hungarian: Ital. = Italian: Kurd. = Kurdish: Lapp. = Lapponic: Lat. = Latin: Lith. = Lithuanian: Lyd. = Lydian: O. Pers. = Old Persian: Osset. = Ossetic: Pers. = Persian: Phryg. = Phrygian: Pied. = Piedmontese: Pol. = Polish: Rhæt-Rom. = Rhæto-Romansch: Sausk. = Sanskrit: Scyth. = Scythian: Serv. = Servian: Span. = Spanish: Swed. = Swedish: Thrac. = (Proper) Thracian: Turk. = Turkish.

ERRATA ET ADDENDA.

p. 15, l. 4 from bottom, for *okro* read *ochro*.
p. 17, l. 13, for *kikka* read *kikkas*.
p. 30, l. 23, for *etak* read *etag*.
p. 36, l. 5, for μούσαν read μοῦσαν.
p. 74, l. 7, for ουερἀτρουμ read οὐερἀτρουμ.
p. 75, l. 4, for ρούβουμ read ῥούβουμ.

Kindred terms to the Arm. *etag*, 'fossa,' and perhaps to the Phryg. *lachit* (p. 30) and the Etrusc. *zi-lach-nke* (p. 115), would be the Ital. *lacca*, 'descensus, cavum, fossa,' and the Gael. *lag*, 'cavum, specus.'

In p. 137, l. 9 from bottom, after *gith*, 'imber,' add *cè*, gen. *cèithe*, 'flos lactis.'

THE

ARMENIAN ORIGIN OF THE ETRUSCANS.

THE subject of the following pages is an extension of the argument in the latter part of my *Contributions to the Ethnography of Italy and Greece*. Upon the earlier part I need not enter here: it will merely be necessary to recapitulate the views I entertain upon the peopling of Europe.

The Indo-Germanic, or, to adopt the shorter and now well-established term, the Aryan race, may be divided into two great divisions: the Northern or European Aryans, and the Southern or Asiatic Aryans. The European Aryans are sub-divided, reckoning by language, and overlooking smaller members, into three great branches: the Latin, the German, and the Slavonian branch. But the Latin is an intrusive language, derived from a single city or a very small district, and having spread over countries mainly occupied by Celts, who are also Aryans. The three great branches of European Aryans would therefore become, when considered ethnically, the Celts, the Germans, and the Slavonians.

The Southern or Asiatic Aryans may be similarly divided into three principal branches: the Armenians, the Persians, and the Indians. The Kurds and Afghans are of less ethnical importance. The Armenians, like the Celts, are now few in number. It will be my endeavour to prove that the race to which they belong once occupied a much greater extent of country, and were spread westward from Armenia to Italy under the names of Phrygians, Thracians, Pelasgians, Etrus-

B

cans, and other designations. As the expansion of the Latin language from its original seat at Rome obliterated in its advance the greater number of the Celtic dialects, so the expansion of the same language in part, but yet more the expansion of the Greek, obliterated in Europe and Asia Minor the dialects akin to the Armenian, until it was only in the original seat of the race, in Armenia itself, that a representative of those dialects survived.

The only members of the Aryan stock with which I shall have to deal, will be the Thracians, *i.e.*, the race of which the Armenians are a part, and the Celts: or with the western branch of the Northern Aryans, and the western branch of the Southern Aryans. These two branches would, by their position, be the first settlers in Europe of the divisions to which they belong. The Celts, I conceive, entered Europe chiefly through Scythia or Russia; and the Thracians, at least mainly, through Asia Minor and Turkey. Having entered Europe, one portion of the Celts would turn to the S. W., and eventually settle in Italy. To these would belong the Umbrians, said by some to be a branch of the *old* Celts, *i.e.*, the Celts who were in Italy before the Celtic invasion which ultimately terminated in the capture of Rome. The Thracians, on the other hand, advancing W. and N. W. from Asia Minor, would form the original Aryan population in Turkey and Greece, would come in contact with the Celts along the line of Dacia, Pannonia, Noricum, and Rhætia, and would pass into Italy, mostly under the name of Tyrrhenians, at a period subsequent to the date of the Celtic settlements in that peninsula.

But there would have been two races in Europe before the arrival of any Aryan settlers. One of these races would have been the Basque or Iberian race, with which I shall have little to do. The other is more important. If there were a race in Europe, not Basque, and earlier than the Celtic, it is almost a direct ethnological consequence that it must have been Fin

Of this race I consider the Ligurians to have been the remnant in Italy, and that the Fins, or some kindred Turanians, formed the substratum over all Italy, Greece, Turkey, the Austrian States, and Asia Minor. Thus the representatives of the three Italian races and languages, the Ligurian, the Umbrian, and the Tyrrhenian or Etruscan, would now, I believe, be found respectively—in Lapland, Finland, and Esthonia; in Brittany, Wales, Ireland, and Scotland; and in Armenia. To substantiate the last of these points is my present object. The representatives of the fourth of the earliest European races, the Iberian, would in like manner be found in Biscay.

Historical evidence of the extension of the Thracian race from Armenia to Etruria.

In endeavouring to determine the family of nations to which the Etruscans belonged, it is necessary first to inquire from what nation they are traditionally derived, or with whom they have been identified. With regard to the former of these points there is great unanimity. The general voice of antiquity derived them from the Lydians, an opinion which the Etruscans themselves were also willing to accept. The Etruscans were also generally identified with the widely spread race called Pelasgian, although the Tyrrhenians and Pelasgians in Etruria, and also in Campania, are usually spoken of as distinct peoples, but continually associated together. The Etruscans would thus appear to be akin to the Lydians and the Pelasgians.[1] Of this last race, which was

---

[1] These affinities are disputed by one ancient writer, Dionysius of Halicarnassus (lib. i, cc. 29, 30). He says: 'In my opinion, however, all are in error, who believe the Etruscan (Τυῤῥηνικὸν) and Pelasgian nations to be the same.' Then follows an argument in proof of this, which is grounded on the well-known mistake of *Crotoniates*, i.e. *Cortoniates*, for *Crestoniates* in Herodotus. Dionysius then proceeds: ' For this reason, therefore, I believe the Etruscans to be different from the Pelasgians. Nor do I think that the Etruscans were Lydian colonists. For they do not use the same language as the Lydians: nor can it be said that,

almost entirely extinct *in same* in the time of Herodotus, scarcely anything is known, and nothing need yet be said. We have now to enquire to what family the Lydians belonged: for the story of the descent of the Etruscans from the Lydians can hardly be regarded as rigidly historical, but merely as implying that both nations belonged to the same family; an ethnical fact which appears in the historical form of a migration from Lydia to Etruria.

The Lydians are in the first instance connected with the Mysians and Carians. It is mentioned by Herodotus that the Mysians and Lydians were κασίγνητοι to the Carians, and that the mythic Mysus, Lydus, and Car, were brothers.[1] He also says that the Mysians were Lydian colonists.[2] In reference to the more general affinities of the Lydians and Carians we have no particular statements, but are left to deduce them from those of the Mysians, who are described as Thracian colonists.[3] We may therefore infer that the Lydians and Carians belonged also to the Thracian family.

We have now probably arrived at the name of the great family to which the Etruscans belonged, *i. e.*, the Thracian. For the Thracians were not a single tribe or people. The name, like that of Celt or German, describes one of the Aryan families, which was, according to Herodotus, the most nume-

---

although they are not indeed like (the Lydians) in speech, yet they still retain some indications of their mother-country. For they do not worship the same gods as the Lydians, nor do they resemble them in their laws and customs; but in these things they differ yet more from the Lydians than from the Pelasgians. Their account, therefore, seems to be more probable, who declare this (Etruscan) nation not to be foreign, but indigenous (in Etruria); since it is very ancient, and is not found to be like any other, either in speech or manners.' There were, therefore, three opinions concerning the Etruscans. They were considered as—
1. Pelasgians, a race which was a mere name in the time of Dionysius;—
2. Lydians;—3. An isolated race allied to no other (a proposition affirmed of the Armenians half a century ago). The solution, I believe, is, that the Pelasgians, Lydians, and Etruscans derived their origin at a remote period from Armenia.

[1] i. 171.   [2] vii. 74.   [3] Strabo, pp. 542, 566.

rous of all races next to the Indian.¹ The Thracians may indeed be traced from the frontiers of Media to Italy and the Alps, and would have included the Armenians on the east, and the Rhætians and Etruscans on the west. The following are the chief indications of a chain of kindred nations within these limits, which the ancients have transmitted to us.

The most easterly of all the tribes expressly said to be Thracian were the Saraparæ, who are mentioned by Strabo as a Thracian tribe dwelling beyond Armenia, near the Medes and the Guranians.² In the Armenian province of Persarmenia, a district bordering on or containing the Lake of Ourmia, the Armenian Geography attributed to Moses of Chorene mentions a part called *Thraki*.³

The Armenians themselves belonged to the same family as the Phrygians, from whom they were said to be descended, and to whose language their own bore much resemblance. Ἀρμένιοι . . . . . Φρυγῶν ἄποικοι:⁴ Ἀρμένιοι τὸ γένος ἐκ Φρυγίας καὶ τῇ φωνῇ πολλὰ φρυγίζουσιν.⁵ But the Phrygians were well known as a Thracian tribe:⁶ the Armenians, therefore, probably belonged to the same family. Continuing westward from Armenia, we come to Cappadocia, a country possessed by a Syrian race, who probably advanced from the south at some remote period, and separated the Armenians from the kindred race of the Phrygians. The eastern part of the province called Cappadocia was, however, Armenian, and formed the district of Armenia Parva. Cappadocia forms the only break in the chain of Thracian countries between Media and Helvetia.

The Phrygians, as just noticed, were a Thracian race: οἱ Φρύγες Θρᾳκῶν ἄποικοί εἰσι. The Mysians, Lydians, and Carians belonged likewise to the same family. So, also, according to Strabo, did the Mygdones, Bebryces, Medobithy-

---

¹ iv. 3. ² p. 531. ³ Mos. Chor. p. 359. Ed. Whiston.
⁴ Herod. vii. 73. ⁵ Eustath. on Dion. v. 694. ⁶ Strabo, pp. 295, 471.

nians, Bithynians, Thynians, and Mariandynians, as well as the Mœsians on the Danube and the Getæ.[1] He says, moreover, that the Getæ were ὁμόγλωττοι with the Thracians,[2] who thus extended to the frontiers of Macedonia, Illyria, and Pannonia. But the Pierians in Macedonia were a tribe of Thracians,[3] and the Macedonians also stated that Phrygians formerly dwelt in their country under the name of Briges.[4] Strabo, again, speaks of Brygi in the south of Illyria;[5] so that we should find Phrygians in Macedonia and Illyria, as well as Asia, and thus trace the Phrygian name from Armenia to the Adriatic.[6]

There were then, it appears, Thracians in Illyria. The Istrians, also, are described as Thracians.[7] The Veneti, again, are classed by Herodotus among the Illyrians,[8] and were reported by one writer to have come from Cappadocia, and to

---

[1] p. 295.   [2] p. 303.
[3] Strabo, p. 410.   [4] Herod. vii. 73.   [5] p. 326.
[6] For a full and excellent account of the Phrygians, see the art. Phrygia in Dr. Smith's Geography. The writer has, however, fallen into one error, which was also made by Dr. Hahn in his *Albanesische Studien*, and through him by myself. The words, Δαλμάται 'Αρμάτοι είναι μοι δοκούσι καί Φρύγες (Cramer. *Anecd. Gr. Oxon.* v. iv. p. 257), do not refer to men, but to horses. It appeared that the Dalmatian breed of horses was the same as that found in Phrygia and Armenia, and also in Cappadocia (ib.), the horses of the two latter countries being in high repute among the ancients.

Three Illyrian chiefs bore the name of *Bato*. One was a Dardanian, one a Dalmatian, and the third a Pannonian. This gives rise to a conjecture that *Bato*, like *Brennus*, signified 'chief.' The Arm. *pet*, = Sansk. *pati*, 'dominus,' = Zend *paiti*, = Pers. *bad*, has this signification. Herodotus mentions that the Scythians called themselves *Scoloti*, and we find a Scythian king called *Scolo-pitus*. This looks as if *pit* may have signified 'chief' in Scythian. Another Scythian king, mentioned by Herodotus, was *Ariapithes*, which might be explained from the Arm. *ayr*, 'man,' and *pet*, 'chief,' 'chief of men.' Herodotus also mentions a king of the Agathyrsi, called *Spargapithes*, and a leader (στρατηγόντα) of the Massagetæ, the son of Tomyris, called *Spargapises*. These names resemble the Arm. *sparapet*, 'general, chief.' Compare also, Arm. *zôr*, 'army,' *zôrapet*, 'general,' *azg*, 'nation,' *azgapet*, 'prince,' *karapet*, 'leader,' *wardapet*, 'teacher.' The remains of the Scythian language will be subsequently noticed.

[7] Scym. Ch. v. 390.   [8] i. 196.

have settled in company with Thracians on the Adriatic, *i.e.*, in Venetia.¹

Thracians were likewise to be found in Pannonia and Noricum. The three Celtic, or mainly Celtic nations, the Boii, Taurisci, and Scordisci, cover the whole area of these two countries. But all these three tribes are said to have been mixed with Thracians,² and the Scordisci, also, with Illyrians.³

When the Etruscan people possessed the plains of the Po, before the Gallic invasion, their frontier would have extended to Venetia and Rhætia. We have already traced the Thracians into Venetia and Noricum, the countries bordering upon Rhætia and the older Etruria. The addition of the kindred nations of the Rhætians and Etruscans, the one directly, and the other indirectly, derived by tradition from the Lydians, completes the list of Thracian nations stretching from the Caspian to the Tyrrhenian Sea.⁴

Two other important ethnical names, Tuscans and Dardans,

---

¹ Strabo, p. 552.   ² Ib. p. 296.   ³ Ib. p. 313.
⁴ The Vindelicians are even by one writer, of indifferent authority, ranked among the Thracians. 'Kaum Erwähnens werth ist, was Scholiasten von der Abstammung der Vindelici träumen, Servius, der im Commentar zu Virgil (*Aen.* i. 244) aus seinem Dichter findet, sie seien Liburnen, und in ihnen wegen des Horaz (iv. 4) Abkömmlinge der Amazonen sieht, und Porphyrio zum Horaz, in anderer der vorigen gleichwerthen Ansicht, sie seien von der Amazonen vertriebenen Thraker gewesen.'—*Zeuss, Die Deutschen*, p. 231. These opinions are doubtless of little value: and yet it is remarkable that they should be so nearly confirmed by the evidence of language in their intimation of the original seats of the nations in these parts. For they merely substitute Cappadocia, from which Thracians *had* in all probability been expelled, when the Armenians were divided from the Phrygians, in the place of Armenia. In the different accounts, there is also much consistency. One writer reports the Veneti to have come from *Cappadocia*, and to have settled in company with *Thracians* on the Adriatic; another derives the Vindelicians (considered by a third as Liburnians, while the Veneti are ranked by a fourth among the Illyrians) from the Amazons, *i.e.*, from *Cappadocia*; while a fifth considers these same Vindelicians as *Thracians* expelled by Amazons, in all probability from some part of Asia Minor, if not from *Cappadocia*. The *Lydian* extraction of the Rhætians and Etruscans is an extension of the same belief to the origin of two other contiguous nations.

have nearly the same extent. Both are connected with Etruria, the Dardans, however, only through the mythic Dardanus. Yet the name is Italian, as Dardanus was the name of an Apulian town in the marshes of Salpi,[1] and Dardi of an old Apulian people.[2] Both these names seem Illyrian; for the Dardanii or Dardaniatæ were an Illyrian nation, and there was a country extending into Mœsia, called Dardania. A large part of the modern Albanians are called Toscans. In Asia these names occur again. There was a Dardanus in Mysia. Herodotus speaks of Dardans in what is now Kurdistan.[3] Ptolemy mentions Tusci in Asiatic Sarmatia, and there is still a tribe called Tuschi or Tuschethi at the head of the river Alazan, a tributary of the Cyrus.

These are the chief historical or traditional indications of the extension of one great family of nations, to which the name Thracian may be applied, from Armenia to Etruria.[4] The languages of the different branches of this family would have been distinguished from one another by dialectic variations; and the discrepancy arising from such a cause would also have been increased by admixture with other races in the countries which the Thracians occupied. In Asia their language might have been partially affected by Semitic elements from the south. The European Thracians, on the

---

[1] La Martinière, *Geog. Dict.*   [2] Plin. *H. N.* iii. 16.
[3] i. 189. The root might be the Arm. *dar,* 'height,' or the Osset. *dard,* 'distant,'
[4] The passages in the Greek, which would prove or imply an affinity between the Etruscans and Armenians, are these, the links of connexion being—Etruria, Lydia, Mysia, Thrace, Phrygia, Armenia:—

Φασὶ δὲ αὐτοὶ Λυδοί, ... ἅμα δὲ ταῦτας τε ἐξευρεθῆναι παρὰ σφίσι λέγουσι, καὶ Τυρσηνίην ἀποικίσαι, κ. τ. λ.—Herod. i. 94.

'Αποδεικνῦσι δὲ ἐν Μυλάσοισι Διὸς Καρίου ἱρὸν ἀρχαῖον, τοῦ Μυσοῖσι μὲν καὶ Λυδοῖσι μέτεστι, ὡς κασιγνήτοισι ἐοῦσι τοῖσι Καροί. Τὸν γὰρ Λυδὸν καὶ τὸν Μυσὸν λέγουσι εἶναι Καρὸς ἀδελφεούς. Τούτοισι μὲν δὴ μέτεστι· ὅσοι δὲ, ἐόντες ἄλλου ἔθνεος, ὁμόγλωσσοι τοῖσι Καροὶ ἐγένοντο, τούτοισι δὲ οὐ μέτα.—Herod. i. 171.

Μυσοὶ δὲ εἰσι Λυδῶν ἄποικοι.—Herod. vii. 74.

Πρὸς δὲ τούτοις, ὅτι τοὺς Μυσοὺς, οἱ μὲν Θρᾷκας, οἱ δὲ Λυδοὺς εἰρήκασι, . . .
. . . μαρτυρεῖν δὲ τὴν διάλεκτον· μιξολύδιαν γάρ πως εἶναι, καὶ μιξοφρύγιον.

other hand, as we find from Strabo, were mixed with Celts and Scythians,[1] while the Etruscans would have been associated with Umbrians, a nation of reputed Celtic origin. Finally, all the Thracian nations would have been more or less affected by the presence of Finnish or Turanian tribes, the predecessors of the Aryan Celts and Thracians in probably all the countries over which the Thracians at any time extended themselves.

Linguistic evidence of the extension of the Thracian race from Armenia to Etruria.

The inference, that there was one family of nations extending from Armenia to Etruria, must now be put to the great test, that of language. We must endeavour to ascertain whether it can be shown that there was one language spoken in the countries which lie between those limits—one language, that is to say, in a wide sense, as English, German, Swedish, Dutch, and other Teutonic dialects, all form one language. Now a complete chain of nations, for the extent required, would be formed by Armenia, Cappadocia, Phrygia, Mysia, Thrace, Illyria, Rhætia, and Etruria; as Illyria and Thrace completely fill the space between Rhætia and Italy on the one

---

—Strabo, p. 572. Xanthus the Lydian, and Menecrates of Elæa, Strabo's authorities for the character of the Mysian language, were, as Mr. Grote observes, competent judges of the fact.

Εἴρηται δ'ὅτι καὶ αὐτοὶ οἱ Μυσοὶ Θρᾳκῶν ἄποικοι εἰσὶ τῶν νῦν λεγομένων Μυσῶν (the Mœsians).—Strabo, p. 542.

Αὐτοὶ δ'οἱ Φρύγες Βρύγες εἰσὶ, Θρᾴκιόν τε ἔθνος.—Strabo, p. 295.

Αὐτοὶ οἱ Φρύγες Θρᾳκῶν ἄποικοί εἰσιν.—Strabo, p. 471.

'Αρμένιοι δὲ κατά περ Φρύγες ἐσεσάχατο, ἐόντες Φρυγῶν ἄποικοι.—Herod. vii. 73.

Καὶ Εὔδοξος δὲ ἐν γῆς περιόδῳ φησὶν, ''Αρμένιοι τὸ γένος ἐκ Φρυγίας, καὶ τῇ φωνῇ πολλὰ φρυγίζουσι.'—Eustath. on *Dion.* v. 694.

These ἀποικίαι, of the Etruscans and Mysians from the Lydians, of the Mysians and Phrygians from the Thracians, and of the Armenians from the Phrygians, may all be interpreted in the same manner, as imaginary or uncertain migrations founded on the existence of ethnical affinities. Such affinities are likewise expressed, in another manner, by the fraternity of Mysus, Lydus, and Car.

[1] p. 313.

side, and Asia Minor on the other. For Strabo, in the beginning of his seventh book, speaks of Illyrians and Thracians, partly mixed with Celts, as occupying the whole country on the south of the Danube as far as the frontiers of Greece. A little further on (p. 312) he adds the Macedonians and Epirots, who would have been the connecting links between the Illyrians and the Greeks.

Of the eight countries which form the chain between Armenia and Etruria, the language of only one has entirely perished. This is Mysia: but as the Mysian language was credibly affirmed to be half Lydian and half Phrygian, the chain of countries and languages will still be unbroken, if the Lydian language be added to the list. It would be thus composed:

Country.   Language.
Armenia .... Old or literary Armenian; a complete language, still written, but unspoken, and dating from about 400 A.D.
Cappadocia .. Three Cappadocian words.
Phrygia } ... Fifty Phrygian words, and a few inscriptions.
Mysia } ... Thirty-eight Lydian words.
Lydia }
Thrace ..... Twenty-eight Thracian words.
Illyria ..... The residuary element in Albanian, after the elimination of all Turkish, Greek, Latin, and other foreign words.
Rhætia ..... The residuary element in Rhæto-Romansch, after the elimination of all German, Latin, and other foreign words.
Etruria ..... Several words, and a great number of inscriptions.

From this table it appears that we should have only one Thracian dialect left, the Armenian; and that of all the other kindred dialects only some slight relics would have survived. The Armenian would thus be the representative of the Thra-

cian tongue; and if it be true that all the other dialects in
the countries above named belonged, mainly at least, with the
exception of Cappadocia, and that also perhaps in part, to the
same Thracian family, then the relics of all those dialects
ought to exhibit Armenian affinities. This I shall now attempt to prove for each in its order, beginning with the
Cappadocian. And here one circumstance may be adduced at the
outset as tending to show that the existence of such affinities
was a thing which might have been surmised. The Armenian
language stands alone, a distinct branch of the Aryan stock,
and one marked by such decided individuality as to have led
some to consider it as an isolated form of speech, and to exclude it from the Aryan group. Now, when a language holds
this peculiar position, when it is not merely, like the English,
one member of a family, the Teutonic; but when it represents,
alone, and in a small and mountainous area, almost like the
Basque, a complete and peculiar family; the question may not
unreasonably arise—what has become of the other members of
this family of languages? It is this question which these
pages, in their widest scope, will endeavour to resolve.

Cappadocian Words.[1]

1. " Apulejus med. herb. 89 : ' ruta hortensis' apud Cappa-
docas appellata est *moly*, a quibusdam *armala*, a Syris *besasa*.
(Golius Arab. *karmal* præbet)." The Arab. word signifies
' ruta sylvestris.' Arm. *mol*akhot, 'weed;' *mol*akhind, 'hemlock.'

2. "Hesychius: νηιξίς (Is. Voss. qb ordinem ναξίς) ἐν
Καππαδοκίᾳ γενόμενος μῦς, ὃν σκίουρόν τινες λέγουσιν."

This word may be compared with the Sansk. *nakula*, Pers.
nighćah, Gael. *neas*, 'a weasel,' and with the Esth. *nuggis*,
Hung. *nyest*, 'a marten.' To show that animals of the

---

[1] All the Cappadocian, Phrygian, Lydian, Carian, Thracian, and Scythian words in the following pages are derived from Bötticher's *Arica*.
In their examination, whatever is inclosed within marks of quotation is
also borrowed from that work, to which I am under great obligations.

weasel kind are sometimes ranked with mice, cf. Lat. *mus-tela*, and Germ. *ratz*, 'ferret, dormouse, marmot.' " Hesychius: σίμωρ παρὰ Πάρθοις καλεῖταί τι μυὸς ἀγρίου εἶδος, οὗ ταῖς δοραῖς χρῶνται πρὸς χιτῶνας. Pers. *samúr*, Arm. *samoyr*, 'mustela, martes Scythica'" (*Arica*, p. 27). Νηιξίς would likewise be Arm., and also Semitic. For we have in Arm. *kotz*, 'a pole-cat, a marten,' and *kznachis* (= *kovz-nachis*), 'a marten.' *Nachis* differs little from νηιξίς or νιαξίς. In th Arm. *achis*, 'a weasel' (cf. Sansk. *ákhu*, 'a mouse'), the *n* of *nachis* has been lost. This may be readily explained from the Heb. *ach-bar*, 'a field-mouse' (*bar*, 'a field') : for the word נך may represent either *ach* or *ñach*.

3. " Curtius vii., 4: *Siros* vocabant barbari (Bactrii), quos ita sollerter abscondunt, ut nisi qui defoderunt invenire non possunt ; in iis conditæ fruges erant. Plinius, xiii. 73 : utilissime servantur tritica in scrobibus, quos *siros* vocant ut in Cappadociâ et Thraciâ. *Etymol. mgn.*: . . . . . . Εἰσὶ δὲ ὀρύγματά τινα σιροί." Arm. *tirim*, 'a tomb' (cf. τάφος, τάφρος, and θάπτω) ; *sor*, 'a hollow.' Georg. *soro*, 'a hole, a burrow.' The word *sirus*, it appears, was common to Cappadocia and Thrace.[1]

These are all the remains of the Cappadocian language, with

---

[1] The Georgians still keep their corn in subterranean magazines of this kind. 'This pit is about eight feet deep. When it is nearly full, fern is laid over the corn, and the mouth, which has a diameter of two or three feet,'—the floor is about six feet broad,—' is covered with strong boards, and then earth laid over all till it is on a level with the adjacent ground. This is so carefully done, that the place may be passed over without notice by a stranger, and even waggons may be driven across it ; so that these magazines, which are for the most part in the open court-yard, are well secured from thieves.'—Parrot's *Journey to Ararat*, Cooley's translation, p. 67. The form of these magazines must be very like that of the pit-dwellings of the Armenians described by Xenophon, with an entrance like the mouth of a well, but increasing in width towards the bottom. Their descendants dwell in the same manner to this day. ' It is not uncommon for a traveller to receive the first intimation of his approach to a village by finding his horse's fore feet down a chimney, and himself taking his place unexpectedly in the family circle through the roof.'— Layard, *Nineveh and Babylon*, p. 14.

the exception of the names of the months, which closely resemble those of the ancient Persian months, as preserved in the Zend and Pehlvi languages,[1] but which may have been borrowed from the Persians. It would obviously be unsafe to draw any certain conclusions from three words only. Two of them, however, are Armenian, and one of the two, also, Thracian. The third is Semitic, as well as one of the other two. These facts would be in accordance with the supposition, that a Thracian race, to which the kindred tribes of Armenia and Phrygia belonged, once occupied the intervening country of Cappadocia, and that these Phrygians and Armenians were afterwards separated by an advance of the Syrians from the south, which gave origin to a mixed Thraco-Syrian dialect in Cappadocia.

Phrygian Words.

1. 'Αδαμνεῖν, ' φιλεῖν': ἀδάμνα, ' φίλον.' "Pers. *kamdam,* ' socius, amicus, maxime familiaris ;' proprie, ' simul vel una spirans.' " Arm. *hamadam,* ' delicious.'——Gael. *daimh,* ' affection ;' *daimheach,* ' a friend.' Heb. *dam,* ' blood.' Arab. *damm,* ' blood ;' *damg,* ' a friend.' The *form* of ἀδάμνα may be compared with the Arm. *atamn,* ' dens.'

2. "Αζινον, ' πώγωνα.' " Arm. *azelel,* ' barbam secare ;'" *azeli,* ' a razor.' Georg. *tveri,* ' a beard.'

3. 'Ακεστήν, ' ἰατρόν.' Gr. ἀκεστής. Gael. *ic,* ' to cure.' Lapp. *vekke,* ' auxilium.' Arm. *ôgn,* ' aid, support :' *akastan,* ' a strong place,' th. *ak-.* Osset. *agaz,* ' whole, sound ;' *aghaz,* ' aid.' The Arm. *ôgn* may perhaps be found in the Bithynian ὄκνος, ' δίφρου τινὸς γυναικαίου εἶδος.'

4. "Ακριστιν, ' κλεπτρίαν ἀλετρίδα.' " Sopingius ἀλίτριαν, Is. Vossius αὐλητρίδα conjecit." Esth. *wargus,* ' theft.' Lith. *wagis,* ' a thief ;' *wagysté,* ' robbery.'——Arm. *erg,* ' a song, an air ;' *eražišt,* ' a musician.'

5. 'Αργυῖτας, ' λάμιαν.' " Quum ordo literarum hâc glossâ

---

[1] Cf. Benfey und Stern, *Monatsnamen einiger alter Völker.*

interruptus sit, varie restituere conati sunt. Fortasse Arm. *aṛlez*, 'animale chimerico,' doctiores ad indagandam veram lectionem adjuvat. Pers. *árdáv*, 'spectrum in desertis apparens.'" Lapp. *wardáli*, 'spectrum.' Gael. *arrachd*, 'a spectre.' Arm. *aṛaćóch*, 'spectral;' *aṛaćóch tesil*, 'a spectre' (lit. 'spectral appearance'). *Aṛaćóch* is properly the instrumental case of *aṛaćch*, the plural form of *aṛaé*, 'vision,' and *tesil* is derived from *tes*, 'sight.' Perhaps ἀργυῖτας, or whatever may be the correct reading, = *aṛaćates* (*aṛaé-tes*).

6. Ἀρμάν, 'πόλεμον.' Gael. *arm*, 'a weapon.' Arm. *harovmn*, gen. *harman*, 'a blow;' *waṛ*, 'arms.'

7. Ἄττηγος, *attagus*, 'hircus.' "Pers. *takka*, 'caper, hœdus:' Arm. *atakel*, 'valere, posse:' Zend. *takhma*, 'fortis.' Ἄττηγος erit *aititakhma*, 'perquam validus.'" Arm. *tik*, 'a goatskin (Fr. *bouc*).' Georg. *thkavi*, 'a goat,' = Germ. *ziege*, = Osset. *sagh*. Heb. *attud*, 'hircus.'

8. Ἀττάλη, 'φάρυξις.' "Quum præcedat ἀτταλαγώσεται, 'μολυνθήσεται,' bene videtur Is. Vossius correxisse φόρυξις." Arm. *ataḷż*, 'timber, carpentry.'

·9. "Βαγαῖος ὁ μάταιος. ἢ Ζεὺς Φρύγιος. μέγας πολὺς ταχύς. In inscriptionibus Persicis, *baga*, 'deus.' Arm. *bagin*, 'ara.'" Pol. *bog*, 'God.' —— Arm. *pakas*, 'faulty, deficient.'——Arm. *bazovm*; Sansk. *bahu*; 'much, great.' Lyd. ἴβυ, 'τὸ πολύ.' "Βοῦ τὸ μέγα καὶ πολὺ Λάκωνες."—— Arm. *wazel*, 'to run;' *wagṛ*, 'a tiger:' "a *celeritate* Tigris incipit vocari" (Plin. *H. N.* vi. 31). Osset. *bach*, 'a horse:' cf. *Pegasus.*——Here the Arm., by supplying the four words, *pak(as)*, *bag(in)*, *baz(ovm)*, and *waz(el)*, enables us to explain all the discordant senses attached by Hesychius to a single Phrygian word, βαγ(αῖος).

10. Βαλήν, 'βασιλεύς.' Sansk. *pála*, 'king, lord.' Heb. *baal*, 'lord.' Pers. *palwán*, 'a hero.' Lyd. πάλμυς, 'βασιλεύς.' Lith. *walo*, 'power.' Germ. *walten*. *Decebalus* was a *Dacian king.* *

11. Βάμβαλον, 'ἱμάτιον, αἰδοῖον.' Arm. *bambak*, 'cotton.'

Lat. *bombyx*, &c.——Arm. *bambasel*, 'to defame, to speak ill of.' The termination seems to be the Arm. *asel*, 'to say,' which would leave *bamb*, 'reproach.'

12. Βέδυ, 'ὕδωρ.' Arm. *hivth*, *vivth*, 'water, element;' *wét*, 'a wave;' *wtak*, 'a stream.' Eng. *wet*, *water*. Pol. *woda*, 'water.' Lat. *udus*. Macedon. βέθυ, 'air.' Pers. *wád*, *bád*, 'air.' Arm. *ód*, 'air.' Gipsy *wodi*, 'soul.'

13. Βεκός, 'ἄρτος.' Alb. *boukë*, 'bread;' *bak*, 'to make warm.' Eng. *bake*. Arm. *bowch*, 'a furnace.' Rhœt-Rom. *butschalla*, 'a kind of bread.' Dr. Parrot, in his *Journey to Ararat*, mentions a kind of Armenian bread called *bockon* (Eng. Ed. p. 169).

14. Βερεκύνδαι, 'δαίμονες.' Alb. *perndi*, *perendi*, 'God.' Lith. *perkúnas*, 'the Thunder-God.' Arm. *weragoyn*, 'superior, higher, above,' the comparative of *wer*, 'on high,'=Pers. *bar*; *wernakan*, 'celestial,' compounded of *werin*, 'high,' and the adjectival termination *-akan*. *Berecynthus* was a mountain. Compare also Arm. *erkin*, 'heaven,' a word remarkably like the Welsh *erchynu*, 'elevated,' from which Zeuss explains *Hercynius*.

15. Βρικίσματα, 'ὄρχησις φρυγιακή.' See inf. in Thrac. s. v. κολαβρισμός.

16. Γάνος παράδεισος χάρμα φῶς αὐγὴ λευκότης λαμπηδὼν ἡδονὴ καὶ ἡ ὕαινα ὑπὸ Φρυγῶν καὶ Βιθυνῶν. Heb. *gan*, 'a garden.'——Gael. *cain*, 'white.' Esth. *känna*, 'fair.' Lat. *candidus*. Gr. γάνος. Arm. *kanać*, 'green.'——Gael. *caoin*, 'pleasing.'——Arm. *ganćel*, 'to cry.' Lat. *gannire*.

17. Γίλαρος, 'ἀδελφοῦ γυνή.' Esth. *källi*, 'man's brother's wife.' Gr. γάλως, 'husband's sister.' Arm. *óg eibór*, 'θήλεια ἀδελφοῦ.'

18. Γλουρός, 'χρυσός.' Arm. *getavor*, 'beautiful, fair.' Gr. γελίω. Germ. *gelb*. Eng. *gold*.——Georg. *okro*, 'gold.'

19. Δάος, 'λύκος.' Lapp. *djur*, 'lupus;' *tär*, 'canis.' Pers. *tází*, 'a greyhound;' *táz*, 'a running.' The Arm. for 'wolf' is *gayl*.

20. Δαρεῖος, 'ὑπὸ Περσῶν ὁ φρόνιμος, ὑπὸ δὲ Φρυγῶν ἕκτωρ.' Pers. *dárak*, 'a scythe.' Osset. *zürck*, 'sharp.' Esth. *terraw*, 'sharp, cunning;' *terras*, 'steel;' *tark*, 'prudent.' Lapp. *tjarrok*, 'rigidus, asper;' *tjarfo*, 'instrumentum hastæ instar, quo glaciem pertundunt.' Arm. *sayr*, 'edge, point;' *sayr*, 'point, head, top, height;' *dar*, 'height.'

21. "Ελυμος, 'αὐλός.' Arm. *elégn*, 'a reed, a pipe' (κάλαμος, Mark xv. 19). The ancients mention two places in Armenia called *Elegia*: cf. Germ. *Ried*. The Arm. *elégn* appears allied, as Bötticher intimates, to ἔλεγος, a word probably not Greek, but Asiatic. Cf. Müller and Donaldson, *Hist. Gr. Lit.* v. i. p. 142. If it be likely, as Müller thinks, that the Ionians received the word ἔλεγος from their neighbours, then it might be inferred that it was a Lydian, as well as an Armenian word. The Arm. words for 'flute' are, *sring* (= Gr. σύριγξ—cf. also Arm. *sriné*, 'sound') and *elégnaphol* (lit. 'reed-trumpet'). The Arm. *chnar*, 'lyre,' evidently = Gr. κινύρα and Heb. *kinnor*. *Elegium* was a place in Noricum.

22. "Εξιν, 'ἐχῖνον.' Arm. *ozni*, 'echinus.' So Arm. *ōʒ* and *iṡ* = ἔχις, and *ayʒ* = αἴξ.

23. "Εὐοὶ σαβοὶ μυστικὰ μέν ἐστιν ἐπιφθέγματα——ἀφ' οὗ καὶ ὁ σαβάζιος Διόνυσος. *Sabazius* = *ṡávañk yazala*, . . . i.e., 'generator, creator.'" Arm. *zevel*, 'to form.' Εὐοί seems a mere interjection, like the Arm. *ekè !* *oh oh !* *ēh !* &c., and similar words in many other languages. Compare, however, Lat. *ave*, *have*, and Arm. *chaveá*, 'expia!'

24. Ζέλκια, 'λάχανα.' "Russ. *zelen*'; Serv. *zlak* vel *zelie*; Lat. *olus*." Arm. *selkh*, *sekh*, 'a melon;' *sokh*, 'an onion;' *solgam*, 'a radish, a turnip,' = Arab. *salgam*, = Georg. *thalgami*. Alb. *selkyiñ*, *salkyi*, 'a water-melon.' Kurd. *selk*, 'beet.' Gr. σίκυς = Arm. *sekh*, the less perfect form of *selkh*, ζέλκ(ιον), or *selk(yiñ)*. Compare, also, Arm. *salk*, 'a stalk.'

25. Ζέμελεν, 'βάρβαρον ἀνδράποδον.' "Anne ex *kimd* et *anya* (Arm. *ayl*), qui *aliam terram patriam* habet?" Arm. *zamack*, 'land,' = Pol. *ziemia*; *ayl*, 'other.' But the Arab.

zamm, 'binding,' zimmí, 'a client, a subject,' seem to give a better derivation. If we take into Arm. the root zam or zem, 'lig(are),' we may form the participle zemeal, 'ligatus, a bondman, ἀνδράποδον,' in the acc. zemealn. The root of ζέμελεν, like the person it described, may have been *barbarous* or foreign.

26. Ζίρνα, 'πύλη.' Arm. zal, yayt, yaytni, 'open.'

27. Ζευμάν, 'πηγήν.' "Arm. zow, 'sea, lake, reservoir.'" Pers. tay, 'reservoir;' zawán, 'water.' Arab. zamzam, 'a well.' Georg. zghwa, 'sea.'

28. Κίκλην, 'τὸν ἄρκτον τὸ ἄστρον.' "Quum nos gallinam cælestem habeamus, quid ni κίκλην ad Sansk. *kukkuta* revocemus." Esth. kikka, 'a cock.' Cf. Gr. κίχλη. The Latins called this constellation *temo*, and we call it the *wain*. Now *temo* is in Arm. cheti, which would be pronounced χίχλι, and might = κίκλη.

29. Κίμερος, 'νοῦς.' Arm. chimch, 'the palate, caprice, fancy;' kamch, 'will, design, judgment.' Chimch and kamch are both plural forms: their singular would be chim and kam. Pers. kám, 'desire, design, the palate.'

30. Κυβήκη, 'ὑποδήματα.' Arm. kóšik or kavšik; Pers. kafš; 'a shoe.' Κυβήκη also signified 'the mother of the Gods,' and 'Aphrodite.' See *Arica*, p. 35.

31. Λιτυέρσας, 'Φρυγῶν ᾆσμα.' Perhaps an ἔρσας for the *lituus*. Arm. erg, 'a song, an air;' eražišt, 'a musician.' The name of the lituus is supposed to be derived from its bent form. Eng. *lithe*. Arm. klov, 'pliable.' Welsh *lleddy*, 'pliable.'

32. Μᾶ, 'πρόβατα.' Arm. mayel, 'to bleat;' machi, 'an ewe.' Lesgi mazza, 'a sheep.'

33. "Plutarchus *de Iside et Osiride*, p. 360 B:——
Φρύγες δὲ μέχρι νῦν τὰ λαμπρὰ καὶ θαυμαστὰ τῶν ἔργων μανικὰ καλοῦσι διὰ τὸ Μάνιν τινα τῶν πάλαι βασιλέων ἀγαθὸν ἄνδρα καὶ δυνατὸν γενέσθαι παρ' αὐτοῖς, ὃν ἔνιοι Μάσδην καλοῦσιν. Gravissimus hic locus veram Ahuramazdæ

etymologiam tandem indigitat. Zend *mazda* nihil aliud quam quod *mainyu* significat ac sicut Sansk. *mastaka*, 'caput,' dictum a *man*, ita Arm. *imast*, ' intellectus,' ab *imanal*, 'intelligere,' et Phrygice *Manis* idem qui *Masdes*." Compare also Arm. *mazdezn*, ' a hero'——*moyn*, 'beauty, grace.' Lat. *amœnus*. Gr. ἀμείνων. Etrusc. (prob.) *manus*, ' good.'

34. *Mitra*, 'pileum Phrygium.' Arm. *mithr*, 'mitre,' probably a borrowed term. Arab. *midray*, ' a horn;' *midrah*, ' a prince.'

35. Ναὶ μήν, '*nal*.' Arm. *na*, ' but, however, rather, in fact;' *imn*, 'really, in fact.' *Imn* appears to identify μήν, μὲν, with *immo*, *imo*.

36. Νηνίατον, νινήατος, ' Φρύγιον μἒλος.' " *Nænia* Romanorum in mentem venit, et radix *nu*, 'laudare.' " Arm. *novag*, ' a song;' *noval*, 'to mew:' th. *nov* (*nu*). Pers. *nánú*, ' a lullaby song;' *nay*, ' a reed, a flute;' *naw*, 'crying;' *nuwd*, ' voice, modulation;' *nuwdg*, ' a singer.' *Nánú*, *nænia*, and νηνία-τον, appear to be the *nay-nu* or *nay-nuwá*, ' the flute-song;' and thus *nænia* and ἔλεγος would have nearly the same meaning etymologically, just as they have in fact. We know that the flute was the proper instrument, both for the *nænia* and ἔλεγος.[1]

37. Νόρικον, νώρικον, ' ἀσκόν.' Pers. *nahrah*, ' a jug, a jar, a basin.'

38. Ὄρου, ' ἄνω.' Arm. ʼ*i wer*, ʼ*i weray*, ʼ*i weroy*, ' above.'

39. Οὐανοῦν, ' vulpem.' Arab. *áways*, ' a wolf.' Arm. *yowaz*, ' a panther.' Esth. *hunt*, ' a wolf.' Germ. *hund*. Eng. *hound*.

40. Πικέριον, ' βούτυρον.' " Radix *pydi*, ' pinguescere.' " Pers. *pih*; Osset. *fiu*; ' fat, grease.' Arm. *panir*, ' cheese.' Esth. *piim*, ' milk.' Lat. *pinguis*. Gr. πῖαρ, παχύς, πύκα, πυκνός. Πικρολέα seems to have signified in Lydian, πλησίον, i.e., πυκνῶς. See inf. in Lyd. *s. v.* βάσκε.

---

[1] Τάγγις ὁ Φρὶξ αὐλῶν πρῶτοι ηὗρεν.—Marm. Arund. (Bentley's *Phalaris*, p. xcv.) Ἐλεγεῖα καὶ θρῆνοι προσᾳδόμενα τοῖς αὐλοῖς (Pausan. x. 7).

THE ARMENIAN ORIGIN OF THE ETRUSCANS. 19

41. "Apulejus de medicaminibus herbarum 5: *hyoscyamum* Phryges *remenia* appellant." *Hyoscyamus* = Germ. *bilsenkraut* = Esth. *marro rohhi* or *marro hain; marro* signifying 'violent,' *rohhi*, '*kraut*, gras, gewürz, *arnzei* (medicamen),' and *hain*, 'hay, grass (herba).' The same language gives *emmis*, 'a sow,' a word allied to *emma*, 'mother.' *Remenia* might be made up of *ro(hhi)—em(ma)—hain* (medicamen—sus—herba), with the termination *-ia*; but the word is difficult to explain. Compare also Lapp. *ruoiwa*, 'hemp;' *ruomse, remse*, 'moss;' and Arm. *rehan*, 'basil (ocymum),' = Kurd. *riahn*.

42. "In *risco*, cista *pelle* contecta, nomen Phrygium." Gael. *rusg*; Welsh *rhisg*; 'any external covering, rind, skin, husk, bark, fleece.' Ital. *riccio*. *Riscus* looks like a Celtic, and would, perhaps, be a Galatian, or even a Cimmerian word, if the Cimmerians should prove to have been Celts. The Cimmerians often invaded and partly held possession of Asia Minor during the ninth, eighth, and seventh centuries, B.C.

43. Σάβοι ἔθνος Φρυγίας. λέγονται καὶ ἀντὶ τοῦ βάκχοι παρὰ Φρυξίν. *Ante* 23.

44. *Sminthos*, 'mures.' "*Sminthus* terrigenam significat: Sansk. *ksam*, 'terra,' gen. *kimas*, locativus si flexionem pronominum hâc in re antiquiorem sequamur *ksmin* (Zend idem *zemi*, Neopers. *zamin* thema), Sansk. *dhá* apud Græcos τιθέναι, ut *thus* pro *dhita* (= hita) Phrygicum esse potuerit. *Sminthus*, 'in terrâ creatus.'" Arm. *žamach*, 'land;' *dnel*, perf. *edi*, th. *d-*, 'to place.'

45. Σοῦσα, 'λείρια.' Arm. *sovsan*; Pers. *sûsan*; Heb. *šušan*; 'lilium.'

46. Σύκχοι, 'ὑποδήματα.' Arm. *sek*, 'dressed leather, cordovan.' (Cf. Eng. *cordwainer*). Lat. *soccus*.

47. *Tiara*. "Juvenalis vi. 516: 'Phrygiâ vestitur bucca *tiarâ*.'—Isidorus *Orig*. xix. 30: Persæ tiaras gerunt, sed reges rectas, satrapæ incurvas. Reperta autem *tiara* a Semiramide Assyriorum reginâ, quod genus ornamenti exinde usque hodie gens ipsa retinet." Arm. *dar*, 'height.' Pers. *tar*, 'top.'—

c 2

Arm. *tér*, gen. *tearn*, 'lord.' Compare Arm. *thag*, 'crown;' *thagavor*, 'king;' *thagovhi*, 'queen.'

" Plato, *Cratylus*, p. 410 A : ' ὅρα τοῦτο τοὔνομα τὸ πῦρ μή τι βαρβαρικὸν ᾖ. Τοῦτο γὰρ οὔτε ῥᾴδιον προσάψαι ἐστὶν Ἑλληνικῇ φωνῇ, φανεροὶ τ' εἰσὶν οὕτως αὐτὸ καλοῦντες Φρύγες, σμικρόν τι παρακλίνοντες. Καὶ τὸ γε ὕδωρ καὶ τὰς κύνας καὶ ἄλλα πολλά." Arm. *hovr*, 'fire;' *hivth*, 'water;' *tovn*, 'dog.' Germ. *feuer, wasser, hund*. Eng. *fire, water, hound*.

Phrygian inscriptions.

What few Phrygian inscriptions remain are sepulchral. They will be found in Texier's *Asie Mineure*, and have been given and conjecturally interpreted by Mr. Rawlinson in his *Herodotus*, v. i. p. 666. They require especial notice here as genuine relics of the Phrygian language, and also because it appears to be in a great measure on the strength of these inscriptions that the learned translator of Herodotus has disregarded, I cannot but think erroneously, the opinion entertained by the ancients of the affinity between the Armenian and Phrygian nations and languages.[1] Instead of classing the

---

[1] p. 652. 'The statement of Herodotus that the Armenians were colonists of the Phrygians, though echoed by Stephen,' (Mr. Rawlinson should have said, by Eudoxus, who, if of Cnidus, lived 800 or 900 years before Stephen, and was a man of the highest repute,) ' who adds that "they had many Phrygian forms of expression," is not perhaps entitled to great weight, as Herodotus reports such colonisations far too readily (as '——it is said in a note——' when he accepts the Lydian colonisation of Etruria (i. 94) and the derivation of the Venetians' (not the Venetians, but the Sigynnæ) 'from the Medes, v. 9), and his acquaintance with the Armenians must have been scanty.' (This is probably true; yet both Herodotus and Eudoxus lived in Asia Minor, both were travellers, and Herodotus may have passed through Armenia on his way to the East. Cf. v. 52. Thousands of Greeks, again, would have heard Armenian and Phrygian, and also Persian, spoken, in the time of Xenophon, Agesilaus, and Eudoxus.) 'Still, as far as it goes, it would imply that the ethnic change by which a(n) Indo-European had succeeded a Tâtar preponderance in Armenia was prior to his own time, and on the whole there are perhaps sufficient grounds for assigning the movement to about the close of the seventh century before our era.' If the evidence of Herodotus and Eudoxus in favour of the Phrygian affinity of the Armenians be rejected,

Phrygians with the Armenians, as Herodotus and Eudoxus have done, and as I should wish to do, Mr. Rawlinson ranks the Phrygians, as well as the Mysians, Lydians, Cariaus, and Pelasgians, with the Greeks (p. 676), and not with the Armenians. Yet I believe that his own explanation of the Phrygian epitaphs will go far to show that his theory is only partially true with respect to the Greeks, and not tenable with respect to the Armenians; for several of his interpretations are unconsciously Armenian, and not Greek. Nor is this affinity between the Armenian and Phrygian merely in sense, but also frequently in form, though, in this last respect, there are some points of difference. These points chiefly are, that Armenian nouns want the nom. sing. in *s*, the gen. in *s*, and the acc. in *n* or *m;* while the Phrygian, like the Latin and

---

should it be used to prove an Indo-European, afterwards limited to a Medo-Persian, affinity? For Mr. Rawlinson (p. 676) ranks those Aryans, whom he considers to have gained the prevalence over the Tátars in Armenia towards the year 600 B.C., with the Medes, Persians, Bactrians, Sogdians, and Cappadocians, and not with the Thracians, or with the Phrygians and Lydians. If this be true, the Etruscans can hardly have been allied to the Armenians, as the supposition of any westward extension of the Armenian race subsequent to 600 B.C. is inadmissible. Whatever Armenian affinities are found in Europe must be of far earlier introduction: for no Armenian conquests or migrations can have been made so far to the west except in pre-historical, or even pre-traditional times. Nor is it only with respect to the Phrygian affinities of the Armenians that I should put faith in Herodotus. I think that the two other principles derived from him, that the Lydians and Etruscans were of one family, and that the Hellenes and Pelasgians were not of one family, will be eventually found, in conjunction with the affinity between the Phrygians and Armenians, to form the basis on which the true system of ethnology in Italy and Greece is to be founded. Both these principles are generally rejected. Mr. Rawlinson holds (p. 664) that the Greek or Hellenic race was Pelasgian, and that the Pelasgic was 'an early stage of the very tongue which ripened ultimately into the Hellenic;' while (p. 359) 'all analysis of the Etruscan language leads to the conclusion that it is in its non-Pelasgic element altogether *sui generis*, and quite unconnected, as far as it appears, with any of the dialects of Asia Minor. The Lydians, on the other hand, who were of the same family as the Carians, who are called Leleges, must have spoken a language closely akin to the Pelasgic ; and the connexion of Lydia with Italy, if any, must have been through the Pelasgic, not through the Italic element in the population.' With this last decision I should be inclined to concur, be-

Greek, is in possession of them. But this will not make the Phrygian a Classic tongue, as such forms are Sanskrit, or generally Aryan. They are, indeed, Etruscan, which is certainly a foreign language to Greek and Latin, and, in Mr. Rawlinson's opinion, not even Aryan. The Armenian genitive usually terminates in *i*, *ov* (i.e., *u*), or *oy*. As in the 1st, 2nd, and 5th declensions in Latin, the Sanskrit genitive in *as* is replaced by the locative or dative. The Armenian nominative and accusative are without inflexions.

The simplest of the Phrygian epitaphs is the inscription on the tomb of Midas:—

Ates arkiaefas akenanogafos Midai gafagtaei fanaktei edaes; which Mr. Rawlinson renders

Ates-Arciaëfas, the Acenanogafus, built (this) to Midas, the warrior-king.[1]

---

lieving the Italic, or Aboriginal element in Italy, that element to which the Oscans, Umbrians, and Sabines belonged, to be Hellenic; and the Pelasgian, on the other hand, not to be Hellenic, but Armenian, and allied to the Phrygian, Lydian, and other Thracian dialects. As we are not acquainted with the meaning, or certain of the existence, of a single Pelasgian word, the cause of ethnology would probably be advanced by avoiding 'Pelasgian,' as far as possible, as a defining term. *Greek* or *Hellenic, Latin, Græco-Latin* or *Classic, Armenian, German, Gaelic, Celtic*, &c., are terms which have a linguistic, and therefore a determinable ethnic sense. *Pelasgian* has none, unless some previous hypothesis be made. It is generally used in the sense of 'Greek' or 'Classic'; but this involves an assumption, and one of these latter terms might be more definite in investigations of ethnic affinity. Sometimes, however, the obscurity arising from the term ' Pelasgian ' may be partly remedied, as in the two propositions above noticed relating to that unknown race. If 'the Lydians must have spoken a language closely akin to the Pelasgic,' and if 'the Pelasgic ripened ultimately into the Hellenic,' it would then follow that the Lydians must have spoken a language nearly allied to the Greek; a conclusion which admits of being tested, as the Lydian language, unlike the Pelasgian, has left some relics. Yet as these relics, as far as I can judge, are not Greek, I should infer that one of the two propositions relative to the Pelasgians, and in all probability the second proposition, was erroneous; and that Herodotus was right in his opinion, ἦσαν οἱ Πελασγοὶ βάρβαρον γλῶσσαν ἱέντες.

[1] I do not know any analogy for *gafagtaei*, 'warrior': but there can be little doubt that the two other words which are explained, *fanaktei edaes*, are correctly rendered, 'ἄνακτι ἔθηκε.'

THE ARMENIAN ORIGIN OF THE ETRUSCANS. 23

The Armenian would explain the inscription in the following manner:—

Ates . . . . . A proper name, Atys.
arkiaefas . . . Arm. *archay*, 'a king;' *archayazn*, 'a prince.' Gr. ἀρχή, ἄρχων. *Archayazn* is compounded of *archay*, 'king,' and *azn*, 'race.' A synonym of *azn* is *azg*, so that the root is *az*; and *archayaz*(*n*) signifies 'a man of royal race.' But perhaps the termination of *arkiaefas* may be merely formative. Lassen suggests here the Sansk. *arka*, 'reverence,' which = Arm. *yarg*, whence *yargi*, 'respectable.' The name, *tariknafas*, was found on an earthen pot near Este, and *tarchnas* at Cervetri. Compare *tariknafas* and *tarchnas* in form with the Phryg. *arkiaefas* and the Arm. *archayaz*(*n*).

akenanogafos . Arm. *akanavor*, 'illustrious,' primarily, 'having eyes;' a word compounded of *akn*, gen. *akan*, 'an eye,' and of the Arm. termination, *-avor*. Compare Arm. *thag*, 'a crown,' *thagavor*, 'a king.' The last member of *aken-anogafos* might be explained from the Arm. *ang*, 'due, fit;' *angov*, 'worthy of;' *yangavor*, 'proper;' which would give for *aken-anogafos* the sense, 'worthy of note (*merkwürdig*), illustrious.' *Akn*, 'an eye,' enters into the composition of several Arm. adjectives; as *aknazov*, 'respectful;' *aknerev*, 'evident;' *aknkaroyï*, 'regarding attentively.' In another Phryg. inscription we meet with *Bonok akenanogafos* and *Inanon akenanogafos*, so that *akenanogafos* would be in all probability a title of honour.

Midai . . . . 'To Midas.' *Miday* would be the Arm. form of the gen. and dat. of *Midas*.

gafagtaei . . Arm. *gah* (= Pers. *gáh*), *gahak*, 'throne, dignity, eminence;' *gahakiž*, gen. and dat. *gahakži*, 'sharer of a throne, colleague.' The declension of *gafagt-aei* seems to resemble that of the Arm. *archay*, 'king,' gen. and dat. *arch-ayi;* or of *Hermés*, 'Hermes,' gen. and dat. *Herm-eay*.

fanaktei . . . Arm. *nakh*, 'first;' *nakhki*, 'chief.' Gr. ἄναξ. Pers. Inscript. *naqa*, 'king.' In form, *fanaktei* may be compared with the Arm. *anakhti*, gen. and dat. of *anakht*, 'pure;' or with *Anahtay*, gen. and dat. of *Anahit*, 'Anaïtis,' the great goddess of the Armenians.[1] In the Arm. *nakhagah*, 'president,' we find *nakh* and the previous word, *gah*, in combination.

---

[1] I should be inclined to connect the name *Anahit* etymologically with ἄναξ. The Milesian traditions reported by Pausanias may throw some light on this subject. He says (lib. i. c. 26):—

Ἔστι δὲ Μιλησίοις πρὸ τῆς πόλεως Λάδη νῆσος, ἀπερρώγασι δὲ ἀπ' αὐτῆς νησῖδες. 'Αστερίου τὴν ἑτέραν ὀνομάζουσι, καὶ τὸν 'Αστέριον ἐν αὐτῇ ταφῆναι λέγουσιν· εἶναι δὲ 'Αστέριον μὲν "Ανακτος, "Ανακτα δὲ Γῆς παῖδα.

And again (lib. vii. c. 2):—

Μιλήσιοι δὲ αὐτοὶ τοιάδε τὰ ἀρχαιότατα σφίσιν εἶναι λέγουσιν· ἐπὶ γενεὰς μὲν δὴ 'Ανακτορίαν καλεῖσθαι τὴν γῆν, "Ανακτός τε αὐτόχθονος καὶ 'Αστερίου βασιλεύοντος τοῦ "Ανακτος.

The name of *Anax*, the *autochthon* and the son of *Ge*, cannot be better derived than from the Arm. *nakh*, 'primus.' Such a derivation would also be suitable to *Anahit:* the Greeks called their gods ἄνακες; voc. sing. ἄνα. The name *Asterius*, again, is readily connected with the Gr. ἀστήρ. Now, in mythology, Asteria is the daughter of Phœbe, who was the daughter of Terra: and in the Milesian (or Carian) traditions, Asterius is the son of Anax, who was the son of Ge. It is obvious that *Anax* here corresponds to Phœbe, Diana, or *Anahit;* and when we compare together the three datives, the Arm. *anahtay*, the Phryg. *fanaktei*, and the Gr. ἄνακτι, the resemblance is very close. Indeed, *Anahit* may be considered as the same deity as 'Astarte, *queen* of heaven with crescent horns.'

The worship of Anaïtis was not confined to Armenia. She was the

edaes . . . . . Arm. *ed,* 'placed.' Gr. ἔθηκε. The Arm. *dnel,* ' to place,' perf. *edi,* is an irregular verb. Similar verbs, regularly conjugated, like *gnal,* ' to go,' and *gnel,* ' to buy,' make *gnaż,* ' he went,' and *gneaż,* ' he bought.' In general, in the case of the third pers. sing. perf. ind. in Arm., regular verbs have the root and the termination, but not the augment, and irregular verbs the augment and the root, but not the termination. Thus a regular verb, *nital,* ' to contrive,' makes *nit-aż,* ' he contrived;' while an irregular verb, *tal,* ' to give,' makes *e-t,* ' he gave,' the complete form being evidently *e-t-aż,* ' he gave.' A similar complete form, in the *-el* conjugation, would be *edeaż,* instead of *ed,* 'he placed.' Now *edeaż,* as *ea* is a diphthong, is very like the Phryg. *edaes,* which apparently consists of the augment *e-*, the root *-d-*, and the termination *-aes.* Another illustration

---

Lydian Diana, the 'great goddess' of the Ephesians, as well as the great goddess of the Armenians (Pausan. iii. 16, Plin. *H. N.* xxxiii. 4). She was also worshipped in Cappadocia (Strabo, p. 733). We find, again, that *Anu* or *Ana* was one of the three great Assyrian or Babylonian deities. The name signified 'the God,' κατ' ἐξοχήν (Rawlinson, *Herod.* v. i. p. 591). ' One class of his epithets refer undoubtedly to "priority" or "antiquity ",' and thus point to a word like the Arm. *nakh,* 'first,' as a root. The wife of *Anu* or *Ana* was *Anuta* or *Anata* (p. 593), a name which is not far from *Anahit.* ' She had precisely the same epithets as himself.' It is also noticed (p. 603) that the 'great goddess' of the Babylonians was *Mulita* or *Enuta.* Now *Anahit* was the 'great goddess' of the Armenians and Ephesians, and the same as *Mylitta* or *Enuta*, whose dissolute rites her own resembled. She was identified with Venus as well as Diana.

Thus, when we come to consider the word *ana* or *anax,* we trace it in Greece, Caria, Lydia, Phrygia, Cappadocia, Armenia, Assyria, and Babylonia: and its root is Armenian. The word is not found in Latin. The natural inference would be that *that* was a Pelasgian, not a Hellenic term; or, in other words, that it was of Thracian origin, and did not belong to the Classic or Græco-Latin stock.

may be supplied by the Arm. for 'to lick,' which is conjugated in three forms, *lizel*, *lizovl*, and *lizanel*, of which the first makes the perfect regularly, and the two last irregularly. We thus have for '*linxit*,' the forms, *lizeaï*, and *liz* or *eliz*, the complete form being *e-liz-eaï*.

The interpretation of the Phrygian inscription, as derived from the Armenian, would thus be:

Atys, the illustrious prince, made (this tomb) for Midas, the enthroned king.

By comparing the Phrygian inscription with the Armenian, we may see what the latter language has apparently lost—

Phryg. Ates arkiaefas akenanogafos Midai gafagtaei
Arm. Ates archayaz(n) akn-yangavor Miday gahakïi
Phryg. fanaktei edaes.

Arm. $\begin{Bmatrix} nakh \\ nakhki \end{Bmatrix}$ ed.

Neither language seems to have possessed the article, but the Phrygian has the digamma. The Phryg. *fanaktei*, so closely resembling the Gr. ἄνακτι, we are obliged to render in Arm. by '*i nakh* or '*i nakhki*, both *nakh* and *nakhki* being indeclinable, just as we should be obliged to render the Lat. *regi* by the Ital. *al rè*. In like manner, the Phryg. *edaes* is reduced to the Arm. *ed*, as the Lat. *posuit* is reduced to the Ital. *pose*. The Arm. has, however, in general, preserved the ancient inflexions much better than the Ital. Thus the termination of *ed-aes* is, as I have shown, still preserved in Arm., as well as of *fanakt-ei*, though not in the equivalent Arm. words: so that, upon the whole, there is no part of the inscription on the tomb of Midas, whether the root or form of the words be considered, but what appears to exist in the Armenian language.

There are two other Phrygian sepulchral inscriptions. The first of these, which is on the side of the tomb of Midas, is as follows, accompanied by Mr. Rawlinson's interpretation:—

THE ARMENIAN ORIGIN OF THE ETRUSCANS. 27

Baba Memefais   *proitafos*   *kphi ganafepos*
Lord Memefaïs,   son of Prætas,
Πάππας
Sikeman   *edaes.*
a native of Sica,   built (this)

Here we meet again with *edaes*, the meaning of which can thus hardly be doubtful. To explain the rest of the inscription, it is necessary to resort to conjecture. *Proitafos* and *ganafepos* seem to be the titles of *Baba Memefais;* and consequently *kphi*, judging from its position, may signify 'and,' as *afe* will be found probably to do in Etruscan. Cf. also Arm. *kap,* 'junction.' In *proit-afos* we find again the termination *-afos,* as in *akenanog-afos*. There remains as a root, *proit,* which, as the mark of dignity in rulers, governors, consuls, prætors, was a staff, we might perhaps explain from the Arm. *bir, wirg,* 'a stick,' *prtov,* 'a rush;' Gael. *bior,* 'a stick,' *bruid,* 'a stab;' Lat. *virga.* This would make *proit-afos* = Arm. *br-avor,* i.e. *bir-avor,* 'stick-bearing, σκηπτοῦχος.' Strabo says of the Heniochi near Colchis (p. 496): δυναστεύονται δὲ καὶ οὗτοι ὑπὸ τῶν καλουμένων σκηπτούχων· καὶ αὐτοὶ δὲ οὗτοι ὑπὸ τυράννοις ἢ βασιλεύσιν εἰσίν. There was also a σκηπτοῦχος at the court of Persia. For the second title, *ganafepos,* from which the nominative termination *-os*, deficient in Armenian, is to be subtracted, we may form from the Arm. words, *gan,* 'punishment,' and *wép,* 'ἔπος,' the word *ganawép,* 'judge.' Cf. *ju-dex, vin-dex,* and Arm. *bazmawép,* 'one who relates many (*bazoum*) things.' *Baba,* if allied to πάππας, would be so also to the Arm. synonym *pap*, Pers. *báb:* and the whole inscription might be thus interpreted, but with great doubt—

Baba   Memefais   proitafos   kphi   ganafepos   Sikeman
Πάππας Μεμεφαῒς σκηπτοῦχος καὶ δικαστὴς Σικαῖος
edaes.
ἔθηκε.

The remaining inscription is of greater length, and the last few words are not quite clear. I give it as far as Mr. Rawlinson has interpreted it:—

Kelokes fenaftun aftas materes sosesait, materes
Celoces sepulcrum suæ matris extruxit, matris
αὐτῆς μητέρος
Epheteksetis ofefinonoman lachit ga materan aresastin.
Ephetexetis ex Ofefinone. Sortita est tellus matrem amatam.
Ἔλαχε γῆ μητέρα ἐραστήν.
ἀρίστην.
Bonok akenanogafos erekun telatos sostut-
Bonok qui Acenanogafus erat hordeum sacrificii obtulit.
inanonakenanogafosaer. . . . .
Inanon Acenanogafus. . . . .

The Armenian will explain, as interpreted above, several of these words, which I shall take in their order:—

Fenaftun, 'sepulchrum.' Arm. *anóth* or *anavth*, 'vessel, pot, box, piece of furniture.' Another Arm. word, *tapan*, signifying 'box, urn, ark,' and therefore nearly a synonym of *anavth*, means also 'sepulchre,' and is commonly employed in that sense.[1] *Arca* and ἀγγεῖον are similarly used.

---

[1] See the *Journal Asiatique* (Février-Mars, 1855), *Voyage à Sis*, the former capital of the mediæval Armenian kingdom in Cilicia. I subjoin one of the epitaphs (p. 277), correcting some few inaccuracies in the reduction to literary Armenian, and rendering the Armenian letters by their equivalents, with the omission of the diacritical marks of the consonants.

Yays tapanēs kay edeal
In hoc tumulo manet positus
Tēr Michayēl mezn ēntreal.
Dominus Michael magnus electus.
Sa wsemagoyn werabereal
Ille superior elevatus
Yovsakan ē werakoceal.
Desiderabilis est cognominatus.
Thovoys hazar ev erkov harivr
Anno mille et duo centum (A.D. 1751.)
Ē hangēstiv 'i Tēr hangeal.
Est pace in Domino quietus.

The Armenian of the epitaph differs slightly from correct Armenian.

Aftas, 'suæ.' Gr. αὐτοῦ. Arm. *ivr*, 'of him;' *ivroy*, 'of his;' *aysr*, or *aydr*, or *aynr*, 'of this, of that.' Sansk. *etasya*, 'of this.'

Materes, 'matris.' Gr. μητήρ. Lat. *mater*. Gael. *mathair*. Sansk. *mâtṛi*. Pers. *mâdar*. Arm. *mayr*. Osset. *mâd*. Arm. *matak*, 'female (of animals),' = Pers. *mâdak*. The Arm. has, in *mayr*, suffered the same loss as the Lat. in *puer*. Cf. Sansk. *putra* = Zend *puthra* = Pers. *pusar* = Osset. *fürth* = Arm. *ordi* = Lat. *puer*.

Sosesait, 'exstruxit.'

Pers. *sát*, 'furniture'. . . Arm. *sar*, 'furniture.'
 sátidan, 'to prepare.'
 sátid, 'he prepared.'
 sátis, 'contrivance'. . . . *saras*, 'form, shape.'
        sarasel, 'to form, to shape.'
        saraseaz, 'he formed, shaped.'

The Pers. verb, it will be seen, is formed from *sát*, not from *sátis*, which corresponds to the Arm. *saras*. Had it been formed from *sátis*, we should have had Pers. *sátisid* = Arm. *saraseaz* = (prob.) Phryg. *sosesait*. The termination of *sosesait* seems = that of *ed-aes*. Compare *lives*, *liveth*, and Germ. *lebt*; *has*, *hath*, and Germ. *hat*. The Arm. *z* = *tz*. In the Gael. *sas*, 'an instrument,' another kindred root to the Phryg.

Thus *tér* is written *tr*, and *edeal*, *etheal*. The terminations in *l*, so common in Etruscan, are here exemplified in Armenian. *Edeal*, 'positus,' is the participle of *·ed*, 'posuit,' = Phryg. *edaes*. The terminations of *tapanës*, *mezn*, and *thovoys*, are not inflexions, but superfluous additions. These final letters in Armenian, consisting of *s*, *d*, and *n*, originally indicated a reference to the first, second, or third person, being really parts of the pronouns, '*I*,' '*thou*,' '*he*.' The *s* in *sa* and *yays* is in like manner borrowed from *es*, 'I;' the actual demonstrative pronoun being *a* or *ay*, though it is never used without one of the letters, *s*, *d*, *n*. The initial letter in *yays* is the preposition '*i*, before a vowel *y*. In *hangstiv*, pronounced, and written in poetry, *hangëstiv*, the instrumental case of *hang-ist*, of which the th. is found in *hang-eal*, we may perceive a form like the Phrygian *aresast(in)*. The Arm. *hazar*, 'thousand, *mille*,' is found in Sanskrit, Zend, Persian, Gipsy, Crimæan Gothic, Hungarian, and the Slavonian of Carniola, Styria, and Carinthia. See Diefenbach, *Lex. Comp. s. v. hazer*.

sos- might be found, as well as in the Arm. *sösaphel,* 'to handle,' a verb in *-aphel* from a root *sös.* Dealing with *sös* as the Arm. has done above with *sar,* we should obtain *sösaseaž,* 'be handled,' *i.e.,* 'managed, made,' a word very like the Phryg. *sosesait.* The verb *sösaphel* forms *sösapheaž.*

Ofefinonom*an,* 'ex Ofefinone.' Sikem*an,* 'a native of Sica,'[1]

Armenian.

  ayd, 'this, that' . . . . . da, 'this, that.'
  aydr, 'of this' . . . . . . dora, 'of this.'
  (y)ayd*mané,* 'from this' . d*mané,* 'from this.'
    ayg, 'morning.'
  (y)ayg*man,* 'in the morning.'

Osset. *ay* or *a,* 'this;' *aman,* 'to this;' *amiy,* 'in this;' *ama,* 'at this;' *amey,* 'from this.'

Lachit, 'ἔλαχι.' This sense cannot be obtained from the Armenian. The Arm. word which most nearly resembles *lachit* is *lakeaž,* '(it) consumed, swallowed, absorbed.' But *lachit,* as the Phryg. perfect seems to terminate in *-aes* or *-ait,* should, perhaps, rather be taken as a present tense. The Arm. present of *lakel,* 'to consume,' is *laké,* 'it (*i.e.,* the earth) consumes, swallows.' If the Pers. had a corresponding verb from a root *lák·,* the pres. would be *lákad,* and the perf. *lákid.* *Lachit* might also be compared with the Arm. *etak,* 'fossa,' and be interpreted 'sepelit.'

Ga, 'earth.' Gr. γῆ = Gael. *ee* = Sansk. *go.* Arm. *kav,* 'clay.' Germ. *gau* = Arm. *gavaṛ.* *Lachit ga,* 'devorat tellus,' or 'sepelit (Celoces) in tellure.'

These seem to be the chief points requiring notice. In the nouns, as I said before, the Phrygian, like the Latin and Greek, has preserved the Sanskrit or Aryan terminations where they are deficient in Armenian: thus the Phryg. *fenaft*un *aftas materes sosesait* appears = Arm. (*z*)*anavth mavr ivroy saraseaž.* It is only in the past and future participles, and then not in-

---

[1] I do not know any place called *Sica* in Asia Minor. We have *Sicum* in Illyria, and *Siculi* in Italy.

variably, that the Arm. acc. sing. presents the termination -*n:*
e.g. *sirealn,* 'amatum;' *sirelin,* 'amandum.' The Etruscan
possesses both the gen. in -*s* and the acc. in -*m.* Many Arm.
pronouns, however, form the dat., though not the acc., in -*m* or
-*ovm*(*um*): as *ayd,* 'this;' gen. *aydr;* dat. *aydm;* acc. (*z*)*ayd*
——— *im,* 'my;' gen. *imoy;* dat. *imovm;* acc. (*z*)*im;* abl.
(*y*)*imoy;* instr. *imow* (*ow* = Gr. ω). Here *im* seems = ἐμός or
meus; imoy = ἐμοῦ or *mei; imovm* = ἐμόν or *meum;* and *imow* =
ἐμῷ or *meo.* The locative of nouns may also be formed in
-*ovm,* as '*i mard* or '*i mardovm,* ' in man.'

Mr. Rawlinson has noticed the resemblance in form between
the Phryg. *ares-astin,* and such Gr. words as ἀρ-ίστην and
ἰρ-αστήν, and has even translated *aresastin,* 'amatam,' which
would require that the Phryg. *ares*- should = Gr. ἰρ-. Similar
forms appear also in the Phrygian vocabulary, in ἀκ-εστήν and
ἄκρ-ιστιν; though the first, being actually Greek, may have
been a borrowed word, if not modified by the Greek reporter.
The same forms are found in Arm., with the exception of the
acc. termination in *n:* e. g.

Phrygian.	Armenian.

ares-ast(*in*) . . ⎰ *im-ast,* 'intelligence:' th. *im*(*anal*) 'to understand.'
⎨ *nav-ast* ⎱ 'a sailor:' th. *nav,* 'a ship.'
⎨ *nav-asti* ⎰
⎨ *ovr-ast,* 'a denier:' th. *ovr*(*anal*), 'to deny.'
⎩ *tap-ast,* 'fallen, laid down:' th. *tap*(*al*) 'to fall.'

'ἀκ-εστ(ήν) . . ⎰ *gow-est,* 'praise:' th. *gow*(*el*), 'to praise.'
⎨ *ovt-est,* 'food:' th. *ovt*(*el*), 'to eat.'
⎩ *pah-est,* 'reservation:' th. *pah*(*el*), 'to reserve.'

ἄκρ-ιστ(ιν) . . ⎰ *erat-ist,* 'a musician.'
⎨ *hang-ist,* 'repose:' th. *hang*(*eal*), 'quiet.'
⎩ *nat-ist,* 'a female servant.'

⎰ *ber-ovst,* 'tendency:' th. *ber*(*el*), 'to bear.'
⎨ *gal-ovst,* 'arrival:' th. *gal,* 'to come.'
⎩ *thag-ovst,* concealment:' th. *thag*(*ovn*) 'hid.'

In order to explain the word *aresastin*, we may take the Arm. *yaṟaǵanal*, 'præire,' th. *aṟaǵ* or *yaṟaǵ*, 'præ;' and form *yaṟaǵast* in precisely the same manner as *imast* and *ovrast* are formed from *imanal* and *ovranal*. This would give—

Phrygian.   Armenian.
ares-ast(*in*) . *yaraǵ-ast*, ' præcellens, præstans :' th. *yaraǵ*(*anal*),
                              ' præcellere,'

and the meaning of *lachit ga materan aresastin* would be, ' devorat tellus matrem præstantem.' *Imast* is declined —— nom. *imast;* gen. and dat. *imasti;* acc. (*z*)*imast;* abl. (*y*)*imasté;* instr. *imastiv*. The other forms ending in -*st* or.-*st* are mostly declined in the same manner. *Aresastin* might also be explained, ' departed,' from the Arm. *hrażest*, ' abdication, resignation, farewell.'

The meaning of the remainder of the inscription is extremely doubtful. There are two proper names in the nominative, each bearing the title of *akenanogafos*. The rest is uncertain, except perhaps in construction. All that can be done in such a case, when comparing the Phrygian with any other language with a view to prove affinity, is to select such words in that language as resemble the Phrygian, and see if they will give a satisfactory meaning. The first clause to consider will be, *Bonok akenanogafos erekun telatos sostut*. The first two words being known, the Arm. suggests for the remaining three, consisting apparently of an acc. in -*un*, a gen. in -*os*, and a verb—

Erekun. Arm. *erk, erkn, erkch*, 'ἔργον;' *herk*, 'cultivation.'

Telatos. Arm. *thatovmn*, 'burial;' *thal*(*el*), ' to bury;' *thalar*, ' an earthen vessel, a basin;' *thal*, ' a territory;' *teli*, ' a place.' Sansk. *tal*, ' condere;' *tala*, ' solum, fundus.' Gr. θάλαμος. Lat. *tellus*. Gael. *talamh*, ' earth.' Etrusc. (as will afterwards appear) *tular*, ' a tomb.' Arab. *talhíd*, ' burying.' For the form of *telat*(*os*) from a root *tel*, compare Arm. *armat*, ' root,' th. *arm; šinaz*, ' a building,' th. *šin*(*el*), ' to build;' and for its declension, Gr. τέρας, τέρατος, or Arm. *kin, knoǵ*, ' γυνή, γυναικός.'

Sostut. Arm. *sasté,* 'he reprehends, ἐπιτιμᾷ' (Matt. viii. 26), th. *sast* = Pers. *zust,* 'strong, severe.' Sansk. *çás,* 'jubere, regere, docere, punire.' *Sostut* and *lachit* would respectively belong to conjugations like the Arm. *hetov,* 'he pours,' and *kami,* 'he wishes.'[1]

The whole clause becomes, 'Bonok the Illustrious forbids work of sepulture;' *i. e.,* no other interments were to be allowed in the same place, a common prohibition with respect to ancient tombs.

The remaining clause begins with another proper name, which Texier reads *Inanon.* Steuart reads it very differently, which is of no importance in the case of a proper name.

The two readings of the remainder are—

Tex. *akenanogafos aer atanisen kursaneson tanegirtog.*[2]
Ste. *akenanogafos atanisen kursaneson tanegertos.*
I shall take the reading to be—
akenanogafos aer atanisen kursaueson tanegertos.

The last two words seem to be an acc. and gen. As no verb appears, *sostut* is probably understood from the preceding clause. *Akenanogafos* is a known word: for the rest the Arm. would give—

Aer. Arm. *ayr,* 'man.'

Atanisen. Arm. *atean,* 'a tribunal, a magistrate, a senate;' *atenakan,* 'belonging to a tribunal, a magistrate, a judge.' I am not clear as to the termination *sen.* It might be compared with the Arm. suffix *-sén* (see *inf.*), but that ought rather to be represented in Phrygian by *-senos.*

Kursaneson. Arm. *korzanovthivn,* 'ruin, destruction,' th. *korzan.* The termination of *kursan-es(on)* might perhaps be compared with the Alb. and Arm. suffixes, *-es* and *-ié.* See *inf.* in Alb. s. v. *lezoues.*

Tanegertos. Arm. *tovn,* gen. *tan,* 'a house;' *kert,* 'a build-

---

[1] We have in Arm. both *lizé* and *lizov,* 'lingit, λείχει.'
[2] In his text, *tageirtog.* The reading of the plate is to be preferred.

ing.' *Tanegert(os)* would be a compound like *Tigranocert(a)*, 'the building of Tigranes.' Compare also Arm. *gomakert*, 'who builds (*kerto*) a stable (*gom*);' *tnasén*, 'who builds (*siné*) a house (*tovn*);' and *mezasén*, 'great (*mez*),' *archayasén*, 'built by a king (*archay*), royal, magnificent,' where *sén* = *kert* has a passive sense equivalent to *factus*. Thus the Arm. might form *tnakert*,' οἰκοδόμος, οἰκοδομή.' Compare *mezasén* and *atanisen*.

By this last clause, 'Inanon the Illustrious, a man with judicial power, forbids any injury to the sepulchre;' which coincides with the second prohibition continually found in sepulchral inscriptions.

For the whole epitaph, the actual Armenian, unmodified, would correspond with and explain the Phrygian in the following manner :—

Phryg. Kelokes fenaftun aftas materes sosesait,
                                     (2)   (1)
Arm.   Kelokés (z)anavth ivroy mavr saraseaž,
Lat.   Celoces sepulcrum suæ matris exstruxit,

Phryg. materes Epheteksetis Ofefinonoman. Lachit
Arm.   mavr Ephetéchsetay yOwewinoneay. Laké
Lat.   matris Ephetexetis ex Ofefinone. Devorat

Phryg. ga materan aresastin. Bonok akonanogafos
Arm.   kav (z)mayr arajin. Bonok akanavor
Lat.   tellus matrem præstantem. Bonocus Illustris

Phryg. erekun telutos   sostut; Inanon akenanogafos,
Arm.   (z)erkn { thalman / thalari / telvoy } sasté; Inanon akanavor,
Lat.   usum { sepulchri / urnæ / loci } vetat; Inanon Illustris,

Phryg. aer atanisen, kursaneson   tanegertos.
                                            (2)   (1)
Arm.   ayr atenakan, (z)korzanovthivn tan-kerti.
                                              (2)   (1)
Lat.   vir judicialis, destructionem domûs-structuræ.
                                                   (ædificii)

The advantage of the Armenian over the Greek in the interpretation of the Phrygian epitaphs seems sufficiently clear. It is true that one or two words are more nearly Greek than Armenian. *Aftas* is nearer to αὐτοῦ than it is to *ivroy*, and *materes* is nearer to μητρὸς than it is to *mavr*. But such partial resemblances would be frequently delusive, if relied on, and lead to very erroneous ethnological results. Thus, to take exactly parallel cases, the Germ. *sein* and *seinige* are nearer to the Fr. *sien* than to the Eng. *his;* and the Lat. *mater, matris*, are nearer to the Eng. *mother, mother's*, and the Germ. *mutter, mutters*, than they are to the Fr. *mère, de la mère*. It must also be remembered that, while the Phrygian and Greek are ancient languages, the Armenian, in the oldest form that we possess it, is comparatively modern.

The conjugation of Phrygian verbs is Armenian rather than Greek, as appears in *edaes* and *sosesait;* but the declension of Phrygian nouns, on the other hand, is more Greek than Armenian. Yet what the Armenian is here deficient in, are merely such Aryan characteristics as are easily lost, as will appear by the following table of declensions. Here I have illustrated the Phrygian declensions, by comparing them with Armenian, Sanskrit, Etruscan, Greek, and Latin declensions. From the Armenian declensions, which are very numerous, I have selected the most common, as exemplified in *Movzay,* 'Musa,' which is regularly declined, though a borrowed word; *san*, 'a nurseling, a godson;' *Levonidés*, 'Leonidas;' *Anahit,* 'Anaïtis;' *anakht*, 'purus;' *armat*, 'radix;' *kin*, 'femina;' *ayd,* 'is, ea, id;' *sireli*, 'amandus, -a, -um;' and *nav,* 'navis.' In the Sanskrit, I have taken the two regular types, *nau,* 'navis,' and *harit,* 'viridis.' As we do not seem to meet with any Phrygian plurals, I have not given any in Armenian. The Armenian plural is usually formed thus: in the nom. and instr., *ch* (χ) is added to those cases in the sing.: iu the acc., *s* is added to the nom. or acc. sing.: and in the gen., dat., and abl., *z̄*, preceded by some vowel or diphthong, is added to the nom. sing.

	Sanskrit.		Latin.		Greek.		Etruscan.	
Nom...	navs	haris	navis	nusa	ναῦς	μοῦσα	Velthina	Ramtha	nav
Gen...	nâvas	harilas	navis	musae	νηός	μούσης	Velthinas	Ramthai	navi	lisisi
Dat...	nâve	harile	navi	musae	νηΐ	μούσῃ			navi
Acc...	nâvam	harilam	navem	musam	ναῦν	μοῦσαν	Velthinam	Ramthn	nav
Abl...	nâvas	harilas	nave	musâ	νηός	μούσης			nave	gonafepos
Inst...	nâvâ	harilâ	nave	musâ		μούσης			navav

			Phrygian.					
Nom...	ga	Ales	Kelokes			telaios	armat	kin	ayd
Gen...	aflas		gofaglaci	Midas	fanaktei	femaftun	armatos	knof	aydr	crekus
Dat...					areaustin		armatoy	knof	aydm	sireli nav
Acc...							armat	kin	ayd	sirelog navi
Abl...	Sikeman						armatos	knofé	aydmané	sirelog navi
Inst...					Ogfnomomas		armatov	knav	aydov	sirelin nav
										sireleav navav

			Armenian.					
Nom...	Movzay	san	Levonidés	Anahit	Anahlay				
Gen...	Movzayi	sanov	Levonideay	Anahlay	Anakhti				
Dat...	Movzayi	sanov	Levonideay	Anahlay	anakhti				
Acc...	Movzay	san	Levonidés	Anahit	anakhit				
Abl...	Movzayé	sané	Levonideay	Anahlay	anakhté				
Inst...	Movzayiv	sanov	Levonideav	Anahlav	anakhtiv				

Although the resemblance between the Phrygian and Armenian languages may not be always perfect, yet it is, I think, sufficiently close to confirm the opinion of the ancients, that the Phrygians and Armenians were of the same race, and that the Armenian language was like the Phrygian in many points. The Latin would hardly, under similar circumstances, approach the Greek more nearly than the Armenian does the Phrygian, as may be readily tested by the aid of the Phrygian inscriptions and vocabulary. Take, for instance, the meaning of the first six words in the vocabulary, φίλον, πώγωνα, ἰατρόν, κλεπτρίαν ἀλετρίδα, λάμιαν, and πόλεμον. The affinity to the Latin is here by no means complete or remarkable. So, on the other hand, if we take what seems the correct interpretation of the Phrygian *Kelokes fenaftun aftas materes sosesait*, i.e., *Celoces sepulchrum suæ matris exstruxit*, we shall perceive little obvious affinity in these Latin words to the Greek, either in root or form, except in *matris*.

There appears to be no other language but the Armenian so near the Phrygian as to claim to belong to the same Aryan family. The next in order of affinity would probably be the Persian. Yet both the classic languages exhibit some signs of affinity to the Phrygian, although of a different family; such instances of affinity being probably either Aryan generally, or Thracian words borrowed from the Pelasgians and Etruscans by the nations of the Classic or Old Italian stock, the Latins, Oscans, and Hellenes. Ἄναξ I have already noticed. *Nænia* and *lituus* are Phrygian, but not really Greek. *Soccus* is Armenian, Phrygian, Greek, and Latin. Ἔλεγος is Greek, Armenian, Phrygian, and probably also Lydian. The roots of *soccus* and ἔλεγος are Armenian. The Phrygian words, *mater* and *ga*, are Aryan generally. From these affinities we may begin to perceive the position which the Thracian race once held in Europe, and its influence upon the other inhabitants of Greece and Italy.

The Phrygian language is succeeded by the Lydian, which

represents, in addition to itself, and in conjunction with the Phrygian, the Mysian language also, which is described as μιξολύδιον καὶ μιξοφρύγιον. Some of the words transmitted as Lydian are of a doubtful character, and their interpretation is not always obvious. Others, on the contrary, are of peculiar weight in an ethnological disquisition. Two may be especially mentioned, κανδαύλης and πανδούριον; both of which, besides being Armenian, and one of them Assyrian, appear to have travelled far westward into Europe, where the first may be recognised in Rhætian Switzerland, as well as in Albania, and the second in Spain, a country still more remote from Assyria and Armenia. Σάρδις is another Lydian word which may deserve more particular attention, as it intimates that there was an ancient form of the Armenian language still closer to the Lydian than the literary Armenian is, which, although it is the oldest form we possess, only extends back about 1500 years.

Lydian Words.

1. 'Αγκών, 'τείχους γωνία.' Arm. *ankivn,* ' corner, angle.' Gr. ἀγκών. Lat. *angulus.* Germ. *winkel.*

2. Ἄκυλον, ' βάλανον πρινίνην.' Arm. *katin,* ' an acorn.' Germ. *eichel.* Lat. *galla.* Pers. *gulúk,* ' pease, a ball.'

3. 'Αρφύταινον, ' δίσκος.' Rhæt.-Rom. *arfüdar;* Pied. *arfudè;* ' to reject.' Lat. *repudio.* Macedon. ἀρφύς, ' ἱμάς.' Arm. *phouthal,* ' to hasten ' (ἵημι); *ar,* ' to '; *ar-achel,* ' to despatch ' (*ach,* ' a leg '); *arkanel,* ' to throw ;' *ar-arkanel,* ' to oppose.' *Ar-phouthal,* therefore, = ' *accelerare.*'

4. " Hesychius: 'Αστραλίαν τὸν Θρᾷκα Λυδοί. Sequitur: ἀστραλὸς ὁ ψαρὸς ὑπὸ Θετταλῶν.——Thruces a loquacitate et garrulitate vel quod lingua uterentur Lydis non intellecta sturnaceos appellatos crediderim. Pers. *bástarak,* ' a starling.' " Arm. *sareak, tarm,* ' a starling ;' *sarel,* ' to cry ;' *sarol,* ' crying.' Alb. *tserlë,* ' a blackbird.'

5. Ἄτταλος, ' παῦσις.' Arm. *kateal,* ' cut ' (cf. κόμμα) ;

ënd-katel, 'to interrupt, to cease,' pres. and past part. ënd-katol and ënd-kateal. Lapp. ajetet, 'detinere;' ajeteje, 'morator.'

6. "Attis, 'scitulus.' Vide ii. (i. e. Phryg.) 7. Quum ex Hesychio glossa ceteroquin sat obscura id eluceat nomen etiam Hattes pronunciatum fuisse, Arm. kat, 'sectio, pars, granum,' hatanel, 'secare, perrumpere, decidere,' hatanil, 'secari, cessare, micare, desperare,' in auxilium voco."

7. "Hesychius: βαϑνρρηγάλη ἰκτῖνος ὑπὸ Λυδῶν. Quum nos avem aliquem rapacem nominemus entenstösser, inesse putarim Pers. bath vel bat, Arm. bad, 'anas.' De parte altera nihil definio, licet βρηγάλη emendare suadeam." The termination of this Lydian word may be explained from the Arm. arag, 'swift;' aragil, 'a stork:' Etrusc. aracus, 'ἱέραξ.' See inf. in Etrusc. s. v. aracus.

8. "Hesychius: βάκκαρις μύρον ποιὸν ἀπὸ βοτάνης ὁμωνύμον, ἔνιοι δὲ ἀπὸ μυρσίνης, ἄλλοι δὲ μύρον λύδιον. Ἔστι δὲ καὶ ξηρὸν διάπασμα τὸ ἀπὸ τῆς ῥίζης. Pollux vii. 104: μύρα ᾔδεσαν καὶ βάκκαριν καὶ ἀμάρακον καὶ ἴρινον." Pers. bukhár, 'perfume, odour.' Arab. bukhár, 'vapour.'——Lat. bacca. Gael. bachar, 'an acorn.' Arm. baklay; Pers. bakhlah; Arab. báklây; 'a bean.' Pers. bakhkalah, 'a walnut.'

9. "Hesychius: βασανιστὴς λίϑος οὕτω λέγεται λυδικοῦ λίϑον γένος καὶ λίϑος βάσανος, ᾧ παρατρίβοντες τὸ χρυσίον ἐδοκίμαζον. Sansk. pásáña ('lapis')." Arm. yesan, 'a grindstone,' = Pers. asyánah, = Sansk. çáña.

10. Βασάρα. See inf. in Thrac. s. v. bassara.

11. "Hesychius: βάσκε πικρολία πλησίον ἐξεϑόαζε λυδιστί et βάστιζα κρόλεα ϑᾶσσον ἔρχου λυδιστί. Utrumque corruptum.——Sansk. vága, 'festinatio.'" Arm. wazel, 'to hasten.' Arab. baskay, 'going fast.' For πικρολία, see ante in Phryg. s. v. πικίριον.

12. Βρένϑιον, 'μύρον.' Arm. bovrel, 'to exhale, to smell;' bovroumn, 'odour.' Rhæt.-Rom. brainta, 'mist.' Eng. breath.

13. Βρίγες, 'ἐλεύϑεροι.' Arm. phrkel, 'to deliver.' Eng. free.

14. "Festus viii. p. 99: '*helvacea* genus ornamenti lydii dictum a colore boum, qui est inter rufum et album appellaturque *helvus*.' Non est lydicum quia si esset per ζ inciperet, cf. Sansk. *harit*, Lith. *żalas*, Pers. *zird* ('viridis')." Esth. *hal*, 'grey;' *haljas*, 'green, bright, shining.' Arm. *aluv, alovakan*, 'soft, tender, delicate;' *alót*, 'feeble, indistinct, obscure, less bright;' *alorés*, 'a fox.'

15. "Hesychius: ἴβρι (read ἴβυ) τινὲς τὸ βοάν, οἱ δὲ τὸ πολύ. Ἔστι δὲ Λυδῶν." See *inf.* in Scyth. s. v. *ἄβις*, and *ante* in Phryg. s. v. βαγαῖος.

16. Ἴμβους. See *inf.* in Thrac. s. v. ζόμβρον.

17. Ἴωπι, 'δεῦρο.' Arm. *hovp*, 'near;' *hovp linel*, 'to approach.'

18. Κανδαύλης, 'σκυλλοπνίκτης, κυνάγχη.' "Arm. *khendel*, 'πνίγειν,' et *khendol* (otherwise *khendavl* and *khendól*), 'πνίγων.'" Aucher gives *kheldel*, instead of *khendel*, as does also the great *Arm. and Lat. Dict.;* but *l* represents *n* in the kindred Asiatic languages (*Arica*, pp. 90, 91. See also Rawlinson, *Asiat. Journ. Behist. Inscript.* p. 34). Alb. *kyendis*, 'I choke.' Rhæt.-Rom. *candarials*, 'a disease of the glands, which severely oppresses the breathing' (eine Art Drüsenübel, das das Athmen sehr erschwert). By this word, the languages of Armenia, Lydia, Illyria, and Rhætia are connected together. The Arm. participial termination, *avl, ól, or ol*, may also be recognised in κανδ-αύλ(ης). Similar forms in *l*, so characteristic of the Armenian and Etruscan languages, may not improbably be discerned in the Lydian words, ἀστρ-αλ(ία), ἀττ-αλ(ος), βαθυρρήγ-αλ(η), and πικρ-ολ(ία). There is another derivation of κανδαύλης from the Sansk. *çvan*, 'canis,' and *dhú*, 'agitare, vexare.'

19. "Athenæus xii. p. 516 CD: κάνδαυλόν τινα ἔλεγον οἱ Λυδοὶ οὐχ ἕνα ἀλλὰ τρεῖς, οὕτως ἐξήσκηντο πρὸς τὰς ἡδυπαθείας. Γίνεσθαι δ'αὐτόν φησιν ὁ ταραντῖνος Ἡγήσιππος ἐξ ἐφθοῦ κρέως καὶ κνηστοῦ ἄρτου καὶ φρυγίου τυροῦ ἀνήθου τε καὶ ζωμοῦ πίονος. Pollux vi. 69: εἴη δ'ἂν προσῆκον τοῖς ἡδύ-

σμασι και ὁ κάνδυλος ἐξ ἀμύλου και τυροῦ και γάλακτος και μέλιτος." Perhaps from the same root as κανδαύλης : or the Arm. *kandal*, 'to desire greatly,' might be suggested.

20. "Athenæus xii. p. 516 C: πρῶτοι Λυδοὶ τὴν καρύκην ἐξεῦρον. Suidas: καρύκη ἔδεσμα ἐκ πολλῶν συγκείμενων. βρῶμα λύδιον ἐξ αἵματος και ἄλλων ἰδεσμάτων . . . και καρυκοποιεῖν τὸ κοσμεῖν ποικιλίᾳ τινι ῥημάτων τὸν λόγον. Sansk. *krī*, 'κιρᾶν,' unde Sansk. *karbura* et Arm. *kharn*, 'varius.'"

21. "Stephanus Byzantinus: Καστωλοὺς Δωριεῖς οἱ Λυδοί φασιν. Augurer nomen litoris accolas significare." Arm. *kovsht, koys*, 'side.' Lat. *costa*. Eng. *coast*. The termination -ωλός might be explained as in κανδ-αύλης.

22. Κοαλαδεῖν, 'βασιλέα.' "Quum habeamus apud eundem (Hesychium) κοαλιεῖν, 'βάρβαρον ἔθνος,' et κόαλοι, 'βάρβαροι,' si notissimi illius δεῖνος, 'βασιλεύς,' memineremus, 'populi regem' interpretari possumus." Gael. *cuallas*; Arm. *žołow*; 'an assembly;' Arm. *žołovovrd*, 'people, multitude.' Osset. *koar*, 'company, multitude.' Pers. *galak*, 'a crowd.' —— Gael. *dion*, 'præsidium;' *dein*, 'fortis.' Pers. *tanu*, 'power.' Arab. *dīn*, 'faith, religion, decree, empire, king.' Arm. *den*, 'faith, religion.' Arm. *atean*, 'a tribunal, a magistrate.'[1]

23. Λάβρυν, 'πέλεκυν.' Lapp. *labtet*, 'findere;' *labmet*, 'verberare.' Pers. *lab*, 'a blow.' Arab. *labt*, 'striking.'

24. Λαῖλας, 'ὁ τύραννος, ὁ μὴ ἐκ γένους τύραννος.' Hindustani *lālā*, 'a master.' Pers. *lālak*, 'a crown.' Arm. *lav*, 'good, fine, better.'——Esth. *läila*, 'bad, severe.' Gr. λαῖλαψ. Arm. *llkel*, 'to vex, torment.' Sansk. *lul*, 'agitare, perturbare.'

25. Μαυλιστήριον, 'λύδιον λέμισμα λεπτόν τι.' "Varie emendaverunt νόμισμα, λέπισμα, μέλισμα." Arm. *matzmay*, 'a plate.'

---

[1] Compare Gael. *basal*, 'a judge,' with βασιλεύς.

26. Μηδεύς, 'ὁ Ζεύς.' "Sansk. *medhas*, in Vedis dei excelsi titulus, *medhira*, ' sapiens.'" Arm. *mtaẃi, mtavor*, ' sapiens.'

27. Μυσός, 'ὀξύη.' Georg. *mukhi*, 'an oak.' Arm. *motay*, 'a tamarisk,' = Gr. μυρίκη. Kurd. *mitẃk*, 'a box-tree.' The name of *Mysia* was supposed to be derived from μυσός. If we may trust Homer, the tamarisk was common in the Troad. See *Il.* vi. 39; x. 466; xxi. 18, 350.

28. Μῶλαξ, 'εἶδος οἴνου.' Gipsy *mol*, 'wine.' Pers. *mul*, 'wine.' Arm. *moli*, 'intoxicated.'

29. Μωύς, 'ἡ γῆ.' Esth. *ma*, 'earth, land.' Lapp. *mdiwe*, 'pulvis.' Georg. *miža*, 'earth.' Lesgi, *misa*, *mussa*, 'earth.'

30. " Photius s. v. Νύμφαι : καὶ αἱ Μοῦσαι δὲ ὑπὸ Λυδῶν νύμφαι. Stephanus Byz. s. v. Τόρρηβος : φθογγῆς Νυμφῶν ἀκούσας, ἃς καὶ Μούσας Λυδοὶ καλοῦσι. Utrum verum alii dicant." Cf. Arm. *novag*, 'a song;' *noval*, 'to mew;' Pers. *nuwá*, 'voice, modulation;' *nuwág*, 'singer, musician.'

31. Νύχμα, 'ὄνειδος.' Arm. *nakhat*, 'reproach, disgrace.' Pers. *nákas*, 'worthless, base.' Arab. *nakúh*, 'contempt.'

32. Πάλμυς, 'βασιλεύς.' See *ante* in Phryg. s. v. βαλήν.

33. " Πανδούριον, ' λύδιον ὄργανον χωρὶς πλήκτρου ψαλλομένου.' Pollux iv. 60 : τρίχορδον 'Ασσύριοι πανδοῦραν ὠνόμαζον. Arm. *phandirn*. Osset. *fandur*. Ital. *mandora*." *Phandirn* signifies 'a trumpet.' The Arm. has also *bandirn* or *bambirn* or *phambirn*, 'castanets,' and *bamb*, 'thorough-base.' Span. *pandero*, 'a tabor,' *pandorga*, 'a concert.'

34. Παραμήνη, 'ἡ τῶν θεῶν μοῖρα.' " Sansk. *parimá*, ' destinare, decernere;' subst. *parimáña*. Etiam apud Armenos *para* quod Sansk. *pari*; sic (Sansk.) *paridhí* = (Arm.) *paraditel* et περιφέρεια = (Arm.) *paraberouthivn*." Arm. *hramayel*, 'to ordain;' *kraman*, 'a decree,' = Pers. *farmán*, = Sansk. *pramáña*.

35. " Servius *Æn.* x. 179. Alii incolas ejus oppidi Teutas fuisse et ipsum oppidum Teutam nominatum, quod postea *Pisas* Lydi lingua sua lunarem (al. singularem) portum significare dixerunt, quare huic urbi a *portu lunæ* nomen im-

positum." If we read *pis-æ*, the Turkish would give *ay*, 'luna;' and if we read *pi-sæ*, the Mantschu would give *pia*, 'luna,' and also *saia*, 'lebes,' = Lapp. *saja*, = Arm. *san*. Cf. Germ. *hafen*, 'pot, haven, port.' The Arm. has—*aph*, 'the hollow of the hand ;' *aphn*, 'a shore ;' and *aphsé* or *aphseay*, 'a bowl ;' perhaps = *pis-*. The Finnish or Turanian element in Asia Minor, which seems to be discerned beneath the Thracian in Phrygia and Lydia, will appear more plainly beyond the Taurus in Lycia. The Lydians of Servius are evidently the Etruscans.

36. "Johannes Laurentius Lydus mens. 3, 14: νίον σάρδιν τὸ νίον ἔτος ἔτι καὶ νῦν λέγεσθαι τῷ πλήθει συνομολογεῖται· εἰσὶ δὲ, οἵ φασι τῇ Λυδῶν ἀρχαίᾳ φωνῇ τὸν ἐνιαυτὸν καλεῖσθαι σάρδιν." Bötticher notices (p. 26) that *sard* would once have signified 'year' in Arm., as the ancient name of what was formerly the first month in the Armenian year was *Navasard*. It nearly corresponded to our August, and in all probability signified 'New-year,' *Nav-sard*. In Arm., *dar* and *tari* signify 'age' and 'year,' the sibilant in the more ancient form *sard*, having apparently been hardened. *Dar* and *sar* have still the same meaning in Arm., *i.e.*, 'height.' The Chaldæan *sar* (σάρος), in Arm. *sar* (Euseb. *Chron.*), containing a fabulous period of 3600 years (ten kings reign 120 *sari*), may be the same word. Compare also Arm. *sar*, 'series, rank, chain,' = Germ. *schar*, Ital. *schiera*. With regard to the final *d* in *sard*, it is one of the three letters, *s*, *d*, and *n*, which are frequently added in Arm. Thus we have *spand*, 'slaughter,' instead of *span*. In Ossetic, *särd* or *särde* means 'summer.'

The following are the names of the ancient Armenian months[1]:—

1. *Navasard* (Aug.)   Lyd. νίος σάρδις, 'νίον ἔτος.'
2. *Hori* (Sept.)   { Georg. *ori*, 'two,' Cf. Mantschu *oris*, 'twenty,' and Arm. *erkov*, 'two.'
3. *Sahmi* (Oct.)   .   Georg. *sami*, 'three.'

---

[1] I am partly indebted here to an article in the *Journal Asiatique* for 1832, vol. x. p. 527.

4. *Tré* (Nov.)	Cappad. Τίριξ; Pers. *Tír;* Georg. *Tiristini;* Zend *Tistrja;* 'the name of the fourth month.'
5. *Chałoż* (Dec.)	Arm. *chał-el,* 'to gather, to amass, to squeeze, to weed,'——*chałżov,* 'must (of wine).' The root of *Chałoż* ought to be *chał. Chałoż,* '*Vendémiaire.*' (?)
6. *Araż* (Jan.)	Arab. *aríz,* 'frost, hoar-frost;' whence *Araż = Frimaire.*
7. *Mehekan* or *Meheki* (Feb.)	Zend *Mithra* (Pers. *Mihr);* Cappad. Μιθρί; 'the name of the 7th month.' Arm. *Mihir,* 'Mithras;' *mehean,* 'a temple;' th. *meh.* The Arm. *Mehekan* would not be borrowed from the Zend, but derived from a common origin with it.
8. *Areg* (March)	Arm. *areg,* 'the sun.'
9. *Ahekan* (April)	Arm. *ahekan,* 'on the left hand, *sinister.*'
10. *Mareri* (May)	Georg. *mareli,* 'the name of the 10th month.'
11. *Margaż* (June)	Arm. *marg,* 'a meadow;' whence *Margaż = Prairial.*
12. *Hrotiż* (July)	Arm. *hrovt,* 'burning;' *hrat,* 'excessive heat:' whence *Hrotiż = Thermidor.*

Of the twelve names of the Armenian months, six may be known to be genuine Armenian, either by root or form, or by both—*Chałoż, Mehekan, Areg, Ahekan, Margaż,* and *Hrotiż.* Three others, *Hori, Sahmi,* and *Mareri,* are Georgian. *Araż* seems Arabic, though its form is Armenian. *Tré* may be considered as Persian: and *Navasard* would be allied to the Lydian, though probably at the same time ancient Armenian.

37. "Τάργανον, ὄζος· Λυδοί. ἢ τὸ ταράττον. ἢ τὸ ἀπὸ στεμφύλων πόμα. καὶ πόα, ἢ καὶ σκορπιοῦρος. Heinsius et Salmasius ὄξος scripserunt." Pers. *tarkhwánah,* 'thick pot-

tage;' *tarkhan*, 'milk soured;' *tarkh*, 'an orange.' Arab. *darrak*, 'treacle, wine.' Esth. *tarri*, 'grapes, berries.' Arm. *taraz*, 'agaric.'——Pers. *tarsán*, 'timid, fearful.' Arm. *tartam*, 'timid, perplexed.'

38. Τεγοῦν, 'λῃστήν.' Arm. *tég*, 'a spear.' Esth. *tägi*, 'a pike, a sword.' Τεγοῦν, like *latro*, might signify 'swordsman' or 'soldier,' as well as 'robber.'

The affinities of the Lydians appear from their language to be the same as those of the Phrygians. Both nations may be classed in the same family as the Armenians, and the Aryan family next in order of relationship would be the Persian. I cannot perceive that near affinity between the Lydian and Greek languages which Mr. Rawlinson's ethnological system would require. There is, indeed, the word ἀγκών given as Lydian: but the root is common to many languages, the termination goes for little in a vocabulary, the reporter is a Greek, and the Arm. *ankivn*, 'ἀγκών,' would be written ἀγκύν in Greek. If 'the Lydians must have spoken a language closely akin to the Pelasgic,' which 'ripened ultimately into the Hellenic,' we could hardly fail to observe more decided Greek affinities in thirty-eight Lydian words than we are able to discover.

As the Carians are so nearly connected with the Mysians and Lydians, the few words which have been preserved in the Carian language may as well be added here.

Carian Words.

1. Ἄλα, 'ἵππος.' Gael. *al*, 'a horse.' Alb. *ala*, 'quick.' Arm. *wal*, 'quick.' Arab. *walus*, 'going quick' (a camel).

2. Βάνδα, 'νίκη.' Arm. *wan-el*, 'to conquer.' For the -δ-, compare *span-anel*, 'to kill,' and *spand*, 'slaughter.' Pers. *wand*, 'praise.'

3. Γέλα, 'βασιλεύς.' Arm. *gel*, 'beauty;' *gelani*, 'fair, good.' Cf. Gr. γελέω and γελέοντες——Arm. *cheti*, 'temo, gubernaculum.'

4. Γίσσα, 'λίθος.' Arm. *kiǵ*, 'marble.' Γίσσα appeared in Μονόγισσα, the name of a Carian town. Cf. Arm. *moyn*, 'beauty.' *Gissa* was an Illyrian town, *Cissa* a Thracian town, and *Cissus* a Macedonian mountain.

5. Κολαβρισμός, 'Θράκιον ὄρχημα καὶ καρικόν.' See *inf.* in Thrac. s. v.

6. " Machon apud Athenæum xiii. p. 580 D :

κύβδ᾽ ἔφη τριωβόλου.

τίς δ᾽ οὐπετρέψων ἐστί σοι, φησὶν, τάλαν

ὄντα γ᾽ ἐν Ἀθήναις καρικοῖς χρῆσθαι σταθμοῖς;

Forsan cognatum καπίθη: v. Persica."

" Xenophon *Anab.* i. 5, 6 : πρίασθαι οὐκ ἦν εἰ μὴ ἐν τῇ λυδίᾳ ἀγορᾷ ἐν τῷ Κύρου βαρβαρικῷ τὴν καπίθην ἀλεύρων ἢ ἀλφίτων τεττάρων σίγλων. Ὁ δὲ σίγλος δύναται ἑπτὰ ὀβολοὺς καὶ ἡμιοβόλιον ἀττικούς, ἡ δὲ καπίθη δύο χοίνικας ἀττικὰς ἐχώρει. Polyænus iv. 3, 32 : ἡ καπίτις ἐστὶ χοῖνιξ ἀττική. Pollux iv. 168 μέτρων ὀνόματα recensens: καπίθη ὡς Ξενοφῶν." Arm. *kapiǵ*, gen. *kapǵi*, 'a kind of measure (κάβος, χοῖνιξ, χοῦς, congius*), the socket of the eye ;' th. *kap*, = Lat. *cap(ere)* ; *kapel*, 'to fasten ;' *kapovt*, 'plunder ;' *kaptel*, 'to plunder.' Heb. *kab*.

7. Σοῦα, 'τάφος.' Arm. *sovzanel*, 'condere, tegere,' th. *sovz* ; *šov*, 'a ceiling, a roof (*lectum*).'

8. Τουσσύλοι, 'Πυγμαῖοι.' Osset. *tyüsül*, 'little,' = Arm. *doyzn*. Arm. *thzovk*, 'a pygmy,' th. *thiz*, 'a span.' Κάττουζα, 'πόλις Θρᾴκης, ἐν ᾗ κατῴκουν οἱ Πυγμαῖοι.' Arm. *kay*, 'dwelling.' Pers. *kad*, 'house.' Osset. *ghau, qau*, 'village.'

9. " Stephanus : Τυμνησσὸς πόλις Καρίας ἀπὸ τυμνησσοῦ ῥάβδου. Ξάνθιοι γὰρ τὴν ῥάβδον τυμνίαν λέγουσιν." Arm. *tophel*, 'τύπτειν.' Eng. *thump*. Arm. *šorp*, 'stick, rod.'

The Lycians and the Caucasian Nations.

The singular resemblance of the Carian τουσσύλ(οι) to the Ossetic *tyüsül* (where *ty* is a single letter) raises a question of considerable interest, which calls here for a digression. The language of the Lycians, the neighbours of the Carians, cannot be explained from the Armenian, especially in its structure, where in the affluence of vowels the Lycian resembles the Zend, and presents a remarkable contrast to the Armenian. No language, however, of any kind, has hitherto been found to explain the Lycian. In this failure of all ordinary languages, and especially of the Armenian, we may be led, from our finding the Osset. *tyüsül*, rather than the Arm. *doyzn, thiz*, or *thzovk*, in the τουσσύλος of Caria, a country bordering on Lycia, to enquire whether the Lycian language was allied to the Ossetic, or to any other language used in the Caucasus. The Ossetic vocabulary, as we possess it, is not very extensive; but the grammar is well known, as we have an excellent treatise on the language in Sjögren's *Ossetische Sprachlehre*.

The Ossetes are commonly considered, but not incontestably admitted, to be a branch of the Aryan stock. The rest of the Caucasus is occupied, with the exception of some Turkish settlers round Mount Elbruz, by the Caucasian race. This is divided into three branches, differing greatly from each other, and separated by dialects into many subdivisions. The West-Caucasians possess about one-half of the chain: they are divided into Circassians and Abasians. The *Zychi* and *Achæi* of the ancients, two tribes who dwelt in this district on the Euxine, have been supposed to derive their names from the Circassian *zug* or *dzyg*, and the Abasian *agu*, both signifying 'man.' Next in order come the Ossetes, who occupy a small tract on both sides of the chain, in its centre. The sources of the rivers Terek and Aragua, and the intervening great Caucasian pass of Dariel, lie in their country. The two divisions of the *Ossetes*, in language, are the *Digori* and *Tagauri*. These names seem to be found in those of the *Issi* and *Tagori*, two Scythian tribes to the east of the Tanais, mentioned by Pliny. The root of the name *Issi* may be the Osset. *osse*, 'woman,' or rather the Lesgi *oss*, 'people.' In Osset., *ossethä* means 'women.' In the same parts Ptolemy mentions the *Tusci*:

and on the central ridge of the Caucasus, within twenty miles of the Ossetes, and bordering on the Lesgi, who will be mentioned presently, we find a little tribe called *Tuschi*, belonging to the Middle-Caucasian race, the Mizdschegi or Kisti. The East-Caucasian race, the Lesgi, occupy a large portion of the ancient Albania, where, according to Strabo, twenty-six languages were spoken: the dialects of the Lesgi are nearly half as many. These Lesgi, called by the Georgians *Lekhethi*, and by the Armenians *Lékch*, are the *Leges* or *Legæ* of antiquity; and the root of their name would probably be found in the Osset. *läg* or *lag*, or the Lesgi *les*, 'man.'[1] Glossaries of the Caucasian dialects, necessarily scanty, have been formed by Klaproth. Specimens are also given in an *Account of the Caucasian Nations* (London, 1788).[2]

Between the Caucasians and Ossetes on the north, and the Armenians on the south, lies the Iberian or Georgian race, divided into Georgians, Mingrelians, Lazi, and Suani. The last two names are ancient, and the *Lazi* are probably the 'men.' The Suani connect the Iberians with the West-Caucasians, and the Tuschi and two other little tribes are considered to be Iberian as well as Middle-Caucasian. A tolerably copious Georgian vocabulary has been published by Klaproth.

The country occupied by the Caucasian nations has a length of about 600, and a breadth of about 100 miles. The area would be equal to that of England. The Armenian area would be about the same, and the Georgian nearly that of Ireland.

---

[1] So the meaning of the name *Mardi* is given by the Arm. and Pers. *mard*, 'man,' i.e. βροτὸς: Osset. *mard*, 'death.'

[2] Can the name of the *Ossetes*, if = *ossethā*, 'women,' in any way explain the story of the Amazons, who are placed nearly in the country of the Ossetes (Strabo, p. 503)? The fabulous Amazons in Asia Minor, who are said to have founded Ephesus, Smyrna, and other towns, might then be the mythic representatives of the Caucasians in that country. Some of the Amazonian traditions are noticed above, p. 7, note 4.

Lycian inscriptions.

The Lycian inscriptions have been elucidated by Mr. Sharpe in Sir C. Fellows' *Lycia* and in Spratt and Forbes' *Lycia*, by Grotefend in the *Zeitschrift für die Kunde des Morgenlandes*, v. iv., and by Lassen in the *Zeitschrift der Deutschen morgenlandischen Gesellschaft*, v. x. A resemblance has been traced between the Lycian and the Zend, but Lassen considers that the two languages have no intimate affinity (*innigere Verwandschaft*). This limits the field of enquiry towards the east, and the obviously un-Semitic character of the Lycian will exclude the Syriac and other cognate languages. There remain, in the immediate neighbourhood of Lycia, on the west the Greek language, and on the north of Greece and Lycia various Thracian dialects. As neither Thracian, *i. e.*, Armenian, nor Greek will explain the Lycian, and as no Aryan European, as well as Asiatic, language seems likely to do so, and as on the south of the Aryan country we fall into Semitic dialects, it is therefore to the north of the Aryans that we are induced to look for the ancestors of the Lycians.

The *data* for the determination of the Lycian language are singularly good. We have three bilingual, as well as a number of other epitaphs. These contain words of the greatest importance, such as terms of relationship, besides a variety of expressions for 'tomb.' In the three bilingual epitaphs, which here follow, the Lycian epitaph is in the original completely given, and then followed in like manner by the Greek. I have altered this arrangement for the sake of comparison.

I. *ewéeya   érafazeya   méte   prinafatu   Sederéya*
               το μνημα τοδε   εποιησατο   Σιδαριος
    this   tomb   here   made   Sidarius

Pé . . . neu   ledéeme   urppe   étle éuwe sé   lade
Παρμεντος   υιος   εαυτωι   και τηι γυναικι
of Parmens   the son   for   self his and   wife

50   THE ARMENIAN ORIGIN OF THE ETRUSCANS.

éwwe   *sé ledéeme*   P . é . léyé.
        και   νιωι   Πυβιαληι.
his   and   son   Pybiales.

II. *éwuinu   italu   méné   prinafútu   Polénida*
    τουτο   το μνημα   εργασαντο   Απολλωνιδης
    this   tomb   here   made   Apollonides
Mollewéséu   sé   Lapara   Polénidau   Porewemétéu
Μολλισιος   και   Λαπαρας   Απολλωνιδου   Πυριματιος
of Mollises,   and   Laparas   of Apollonides,   of Purimates
prinézeyéwe   urppe   lada   épitéwé   sé   ledéemé
οικειοι   επι ταις γυναιξιν   ταις εαυτων   και τοις εγγονοις
the domestics, for   wives   their   and children.
sé   eyé   tesé   retúleteé   italu   éwéwe   méeyé
και   αν   τις   αδικησηι   το μνημα   τουτο
and   if   any one   injures   tomb   this   here
(*oéte   ponamakke   adadawa(l)e   ada   4*)
(εξωλεα   και πανωλεα   ιη αυτωι   παντων)

The Lycian and Greek in brackets do not correspond. We find in other epitaphs—the references are to Fellows' *Lycia*—
sé eyé italadu tése meite adadawéle ada II (p. 482).
(and if buries any one here let him pay adas two).
and—
sé eyé italadu meite adadéwale ada O—(p. 483).
and—
sé eyé italútu tése meite adadawale ada III. (p. 486).

There is a fac-simile of the third bilingual epitaph in the Lycian room in the British Museum. In the only part which is of additional importance, the Greek does not enable us to arrive at a literal translation of the Lycian. What I have given as such is therefore partly conjectural.

III. *éwuinu   prinufo   méte   prinafatu   -utta   ulau*
        τουτο το μνημα   ηργασατο   Ιτασλα
        this   tomb   here   made   -utta of Ula
ledéeme   urppe   lade éwe
    Αντιφελλιτης   αυτωι   και   γυναικι
the son,   an Antiphellitan,   for   self   and   wife his

THE ARMENIAN ORIGIN OF THE ETRUSCANS.   51

sé	*tedéemé*	*éuweé*	*sé*	*eyé*	*teéde*	*teké*	*mutu*
και	τεκνοις		εαν	δε	τις		
and	children	his.	And	if	any one makes a purchase

méné	*wastto*	*une*	*ulawe*	*éweyéue*	*séeĉareſéu.téze*
αδικησηι	η αγορασηι		το μνημα		η λητω αυτο. επιτν.
here,	injures	or	tomb		this,

The words in the preceding inscriptions which are most important ethnologically are obviously the words of relationship, *tedéeme*, 'son,' and *lade*, 'wife,' which are neither Aryan nor Semitic. They may, I think, be shown to be Caucasian; and Caucasian terms for 'wife' and 'son' seem also to be found in Armenian by the side of the Aryan words, *kin*, 'γυνή,' and *ordi*, '*putra, puer*.' The chief difficulty in the comparison lies in constructing the perfect form of the Caucasian word from so many different dialects. I have therefore not merely cited the Caucasian terms, but also analysed them, in the more important comparisons of the following list—

éweéya, éwówe, éweyéwe, éwuinu, 'this.' The first term is supposed to be a fem. acc. case, and the fourth a neut. acc. Osset. *ay*, 'this' (nom.), *ay, ayyi, ayyey*, (gen. and acc.: there are no genders). Lesgi *kai, hoi, ua*, 'this.' Kisti *woye*, 'he.' Georg. *ese*, 'this, he.' Kurd. *au, ava*, 'this;' *au, avi*, 'that;' Alb. *aï, ayu*, 'this, he.' Pers. Behist. *kuwa*, 'ille, hic;' *awa*, 'id.'

érafazeya or *arafazeya*, 'tomb.' The root here appears to be some word like *altus*, signifying 'deep' and also 'high.' The word will require analysis and illustration—

Arab.		zamán (pl. azmán), 'time, age, world.'
		dsmán, 'heaven.'
		zamín, 'country, ground.'
Pers.	{ gar ———————————	azmán, 'the highest heaven.' } the same
Arm.	{ ger ———————————	ezman, 'a tomb.' } word
	{ ger }	'up.'
	{ wer }	

Georg.	{ or	——	mi,	'a tomb.'
	or	——	mo,	'a hole, a ditch, a well.'
	ghr	——	ma,	'deep.'
	{ ghr	—iati,	....	'a hole.'
Basque	gar	—aitza,	....	'height.'
Lesgi	{ gwoar	—ida,	....	'depth.'
	ritsh	—adaa,	....	'height.'
Kisti	{ urík			
	yurk	—a }	....	'a hole.'
	irakh	—ua,	....	'a hill.'
Esth.	{ urk,	....	....	'a hole or deep place in a river.'
	urg,	....	....	'a fox-hole.'
Arm.	arph	—i,	....	'heaven, sun.'
Osset.	{ arv,	....	....	'heaven.'
	arf,	....	....	'deep.'
	arf	—ade,	....	'depth.'
Arm.	wirap,	....	....	'a very deep ditch.'
Lycian	éraf	—azeya,	....	'a tomb.'

The Lycian *érafazeya* is the acc. sing. The acc., and also the gen. sing. of the Osset. *arfade* is *arfadiy*. Mr. Sharpe observes that the Lycian acc., both in the sing. and plur., invariably ends in a vowel. It is the same in Ossetic, where the terminations of the gen. and acc., in both numbers are— *i, y, iy, üy*. The Lycian gen. sing. terminates in *u*. But there are very few Lycian words *not* ending in a vowel.

méné, méeyé, méte, meite, 'here.' Osset. *mänä,* 'here;' *am,* 'here;' *amiy,* 'in this, here;' *ama* or *amä,* 'at this;' *amey,* 'from this,' or 'through this.' The -*te* in *méte* or *meite* may be the Osset. *thä,* an enclitic like *τί* or *δί.* *Méné* would then = *mänä, méeyé* = *amiy, méte* = *amä-thä,* and *meite* = *amiy-thä.*

prinafatu, 'he made;' *prinafŭtu,* 'they made.' For the form of the Osset. perfect, we must go to the auxiliary verb, *fa-un,* 'to continue to be, to complete.' It gives—*fädän, fädä, fäziy, festäm, festuth, festüy,* 'fu-i, -isti, -it, -imus, -istis, -erunt.' 'Erat,' from *un,* 'esse,' is *udiy.* A verb like *füssün,* 'scribere,' makes *füsta,* 'scribebat;' *füstoy,* 'scribebant;' and

THE ARMENIAN ORIGIN OF THE ETRUSCANS. 53

füst fäżiy, 'scripsit.' The form of *fäżiy* is not unlike that of *prinafatu*. As we have *prina-fatu,* ' made ;' *prinu-fo* and *prina-fu,* ' tomb,' and *prin-ézeyéwe,* ' domestics,' with the singular *prinéze* in another place, the root *prin* would be some word like δέμ(ω) or δόμ(ος). It may, perhaps, be found in the Arm. *wran,* ' a tabernacle.' For the change of *p-* into *w-* (*v*), compare Arm. *wrip-*ak, '*prav-*us,' and *wat* = Eng. and Pers. *bad.* We may here compare Lycian and Ossetic forms :—

Lycian
{ *prin-éze*
  prin-ézeyéwe (nom. plur.)
  eraf-azeya (acc. sing.)

Osset.
{ *arf-ade* (nom. sing.)
  arf-adiy (acc. sing.)
  arf-adethä (nom. plur.)
  arf-adethiy (acc. plur.)

tedéeme, ' son, child.' The following words all signify ' son,' ' child,' or ' boy,' in their respective languages. The Arm. *t* is replaced by *khl*, the orthography being here phonetic :—

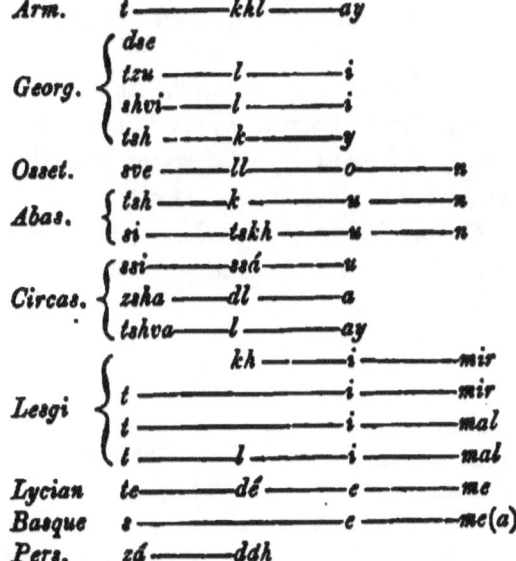

```
Arm.     t————khl————ay
         ⎧ dse
Georg.   ⎨ tzu————l————i
         ⎪ shvi———l————i
         ⎩ tsh————k————y
Osset.   sve————ll————o————n
Abas.    ⎧ tsh————k————u————n
         ⎩ si————tskh————u————n
         ⎧ ssi————ssá————u
Circas.  ⎨ zsha———dl————a
         ⎩ tshva———l————ay
         ⎧   kh————i————mir
Lesgi    ⎨ t————————i————mir
         ⎪ t————————i————mal
         ⎩ t————l————i————mal
Lycian   te————dé————e————me
Basque   s——————————e————me(a)
Pers.    zá————ddh
```

For the variation between the Lesgi *timir* and the Lycian

tedéeme, compare the Lesgi forms, *htlim, htli, chlim*, 'water.' In *chlim*, the *t* is lost and the final *m* preserved, nearly as *timir* has lost the *d* of *tedéeme*, but retained a final *r*. The reverse takes place in *htli*. So again, Osset. *füd* = Arm. *hayr*, for both = Lat. *pater*, Fr. *père*.

urppe, universally considered to mean 'for.' Arm. *ar, ar 'i*, 'for.' Lesgi *iar*, 'of.' Georg. *era*, 'because.' Lassen compares the termination of *ur-ppe* with *nem-pe*. Cf. Arm. *pés*, 'as, like:' *orpés*, 'as according to, on purpose' (lit. 'which-like'); *hipés*, 'as' (lit. 'this-like').

étle, atle, 'self.' Sharpe and Lassen instance the Sansk. *átman*, 'self,' but the Lapp. *ets*, 'self,' and the Alb. *vetë*, 'self,' may be nearer. The Lapp. has also another form, deficient in the nom.; for the gen. of *ets*, in the third person, is *eljes* or *alde*, and the dat. *etje-sas* or *alla-sas*. *Étle* and *atle* would be intermediate to *etje* and *alla*.

éuwe, 'his.' Osset. *uy, oy, ye*, 'he, his.' Kisti *woye*, 'he.' Lesgi *ua*, 'this.' Alb. *aï*, 'he.' *Éue* seems to be the Lycian for 'he' or 'him' (Fellows, p. 486). Pers. Behist. *awahyá*, 'istius.'

épttéwe, 'their.' Osset. *udatthä, yethä*, 'they;' *udättküy*, 'of them.' *Yethä*, 'they,' bears to *ye*, 'he,' nearly the same relation that *éptté(we)* does to *éu(we)*, if we suppose the *u* in *éuwe* to be hardened into *p*. Alb. *ata*, 'they.'

sé, 'and.' Georg. *da*, 'and;' *he*, 'also.' Lesgi *gi*, 'and.' Lapp. *ja*, 'and.' Alb. *e*, 'and.' Arm. *ev*, 'and.'

Lade, 'wife.'

Arm.	e ——	khla ——	r,	'wife.'
Abas.		lkha ——	dza	
Kisti	zye ——	lk,		
Circas.	⎧ t ——	lay ⎫		
	⎨ t ——	leh ⎬	....	'husband.'
	⎩ t ——	lyf ⎭		
Lesgi	⎧	le ——	ss	
	⎩ t ——	l'ya ——	di	'wife.'
Lycian		la ——	de	

For the initial *t*, which distinguishes the Lesgi *tl'yadi* from the Lycian *lade*, compare Circas. *lay*, *l'lay*, 'flesh;' *lay*, *t'klay*, 'blood.' Terms possibly akin to those above may be the Osset. *lag*, 'man,' and *lappu* and *latu*, 'lad,' apparently = Esth. *lats*, *laps*, 'child.'

italu, 'a tomb.' Lesgi *tataul*, 'a ditch.' Circas. *tytska*, *tshitoga*, 'a ditch' (*graben*, *i.e.*, *grave*). The Lycian has two more words for 'tomb,' *gopu* and *goru*. These would be the same as the Arm. *govb* and *kkor*, both signifying 'ditch, hollow.' *Gopu* would also be the Georg. *kubo*, 'tomb,' and the Sansk. *kúpa*, 'a ditch.'

eyé, 'if.' Arm. *ethé*, 'if.' Gr. ɛἰ. Osset. *ie*, *aviy*, 'or.' Lesgi *ivā*, 'or.'

tesé, *tése*, *teéde*, 'τίς.' Osset. *tyi*, *tyizi*, 'who?'

In the three extracts between the second and third of the bilingual epitaphs, there are some instructive points. The verb *itadu* is rendered by Mr. Sharpe 'buries;' *itatadu*, 'allows to bury;' and *itatútu*, 'let' or 'lets bury.' The grammar of the Caucasian languages is too little known, and the languages themselves probably too barbarous, to allow of any comparison with them. The Lycian forms, however, have considerable resemblance to those of Lapponic verbs. Compare—

Lycian. Lapponic.
itadu, 'buries.' . . . . . . *tjodljo*, 'stat.'
itatadu, 'allows to bury.' . *tjodljato*, 'substitit, stare facit.'
itatútu, { 'lets bury.' } . . { *tjodljota*, } 'stare permittit.'
          { 'let bury.' }   { *tjodljotek*, } 'stare permittunt.'

The word *ada* is explained by Mr. Sharpe from the Arab. *ada*, 'payment,' which seems a very good derivation. It might also be connected with the Lapp. *wädja*, 'pretium,' *hadde*, 'pretium,' *haddo*, 'ultio.' *Adadawéle* is regarded by the same writer with apparent justice as a compound of *ada* and *dawéle*, which last he explains from the Arab. *tawan*, 'a fine.' We might also refer it to the Lesgi *tl'e*, 'give' (*da*), *tallel*, 'to give,' without any injury to the sense. The forms, *Moll-ewés-*

ἐυ for Μολλ-ισ-ιος, and *Por-ewem-étéu* for Πυρ-ιμ-ατιος, seem to show that *dawêl* might = *dal*. The numerous Greek inscriptions found in Lycia leave no doubt as to the tenor of the words *adadawéle ada*.

The termination of II. is now reduced to—

sé eyé teté rétideteé itatu éwéwe méeyé oéte ponamakke
and if any one injures tomb this here . . . . . .
adadawale ada 4.
he pays adas four.

The th. of *rétideteé* may perhaps be found in the Arm. *aratel*, ' to sully, to spoil.' The meaning of *oéte ponamakke* must be left to conjecture. It would be consistent with the context if the words were rendered ' for a fine.' Cf. Lat. *ut;* or Esth. *ette,* Lapp. *auta,* ' præ'——Lat. *pœna,* Esth. *pin-ama,* ' punire ' ——Esth. *maks,* = Lapp. *makso,* = Arm. *machs,* = Heb. *mekhes,* ' payment, tribute, toll :' *ponamakke,* ' strafgeld.'

The termination of III., like that of II., is obscure. The analogies which led me to interpret *teké* . . . . *éwcyéue* as I have done, are the following—

teké, ' makes' . . . Lapp. *takk-et;* Fin. *tek-ä;* Esth. *tegg-ema;* ' facere.' Lapp. *takka,* ' facit.'

mutu, ' a purchase'. Osset. *müzd;* Pers. *muzd;* Sansk. *mülya;* ' pretium, merces.' Bötticher will not admit μισθός as akin to *müzd.*

méné, ' here' . . . So interpreted before. The Osset. *amän,* the dative of *ay,* ' this,' might here give a better sense, ' for this.'

*wastto*₄ ' injures'. . Lapp. *waste,* ' turpis, deformis.' Lat. *vastare.* *Wastto* might also be a noun governed by *teké,* and the sense be, ' or (does) injury to this tomb.'

une, ' or ' . . . . . Georg. *anu,* ' or.' Osset. *inne,* ' other ;' *aniu,* ' whether.'

ulawe, ' tomb '. . . Lapp. *joul-et,* ' to bury.' Mantschu *oulan,* ' a . ditch.' This seems to be the sixth

Lycian word for 'tomb.' The others are — *érafazeya* (Osset. Arm.), *itatu* (Lesgi), *goru* (Arm.), *gopu* (Georg. Arm. Sansk.), and *prinafu* (doubtful).

éweyéue, 'this' . . As before. Both *ula-we* and *éweyé-ue* may be datives: *ulawe éweyéue*, 'to this tomb.'

This completes the analysis of the three bilingual Lycian epitaphs, for conjecture seems useless upon the few confused words which remain in III. There are, however, in the Lycian epitaphs which are not bilingual, three words which, as they would be terms of relationship, ought here to be noticed. We find in Fellows' *Lycia* the following passages—

urppe   atle   éuwe   sé   une   éuwe (p. 487).
for   self   his   and ... his

urppe   lade   éuwe   sé   tedéemé   sé   uwélatedeéwa (p. 479).
for   wife   his   and children and . . . .

urppe   lade   éuwe   Ofeité   Gométeyéu   zzemaze   sé   tedéemé
for   wife   his   Ofeite of Gometeye   . . . and children
éuweyé (p. 477).
his.

une. Mr. Sharpe refers to the Arab. *um*, 'mother.' We have Abas. *oan*, Circas. *ana*, Lesgi *enníu*, Hung. *anya*, and Lapp. *edne*, all signifying 'mother.' In Arm. there is *hani*, 'grandmother,' and in Mantschu, *ounga*, 'parents.'

uwéla-tedeéwa. This appears justly considered by Mr. Sharpe as a compound, of which the last member is either allied to *tedéeme*, or is that word badly copied. *Uwéla* he explains from the Arab. *weled*, 'son,' *welad*, 'being born.' In Lapp. *welja*, and in Alb. *wela*, signify 'brother.' The Lesgi has *evel*, *evelyad*, and *ilyud*, 'mother,' and the compound *evel-llimal* would mean literally, in Lesgi, 'mother's child.' The Lycians traced their descent through the mother. Perhaps, we may render the Lycian word, 'κασίγνητοι,' or '*nepotes*.'

zzemaze. This is rendered by Mr. Sharpe, 'daughter,' which is doubtless the most obvious sense, and might bring us back to the Basque *semea*, ' son,' the Georg. *dse*, ' son,' and the Lesgi *timal*, ' child.' But the word might also be explained ' sister,' from the Caucasian and Georgian——

Abas.	{	*tshi*	' brother.'
		khsha	' sister.'
Circas.		*stshí*	' brother.'
Kisti	{	*vasha*	' brother.'
		esha	' sister.'
Lesgi	{	*vaas*	' brother, boy.'
		yas	' sister, daughter.'
		yassi	' girl.'
Georg.	{	*ds———————ma*	' brother ' (*dse*, ' son ;' *mama*,
		dji———————ma	' father.')
Lycian		*zze———————maze*	

One other expression may be noticed. In Fellows, p. 476, we meet with this epitaph :—

ẽwinu gorũ mute prinafatũ ẽsédéplume urppe lade ẽuwe
This tomb here made Esedeplume for wife his

sé tedésaems ẽuweyé woméleyé.
and children his . . . .

The most probable meaning of *woméleyé* is, I think, ' dead.' It may be compared with the Lapp. *james, jabmes, jabma,* ' mortuus ;' *jabm-et,* ' mori ;' *jabmel-et,* ' cito vel mature mori.' That Esedeplume did not make the tomb ' for himself ' as well, is rather in favour of ' his wife and children ' being dead. There is also in Lapp., *áme* or *ábme,* ' old ;' *ábme peiwe* (*peiwe,* ' day, dies ') de defunctis dicitur, quando illorum mentio fit : *e.g. Nila ábme peiwe,* ' Nicolaus defunctus.'

Lycian Words.

Five words are given by Bötticher in his *Arica* as Lycian. They are all names of places, and their affinities are sometimes doubtful :—

1. Κάδρεμα, ' σίτου φρυγμός.' Gr. καίω. Arm. *kizel,* ' to burn ;' *khah,* ' cooked (meat).'——Suani *dier* ; Arm. *torean ;* ' σίτος.' *Eme* would appear from the Lycian coins to be a com-

THE ARMENIAN ORIGIN OF THE ETRUSCANS. 59

mon termination in the nomenclature of towns: thus we find *Fégsérd-eme*, Pegasa or Pedasa, and *Trooun-eme*, Tros or Tlos. Compare *Perg-amus* and *Berg-omum*. The roots of Κάδρ-εμα would therefore probably be, κα and δ-ρ, which are very nearly the Arm. and Suani *khah-dier*, 'roasted corn.'

2. Πάταρα, 'κίστη.' Arm. *pat-el*, 'to envelop;' *pateanch*, 'an envelope, a case, a sheath, a shell;' *patat*, 'an envelope, a bale, a bundle;' *patan*, 'an envelope, a band.'

3. Πίναρα, 'στρογγύλα.' Arm. *pndel*, 'στράγγειν.' (?)—— Arm. *pnak*, 'a plate (cf. Ital. *tondo*), a bowl, a pot,' = Gr. πίναξ, = Osset. *fiñc*, = Georg. *pina*. Sir C. Fellows supposes the city of Pinara to have been so called from a remarkable round crag there, not unlike the Table Mountain in character, and containing 'some thousands' of tombs. He gives a picture of it in his *Lycia*, p. 139, which seems to confirm his opinion. The battle of Issus was fought on a river *Pinarus*.

4. Τύμηνα, 'the name of a certain he-goat.' Lesgi *teng*, 'a he-goat;' *deon*, 'a ram;' *haiman*, 'a sheep.' Abas. *shima*, 'a goat.' Gr. χίμαιρα.

5. Ὕλαμος, 'καρπός.' Esth. *willi*, 'fruit.' Mantschu *ouli*, *oulana, oulouri*, three different kinds of fruit. Georg. *khili*, 'an apple.' In a Lycian inscription (Fellows, p. 479) we find . . . . *ené* oulame *tofeto* oulame *mée toféte teké* . . . . We have here again a termination *-ame*, similar to Κάδρ-εμα, *tedé-eme*, &c. May the Lapp. *áme*, 'thing, res,' be compared?

It is, on the whole, rather difficult to form a judgment upon the affinities of the Lycians: but my impression would be that their kindred lay to the north of Armenia and in the Caucasus, and that they were, in consequence, rather to be classed among the Turanians than the Aryans. Yet there is much difference of opinion as to the classification of the Caucasian and Iberian races, even among the most profound ethnologists. Rask considers them as Ugrians or Turanians, agreeing in substance with Klaproth, who is inclined to rank them, or at least the Lesgi, with the Fins and Samoyedes. Bopp, on the other hand, discerns an Aryan affinity in the Iberians and Abasians, while Pott regards the Georgian language as entirely foreign to the Aryan, although it may have borrowed some Persian words. The Lycians are usually placed without doubt, as by Mr. Rawlinson, among the Aryans, though the linguistic proofs seem hardly so decisive as he considers them in favour of such a conclusion.[1]

There are many names resembling *Lycii*, and mostly lying on the edge of the Thracian area: 1. The *Leges* of the Caucasus, whom Strabo calls Scythians; 2. the *Ligyes* placed by Zonaras near the Caucasus; 3. the Colchian *Ligyes*, mentioned by Eustathius; 4. the *Ligyes* of Herodotus, probably the same as the preceding two, in or near Pontus; 5. the *Ligyrii* of Thrace; 6. the *Ligyrisci* of Noricum, the same as the Taurisci; 7. the *Lygii* of Tacitus, on the Upper Oder or Vistula;[2] 8. the *Ligyes* of Italy, the Ligurians. These last I have previously inferred to be Fins: and many of the other *names*, at least, might be Turanian, indications of an early race which may have been, as it were, swept into corners by the advance of the Thracians from Armenia to Italy. Lycia in Asia Minor, and Liguria in Italy, might correspond to Wales, Brittany, or Biscay, rugged districts where the primitive inhabitants of a

---

[1] Herod. v. i. p. 668.
[2] Not far from the *Lygii* lay the *Osi*, who spoke Pannonian and not German (Tacit. *Germ.* c. 47). The name *Osi* resembles Pliny's *Issi*, the Lesgi *oss*, 'people,' and the name *Ossetes*. One of the five tribes of the Lygii mentioned by Tacitus were the *Arii;* a name which seems like the word *Aryan*, the Ossetic *ir*, 'an Ossete,' the Arm. *ayr*, 'man,' *ari*, 'valiant,' and several kindred terms. Another tribe was the *Elysii*, perhaps derived from the same root as *Lygii* (Osset. *läg*, Lesgi *les*, 'man '), and reminding us of the *Elisyces*, a *Ligurian* nation between the Rhone and the Pyrenees. A third Lygian tribe was the *Manimi*, a name which might be derived from the Teutonic *man*, and which resembles in form the Etrusc. *arimus*, 'a monkey.' The other two Lygian tribes were the *Naharvali* and the *Helvecones*, of which the last might perhaps be partly compared with the Celtic *Helv-ii* and *Helv-etii*. The neighbouring *Gothini* are said by Tacitus to have spoken Gallic.

country have kept their ground against invaders. The descendants of the first possessors of the countries between the Ægean and the Caspian may have been sheltered by the Caucasus and Taurus from the Thracian race, which had deprived their ancestors of the intervening countries. To the same Caucasian stock may have belonged other nations of doubtful origin, and similarly circumstanced to the Lycians, such as the Pæonians. This people, whose country was once nearly conterminous with the later Macedonia, represented themselves as a colony of the Teucrians from Troy (Herod. v. 15). The remains of these Teucrians were called *Gergithes* (ib. v. 22), and probably dwelt at *Gergis, Gergithus,* or *Gergithion* in the territory of Lampsacus (Strabo, p. 589). There was a second place of the same name in the territory of Kyme (ib.) The Teucrian *Gergithes* were afterwards removed by Attalus, and placed in another town called *Gergetha,* near the sources of the Caicus (ib. p. 616), perhaps the same as the second *Gergithion* mentioned above. In the same country Strabo also notices *Pionia* and *Gargaris* as towns of the Leleges (ib. p. 610). Now the *Troes* were a Lycian people, and indeed the Lycian *Tlos* is *Tros,* as the Lycian inscriptions show. *Gergeti,* again, is an Ossetic town, and Strabo (p. 504) speaks of *Gargarenses* on the northern edge of the Caucasus.

To return from the digression on the Lycians—the addition of the Lydians, with their κασίγνητοι, the Carians and Mysians, to the same family as the Armenians, will unite this last nation to that branch of the Thracian race from which the Etruscans were directly derived by tradition. It also brings the Armenian language to the shores of the Ægean and the Hellespont, and half the distance from Armenia to Etruria. We now cross over into Europe, to examine in the first place the language of the nation to which the name of Thracians more especially belonged, and which extended from the Ægean to the Danube.

Thracian Words.

1. Ἀργιλος, ‘μῦς.’ Esth. *hiir, iir,* ‘a mouse.’ Gr. ὕραξ. Lat. *sorex.* Arm. *aṙnét,* ‘a dormouse.’ When we compare *aṙ-nét,* gen. *aṙ-niti,* with the Sansk. *ati-nidrálu,* ‘a dormouse,’ and the Sansk. *nidrá,* Arm. *nirh,* ‘sleep,’ it is sufficiently plain that the *aṙ* of *aṙ-nét* signifies ‘mouse.’ This gives us the first syllable of ἄρ-γιλος; and the termination might be explained from the Arm. *givl,* ‘a field,’ so that ἄργιλος would signify ‘field-mouse, *mus araneus.*’ Cf. Heb. *ach-bar,* ‘field-mouse’ (*ante,* p. 12, s. v. νηεξίς).

2. *Bassara,* ‘a kind of garment, probably made of a fox's hide.’ Also Lydian. Arm. *bas,* ‘hair, mane;’ *maz,* ‘hair;’ *mask,* ‘skin, pelisse, tunic.’ Bötticher notices the rather curious fact that *basor* signifies ‘a fox’ in Coptic. Cf. Heb. *basar,* and the kindred Semitic terms signifying ‘flesh, skin;’ and also Arm. *basavor,* ‘hairy.’

3. Βρία, ‘πόλις.’ "Osset. *bru,* ‘arx, castellum.’" Arm. *berd,* ‘a castle;’ *bourgn,* ‘a tower.’ Gael. *bri,* ‘a hill.’ Germ. *berg, burg.*

4. Βρίζα, ‘a plant, and the seed of a plant, resembling ῥίφη.’ Therefore a marsh-plant. "Radix Sansk. *vṙíh,* ‘crescere;’ *vríhi,* ‘oryza.’" Arm. *brinz,* ‘rice;’ *prisk,* ‘the plant *Thapsia.’* Rhæt-Rom. *ritscha,* ‘grass growing in water.’

5. Βρυγχόν, ‘κιθάραν.’ Arm. *phṙntel, phṙnkal,* ‘to cry.’

6. Γίντα, ‘κρέα.’ Arm. *jamb;* Sansk. *jambha;* Irish *diamann;* ‘food.’ Sansk. *jam;* Basque *jan;* Span. *yantar;* Arm. *jatel;* ‘to eat.’ Lat. *jentaculum.*

7. (Ζάμολξις). Σαλμόν, ‘δοράν.’ Arm. *salovmn,* ‘what envelopes;’ *salil,* ‘ a carcase;’ *gelmn,* ‘a fleece.’ Osset. *zarm,* ‘a hide.’

8. Ζεῖλα, ζίλαι, ‘οἶνος.’ Arm. *zelovl, helovl,* ‘to pour;’ *zelkh,* ‘drunken.’ Gael. *sil,* ‘to drop.’ The Scythians, Pliny says, called the Tanais by the name of *Silis.* They had, indeed,

several rivers of this latter name. We meet with the *Silarus*, now the *Sele*, near Pæstum in Italy.

9. Ζειρά, 'περίβλημα, ζῶμα.' Arm. *hir*, 'around, a circle;' *zrah*, 'a cuirass,' = Pers. *sirah* ; *zir*, 'a circle.'

10. Ζετραία, ' χύτρα.' "Vocabulum græcum et thracicum, ni fallor, ejusdem stirpis." Arm. *kove*, 'a pot, a jug;' *kathsay*, 'a kettle;' *khezi*, 'an earthen vessel, pottery.' Rhæt-Rom. *checla*, 'a pot.' Gael. *soitheach*, 'a pot.' The Mariandynians, a Thracian tribe in Bithynia, called a black fig χύτρα (*Arica*, p. 8). Here we have the Arm. *thovz*, 'a fig,' and a form like ζετ-ραία.

11. Ζιβυθίδες, ' γνήσιοι.' Arm. *zavak*, 'child, blood.' Kurd. *zavà*, ' kind, species.' Ang.-Sax. *sib*, = Germ. *sipp*. Lat. *soboles*, = Gael. *siolach*.

12. Ζόμβρον, 'τραγέλαφον.' "Slav. *zo͵br*, ' urus.' Arm. *zovarak*, ' vitulus, juvencus'"—*dovar*, 'an ox'—*gomés*, 'a buffalo'—*gamphr*, ' a bulkdog, a mastiff'—*zambik*, ' a mare'—*smbak*, 'a hoof.'—Lyd. ἴμβους, ' βοῦς.'

13. Θράττης, 'λίθος.' Arm. *char*, 'a stone;' *kharak*, 'a rock.' Gael. *creag*, *carraig*, 'a rock.'

14. Καπνοβάτας. "Strabo vii. 3, 3. λέγει τοὺς Μυσοὺς ὁ Ποσειδώνιος καὶ ἐμψύχων ἀπέχεσθαι κατ' εὐσίβειαν, . . .
 . . . . διὰ δὲ τοῦτο καλεῖσθαι θεοσιβεῖς καὶ καπνοβάτας. Arm. *khaphan*, ' an obstacle;' *khaphanel*, ' to hinder, restrain, take away' (ἀπέχειν) ; *khaphanovaz*, ' hindrance, interdiction, prohibition.'

15. Κῆμος, 'ὄσπριόν τι.' "Sansk. *kámin*, 'a climbing plant.'" Arm. *kbnil*, ' to cling, to creep along the ground.' Gr. κύαμος.

16. Κολαβρισμός, 'θρᾴκιον ὄρχημα καὶ καρικὸν, ἦν δὲ . . . ἐνόπλιον.' The word divides itself into κολα-βρισμός. Bötticher compares the first part with the Pol. *kolo*, ' circulus, rota,' which would be allied to the Arm. *kolow*, ' rotation, circulation.' The Arm. has also *khalal*, ' to leap, to play.'—βρισμός seems allied to βρικίσματα, ' ὄρχησις φρυγιακή;' which, as the

κολαβρισμός was ἐνόπλιος, may be compared with the Arm. *bir, wirg,* 'a great stick, a club' (cf. Lat. *virga,* Gael. *bior,* 'a stick'), *wér,* 'a wound.'

17. Κτίσταç. The quotation from Strabo in (14) is thus continued: Εἶναι δέ τινας τῶν Θρᾳκῶν, οἳ χωρὶς γυναικὸς ζῶσιν, οὓς κτίστας καλεῖσθαι. "Cf. Hesychium: κάπροντες ἐκαλοῦντο οὕτως οἱ Θρᾷκες." Arm. *khiž,* 'an obstacle,' a synonym of *khaphan* (14); *chežel,* 'to separate, to remove, to take away;' *khéth,* 'an obstacle;' whence *kthal,* ' to afflict one's self,' *gthel,* 'to stumble.' Thus καπνοβάται, κάπροντες, and κτίσται may all be explained in the sense of ' ἀπεχόμενοι ' from the Arm. It is observable that the Greek reporter has made out of the Thracian two genuine Greek words, καπνοβάται and κτίσται.

18. Λίβα, ' πόλις.' Germ. *leben.* Arm. *linel,* 'to be, to live.' Irish *libhearn,* 'a habitation, a ship' (cf. *Liburni* and *liburna*). Arm. *lóray* or *lavray,* 'a dwelling.' Esth. *lin,* 'a town;' *laiw,* 'a ship.' In the Prussian province of Saxony there are a great number of places with the suffix *-leben,* such as *Eisleben* and *Ermsleben.* Λίβα does not appear among Thracian names of places, though *Lebœa* was a Macedonian town: but *dava* must have had nearly the same sense in Mœsia and Dacia. Could Λίβα be an error for Δίβα? *Dava* would be allied to Georg. *daba,* 'village, place;' Arm. *deh,* 'district, part;' Pers. *díh,* 'village;' Gael. *daimh,* 'house, domus.'

19. Μαγάς, ' σανὶς τετράγωνος ὑπόκουφος δεχομένη τῆς κιθάρας τὰς νευρὰς καὶ ἀποτελοῦσα τὸν φθόγγον.' Arm. *makan,* 'a drumstick;' *mahak,* 'a great stick.' Heb. *makal,* 'a twig;' *makkel,* 'a rod.'

20. Ὄλξις, 'a bear.' Arm. *arǰ,* 'a bear.' Lat. *ursus.* Lith. *lókis.*

21. Πέλτης, ' Θράκιον ὅπλον καὶ εἶδος ταρίχου.' Gael. *peall,* 'to cover;' *peall, pill,* 'a hide.' Lapp. *pils,* 'pellis rangiferina aut alia non satis villosa.'——Pol. *bełt,* 'a javelin.' Arm. *bałkhel,* 'to strike;' *petel,* 'to dig.'

22. Πιτῦγιν or πιτύην, 'Θησαυρόν.' Arm. *pitani*, 'profitable, useful, necessary;' *pitoych*, 'what is necessary.' Cf. χρῆμα, χρήματα.

23. 'Ρομφαία, ' Θράκιον ἀμυντήριον, μάχαιρα, ξίφος, ἢ ἀκόντιον μακρόν.' Arm. *roumb*, 'sarissa' (Rivola), 'bombe, grenade' (Aucher—a sense necessarily modern); *rmbachar*, 'pierre (*char*) de baliste.' Kurd. *rhm*, 'a spear.' Heb. *romakh*, 'a spear.' Lat. *ramus*. Gr. ῥάβδος. Gael. *rong, rongas*, 'a staff, a bludgeon.' Esth. *rond*, 'a piece of wood.' Lapp. *rámpo*, 'truncus sive tigillum in quo in frusta carnes aut aliæ res conciduntur.'

24. Σανάπαι, 'μίθυσοι,' compared by Bötticher with the O. Pers. σαννάκρα, 'ἔκπωμα.' Lapp. *saja*, 'situla.' Esth. *sang*, 'a milkpail.' Arm. *san*, 'a cauldron;' *sahil*, 'to flow,' with which may be connected, Lat. *sanguis, sanies*, and Mantschu *sengui*, 'blood.'

25. Σαραπάραι, 'κεφαλοτόμοι, ἀποκεφαλισταί.' Arm. *sar*, 'summit, top;' *sayr*, 'point, edge;' *zayr*, 'summit, head.' Kurd. *ser*, 'head, top.'——Arm. *pharatel*, 'to remove, to take away;' *pharat*, 'distant, removed, far;' *pherekel*, 'to divide;' *pherth*, 'a part.' Osset. *sar*, 'a head;' *farath*, 'an axe.'——Gr. κάρα. Arm. *karaphn*, 'a head;' *karaphel*, 'to behead.'

26. *Sidalcas* or *Sitalcas*. "Xenopho *Anab*. vi. 1, 6, Thracas *Sitalcam* vel *Sidalcam* carmen *popularium* suorum cantantes introducit. Pars vocis altera Sansk. *arka*, Arm. *erg*, 'hymnus, carmen.'" If *Sid-* or *Sit-* imply 'popularis,' it may be compared with the Lapp. *sita*, 'pagus.' Cf. κωμῳδία.

27. Σκάλμη, 'θρᾳκία μάχαιρα.' Lapp. *skalmet*, 'pugnare cornubus.' Arm. *setb*, ' the blade of a knife.'

28. Σκάρκη, 'ἀργύρια.' Lapp. *skarktek*, 'fiscus sive receptaculum pecuniarum, quæ in templo offeruntur sive dantur.' Arm. *skavarak*, 'a plate, a disk.' Goth. *skatts*, 'geldstück, geld, ἀργύριον, δηνάριον.' Germ. *schatz*. Lapp. *skatte*, 'tributum.' Eng. *scot*.

F

The result of the examination of these Thracian words tends greatly to confirm the hypothesis, that the (Proper) Thracians belonged to the same family as the Armenians. Traces also may be discerned, as in Asia Minor, of the existence of a primeval Finnish or Turanian nation in Thrace. It is satisfactory to find that all the Proper Thracian words known seem capable of explanation either from the Armenian or the Finnish.

The course of my argument would now lead me to examine the Albanian; but it may be well, in order that the early ethnography of Europe may be more clearly understood, to make a previous analysis of the remains of the Scythian language. There are also a number of Dacian words, which may be afterwards noticed.

Scythian Words.

1. "Αβις, 'ἔβαλλον.' Gael. *up*, 'to push ;' *ob*, 'to refuse, deny, reject.' Welsh *eb*, 'to send from, to say,' = Gr. ἔπω. Arm. *wép*, 'ἔπος.' Lyd. ἴβυ, 'τὸ βοάν.' Hesych. "Mox sequitur ἰβύει, 'τύπτει, βοᾷ.' " 'They pushed,' would be in Gael. *dh' up iad*, or, omitting the initial *dh'*, as may be done, *up iad*. This bears considerable resemblance to ἄβις. The final consonant in *iad*, the constructive form of *siad*, 'they,' is sometimes omitted in Gael., as in *lia* or *leo*, 'with them' (*le*, 'with').

2. Ἄγλυ, 'κύκνος.' Gael. *ala, eala, ealag, ealadh*, 'a swan, a wild swan.' Esth. *luik*, 'a swan.' Lat. *olor*.

3. Ἀδιγόρ, 'τρωξαλλίς.' Gael. *ithche, itheadh*, 'eating, the act of eating ;' *-or, -oir*, or *-sir*, Gael. termination. Sansk. *adaka*, 'edens, τρώγων.'

4. Ἀλίνδα, 'an oleaginous kind of cabbage-plant growing in the Tanais.' Gael. *ola ;* Arm. *et, ivi ;* 'oil.'——Gael. *aileanta*, 'fragrant ;' *aillean*, 'elecampane.' Lat. *allium*. Gr. ἐλίνιον. Arm. *eléy*, 'endive ;' *elégn, elinğ*, 'a reed, a rush, a nettle.'

5. Ἀβάκης, ἄβαξ, 'ἄφωνος, σιωπηρὸς, καὶ ὄνομα ἀρχιτεκτονικὸν, ὃ Σκύθαι λέγουσιν ἄνδρα καλεῖν.' Sansk. *a*, negative particle, *vač*, 'loqui.' Gael. *o*, 'from,' = Lat. *a, ab; bagh*, 'a word,' = Lat. *vox*.

6. Ἄνορ, 'νοῦς.' Gael. *anam*, 'soul.' Lat. *animus*: &c.

7. Ἄριμα. " Herodotus iv. 27. ἄριμα ἓν καλέουσι Σκύθαι. Errat. Non unum sed primum significat et præstantissimum. Sansk. *aryaman* sensum primarium amisit, retinuit Zend. *airyama*." Gael. *air, aireamh*, 'number;' *aireanach*, 'a beginning.' Lapp. *aremus*, 'primus.' Gael. *arm*, 'origin,' = Arm. *arm, armn*, = Arab. *arum*. Arab. *arím*, 'one, any one.'

8. Βρίξαβα, 'κριοῦ μέτωπον.' Georg. *verzi*, 'a ram.' Pol. *baran*, 'a ram.' Kurd. *berk*; Pers. *barah*; Lesgi *bura*; 'a lamb.' Lat. *vervex*. Lapp. *brekot*, 'balare.'——Lapp. *diwe*, 'caput.' Pied. *abà*, 'caput.'

9. *Groucasus*, 'nive candidus.' Lapp. *grawes*, 'canus;' *kaisse*, 'mons altior, plerumque nive tectus.' Esth. *kahho*, 'frost;' *kasse jäa* (*jäa,* 'ice'), 'ice formed by frost upon snow.' Georg. *qinwa*, 'frost.'

10. Δάνουσις or δάνουβις, 'αἴτιος δυστυχίας.' Gael. *don, donas*, 'mischief,' and perhaps *aobhar*, ' a cause.'

11. Ἐξαμπαῖος, 'ἱραὶ ὁδοί.' "Id Zend. esset *aśavanô páthô*."——" Sansk. *yaǵ*, 'venernri;' Zend. *yaz*; Arm. *yazel*, 'sacrificare;' *yašt*, sacrificium"[1] (hinc Gr. ἅγιος)." Arm. *ǵanapar*, 'a way.'

12. Ἱππάκης, 'βρῶμα σκυθικὸν διὰ γάλακτος ἱππείου σκευαζόμενον.' Lapp. *häpos*, 'equus.' Osset. *yefs, afse*, 'equa.'

13. Κάναμις, 'a kind of odoriferous plant like flax.' Arm. *kaneph*; Gael. *cainb*; Bret. *canab*; 'hemp.' Gael. *canach*, 'cotton-grass, the herb cat's-tail, cotton, a cotton-tree;' *caoineach*, 'stubble.'

14. Καραρύες, καράμη. " Καραρύες οἱ σκυθικοὶ οἶκοι. ἔνιοι δὲ τὰς κατήρεις ἁμάξας. Καράμη ἡ ἐπὶ τῆς ἁμάξας σκηνή. Arm. *karch*, 'plaustrum.'" Gael. *carbad*, 'a chariot.'

---

[1] Cf. Lat. *hostia*: also *ara* (= *asa*) with *yaz-el*.

15. Κόλος, 'a kind of white animal, in size between a stag and a ram, but swifter in running.' Arm. *khalal*, 'to move, to leap.' Gael. *clis*, 'quick.' See *ante*, p. 63, s. v. κολαβρισμός.

16. Κόρακοι, 'φίλιοι δαίμονες.' Gael. *car*, 'friendly.'—— Arm. *ogi*, 'spirit.' Alb. *ago*, 'God.'

17. Ματόας, 'άσιος.' Pol. *mada*; Esth. *mütta*; 'mud.' Arm. *miz*, 'dirt, filth.' Lapp. *mdiwe*, 'pulvis;' *mdiwe tjatse* (*tjatse*, 'aqua'), 'aqua turbida.' *Matoas* was a Scythian name for the Danube, 'turbidus et torquens flaventes Ister arenas.' It might perhaps = *mdiwe tjatse*.

18. Μίσπλη, 'ή σιλήνη,' "proprie luna plena, ni fallor." Sansk. *más*, 'moon, month.' Gael. *mios*, 'month.' Arm. *amis*, 'month;' *makik*, 'the horns of the crescent moon.'—— Arm. *li*; Gael. *lan*; Cornish *len*; 'full.' Lat. *plenus*. Gr. πλέος.

19. Οίόρπατα, όρμάται, 'ανδροκτόνοι.' Gael. *fear*, 'man;' *bat*, 'to beat;' *bas*, 'death.' Arm. *ayr*, 'man;' *mah*, 'death.'

20. Παγαίη, 'κύων.' Pol. *pies*, 'a dog.' Lapp. *piädnak*, 'a dog.' Germ. *petze*. Eng. *bitch*. "Herod. i. 110: τὴν κύνα καλέουσι σπάκα Μῆδοι. Zend. *çpá*; Afghan *spay*; Pers. *sak*; 'canis.'" The sibilant in σπάκα may have passed into an aspirate, and then have been lost, in παγαίη, just as Arm. *spitak* = Sansk. *çveta* = Ang.-Sax. *hvit* = Eng. *white* = Germ. *weiss*. Σπάκα is, however, identical in meaning with the Pol. *sobaka* and *suka*, in which second form the labial has disappeared, as in the Pers. *sak*.

21. Πάρθους, 'φυγάδας.' Arm. *pharatel*, 'to drive away;' *partil*, 'to be conquered.'

22. Σαγάρεις. 'Μασσαγέται τοξόται τε καὶ αἰχμοφόροι, σαγάρεις νομίζοντες ἔχειν.' Arm. *sakr, sakovr*, 'a sabre.' Lat. *securis*.

23. Σανάπτις, 'οίνιώτης.' See *ante*, p. 65, s. v. σανάπαι.

24. Σίσυρνα, 'χιτὼν σκύτινος, ἔντριχος, χειριδωτός.' Lapp. *sasne*, 'pellis depilata;' *sasenek*, 'femoralia ex aluta facta;' *sasse*, 'manica.'

25. Σποῦ, 'an eye.' Arm. *spasel*, 'to observe.' Germ. *spähen*. Eng. *spy*. Lat. *spes, specio*.

26. Τάρανδος, 'a kind of animal, τὸ μέγεθος βοὸς, τοῦ προσώπου τὸν τύπον ἐοικὸς ἐλάφῳ.' Gael. *tarbh*, 'a bull;' *tarbhan*, 'a little bull;' *tarbhail*, 'bull-like;' *tarbhanta*, 'grim, bull-faced.' The Gael. *bh*, = *v* or *w*, is scarcely audible in *tarbh* and its derivatives.

27. *Temerinda*, 'mater maris.' Divide into *temer-inda*. " Sansk. *támara*, 'aqua' (cf. Cornish *Tamar*); *timi*, 'oceanus;' '*tim*, humidum esse.' Arm. *tamovk*, 'humidus.' " Gael. *tabh, tamh*, 'oceanus;' *taom*, 'a torrent, to pour.' Arm. *thavn* or *thón*, 'moisture.' Arab. *tamm*, 'the sea.'——*Inda* is compared by Zeuss (*Die Deutschen*, p. 296) with the Hung. *anya*, Turk. *anya, inya*, 'mother.' Kindred terms would be—Lapp. *edne*, Circas. *ana*, Lesgi *enniu*, 'mother:' and also perhaps the Arm. *hani*, 'grandmother,' and the Lycian *ʞne*, probably 'mother.'

28. Φρίξα, 'μισοπόνηρος.' The analogy of ἀράξα, 'μισοπάρθενος,' the name of a plant in the Araxes, shews that it is the first part of φρίξα which signifies 'wicked,' and the latter part 'hating.' The word is not easy to explain, but Dr. Donaldson seems to have analysed it successfully. He compares the first part with the Germ. *frev-el*, and the Lat. *prav-us*, words which would be allied to the Arm. *vrép*, 'a fault;' *vripak*, 'wicked;' *vripil*, 'to sin;' and also to the Irish *fiar*, 'crooked, wicked;' *freac*, 'wicked.' The same philologist also compares -ξα with the Germ. *scheu*, the primitive idea in which is 'aversion' or 'turning from,' as appears by the Eng. *shy, shun*, and the Germ. *schief, schel*, or *schiel*. The Arm. has *šel*, 'oblique,' = Germ. *schief;* and *šil*, 'squinting,' = Germ. *schel* or *schiel*. In Irish, we find *seach*, 'a turn,' and also *scach*, 'to pass by, to shun.' On the whole, the Irish seems, in the words *freac-seach*, to approach nearest to φρίξα.[1]

---

[1] For the names of the Scythian deities see *Varronianus*, p. 48. I have merely to add their apparent Armenian or Celtic affinities. The names are six in number:—

When we come to compare the Proper Thracian with the Scythian, or the most ancient European language of Turkey with the most ancient European language of Russia, we may discern in each both Finnish and Armenian affinities. The Scythian language is, however, distinguished from the Proper Thracian by the presence of an important, it may even be said a predominant, Celtic element. Now it is very possible that there may have been at one time two distinct races, one Thracian and the other Celtic, in Scythia; the Scythians and the Cimmerians. The Scythians are indeed called ἔθνος Θράκιον by Stephanus of Byzantium; and an affinity between the *Cimmerii* and the *Kymry* has frequently been conjectured. However this may be, the affinity between the Scythian and the Celtic, and the absence of any such affinity between the Proper Thracian and the Celtic, may be used as an argument to prove that the Celtic elements of the population of Europe entered mainly through Russia, and the Armenian (or Thracian) elements mainly through Turkey.

Dacian names of Plants.

The Dacians and Getæ were always considered as Thracians by the ancients, and were both said to speak the same Thracian language. The relics of this language are of a peculiar nature, consisting of the names of plants, and thus only likely to ex-

---

Ταβυτί, 'Ἰυτίη.' Arm. *tap,* 'fire.' Gael. *teas,* 'ardour.'
Παπατες, 'Ζεύς.' Arm. *pap,* 'grandfather.'
'Απία, 'Γῆ.' Irish *ibh*, 'a country.'
Θαμμασάδας, 'Ποσειδῶν.' Gael. *tamh,* 'oceanus.' Arm. *tamovk,* 'moist.'——Arm. *mardern,* 'a hero.'
Οἰτόσυρος, 'Ἀπόλλων.' We find in Arm. *with,* 'a gazelle,' and *withkhari,* 'vast, colossal;' from which might be deduced *with,* 'swift' or 'mighty.' *Zôr* is 'power, force,' in Arm. and Pers. Οἰτόσυρος might possibly be *withazór,* 'greatly powerful,' and thus be equivalent in sense to the Arm. *mezazór;* or else, which is perhaps more appropriate, 'swiftly powerful.' *With,* if interpreted 'swift,' might be allied to the Arm. *shoyt,* 'swift,' and *phoyth,* 'swiftness,' which may likewise be compared with *air.,*
'Αρτίμπασα, 'Οὐρανίη Ἀφροδίτη.'

hibit a partial affinity to another language of the same family. Thirty-two such names have been collected by Grimm, in his *History of the German Language*, from Dioscorides περὶ ὕλης ἰατρικῆς.[1]

1. Βλῆτον. 'Ρωμαῖοι βλίτουμ, Δάκοι βλής. Arm. *blith*, 'bread, cake.' Gael. *bleath, bleth, bleith*, 'to grind.' Welsh *blawd*, 'meal, flour.' The leaves of *orach* are "as if they were overstrown with *meal* or *flour*;" and those of *blite* are "almost like the leaves of *orach*, but not so soft, white, nor *mealy*."[2]

2. 'Αναγαλλὶς ἄρρην, χελιδόνιον, Γάλλοι σαπάνα, Δάκοι κερκεραφρών. Grimm is inclined to consider this as a corrupted Greek name, and is led by the Gr. ἄφρων to compare the Germ. name of the *anagallis, gauchheil (gowk-heal),* 'salus stultorum.' By a rather curious coincidence, the Arm. *aproomn,* from *aprel,* 'salvare,' signifies 'salus;' while *kerkeril,* again, signifies 'to be hoarse.' *Kerkeraproomn,* therefore, which is almost identical with κερκεραφρών, would be Arm. for 'salus rancorum.' Disocorides says of this herb: ὁ δὲ χυλὸς αὐτῶν ἀναγαργαριζόμενος ἀποφλεγματίζει κεφαλήν.

3. Χελιδόνιον μέγα. 'Ρωμαῖοι φάβιουμ, Γάλλοι θῶνα, Δάκοι κρουστάνη. "Lith. *krégżde,* 'χελιδών;' *kregźdyne,* 'χελιδόνιον μέγα.'" (Grimm). The Arm. words for *celandine* have no affinity to the Dacian. They are: *zizernakhot* and *zizernachar,* 'swallow-herb' and 'swallow-stone.' Yet we may derive the Dacian name, *kroost-*, of the 'twittering' swallow, from the Arm. For in Arm., *krit* is 'chirping;' and the change of the suffix *-it* into the suffix *-ost* would give *kroost*.

4. Κενταύριον. 'Ρωμαῖοι φενριφούγιαμ, οἱ δὲ αὔρα μουλτιράδιξ, Δάκοι τουλβηλά. *Centaury* is only defined in Arm. as 'a certain herb (*khot*).' The nearest approach to τουλβηλά in Arm. is *tovlt,* = Kurd. *tólk,* 'ἀλθαία, bismalva, marsh-mallow,' and '*ῥοδόδενδρον,* oleander.' There are also *thalth,* 'sowbread, cyclamen,' and *thovlth,* 'paper.' But τουλ-β(ηλα), 'febrifuge,'

---

[1] For v. r. see *Appendix.*   [2] Dodoens' *History of Plants.*

might be explained from the Esth. *lulli-abbi*, 'fire-help.' The Gael. for τουλ-βηλά is ceud-*bhileach*, ' hundred-leaved.'

5. Δίψακος. 'Ρωμαῖοι λάβρουμ βίνερις, οἱ δὲ κάρδουμ βίνερις, Δάκοι σκιαρή. Welsh *ysgall*, 'a thistle.' Gipsy *karro*, ' a thistle.' Arm. *cher(el)*, Alb. *skyir*, ' to tear.' The Arm. for ' teazle' is *kangar;* for ' thistle,' *ockoz, ekchan*. These last seem allied to the Esth. *okkas*, ' sting, thorn,' and *ohhakas*, ' thistle,' as well as to the Gael. *oighionnach*, ' thistle.'

6. 'Ηρύγγιον. 'Ρωμαῖοι καπίτολουμ κάρδους, οἱ δὲ καρτεραί, Δάκοι σικουπνοίξ. Arm. *sokh*, ' an onion,' *sekh*, ' a melon' : Gr. σίκυς : Alb. *segë*, ' a pomegranate.'—Arm. *phouaj*, ' a plume, a tuft.' "Upon the tops of the branches (of the great Eryngium) come forth round knobby and sharp prickly heads, about the quantity of a nut, set round about full of small flowers;" and at the top of the branches of the small Eryngium "grow round, rough, and prickly bullets or knobs."

7. Θύμος. 'Ρωμαῖοι ϑούμουμ, Δάκοι μόζουλα. Grimm refers to *muscus*, Germ. *moos*. In Alb., *modë* is ' darnel;' *modhoulë*, ' a pea;' and *misir*, ' a wallflower' or ' gilliflower,' both fragrant like thyme. The Arm. for ' thyme' is *zothrin;* for ' moss,' *mamour* or *lór*. In commenting on the Lyd. μυσός, ' ὀξύη,' which I have considered as akin to the Arm. *motay*, ' μυρίκη,' Bötticher expresses the opinion, that it must be compared with μωῦς, ' γῆ,' so that it would have the sense *terrigena*, "ut ad quamvis arborem designaudum aptum sit." If μυσός and *motay* signified ' terrigena,' such a meaning would be equally applicable to μόζουλα, ' thyme.' We have, too, the Kurd. *milék*, ' box, a box-tree.' The termination -ουλ(α) would be Arm., as in *pt-ovt*, ' fruit,' *ovt*, ' a kid.' There would remain μοζ-, ' terra,' which may be explained from the Georg. *miza*, ' terra,' Eng. *mud*, Esth. *mötta*, ' mire,' Arm. *miz*, ' filth.' There is also Arm. *mazar* (cf. Span. *madera* and Lat. *materia*), ' heath, bush, furze, broom, clump of wood;' which appears allied to the Esth. *möts*, ' bush, wood.'

8. "Ανηϑον τὸ ἐσϑιόμενον, οἱ δὲ πολγίδος . . . . Δάκοι

THE ARMENIAN ORIGIN OF THE ETRUSCANS. 73

πόλπουμ. The Arm. for 'dill, fennel,' is *samith*.[1] *Bolk* is 'horse-radish;' and *bothoḡ*, 'a sprout, a bud;' and *pipet*, 'pepper.' In Georg. *balakhi* is 'herb,' *balkha*, 'mallow,' and *boloki*, 'root, turnip.'

9. Ἀρτεμισία. Ῥωμαῖοι οὐαλέντια, οἱ δὲ σιρπύλλουμ, οἱ δὲ ἕρβα ῥέγια, οἱ δὲ ῥαπίουμ, οἱ δὲ τιρτανάγετα, Γάλλοι πονέμ, Δάκοι ζουόστη. I find no name for *mugwort* in Arm.; but ζουόστη readily resolves itself into Arm. *ʒow-ost: ʒow*, 'mare;' *ʒowak*, 'stagnum'—*ost*, 'ramus, germen, palmites, frondes,' = Germ. *ast*. "Mugwort groweth in the borders of fields, and about highways, and the banks of brooks or quiet standing waters." (Dodoens). Ἀρτεμισία φύεται ἐν παραθαλασσίοις τόποις, ὡς τὸ πολύ. (Diosc.) Another of the above names, τιρτανάγετα, resembles the Arm. *thrthnǰork*, 'sorrel.' *Therth* is 'a sheet (*feuille*) of paper.'

10. Ὄρμινον ἥμερον. Ῥωμαῖοι γεμινάλις, Δάκοι ὅρμια. "Evidently formed from the Greek." (Grimm). Or both derived from a common origin. *Clary* is not named in Arm., but there is *warm*, 'a net, a noose,' which may be compared with ὅρμος, ὁρμιά, and ὅρμινον. In Esth., *ormid* is 'goats-beard or meadwort.'

11. Λιθόσπερμον. Ῥωμαῖοι κολούμβαμ, Δάκοι γονολῆτα. Apparently Greek. The Arm. is *charasermn*, which is exactly 'λιθόσπερμον.' Γονολῆτα, if genuine Dacian, might be akin to the Arm. *gonget*, 'turnip, wild turnip or rape, rape-seed.'

12. Ὀνοβρυχίς. Ῥωμαῖοι ὀπακά, οἱ δὲ βριχιλλατά, οἱ δὲ λόπτα, οἱ δὲ ἰουγκινάλεμ, Δάκοι ἀνιασσείξί. No name in Arm., but ἀνιας-σεξέ is not unlike the Arm. *anyaǰ séz*, 'unlucky grass,' or 'mischievous grass.' This is very nearly the French periphrasis for 'weed,' *méchante herbe*. Cf. also 'infelix lolium.'

13. Χαμαιπίτυς. Ῥωμαῖοι Κυπριποῦμ, Δάκοι δοχιλᾶ. In

---

[1] *Semeth* is given in Dioscorides as the Egyptian name of *cress*. In Arab. *shamdr* is 'fennel;' *shdmidh*, 'fruitful (palm);' and *shdmm*, *shdmmat*, 'smelling.' In Pers., *shdmákh* is a kind of millet.

-ελᾶ we may have a word equivalent to the Arm. *elevin*, 'a pine, a cedar,' Gr. ἐλάτη, Arm. *elat*, 'a cedar.' The meaning of δοχ- is less easily conjectured. *Thovkh* signifies 'brown' in Arm., which presents no name for *ground-pine*. But δοχ- would be better referred to the Alb. *tokë*, 'earth, ground,' which is exactly the meaning required.

14. Λειμώνιον. 'Ρωμαῖοι ουεράτρουμ νίγρουμ, οἱ δὲ τιν- τιννάβουλουμ τέρραι, Γάλλοι ἰουμβαροὺμ, Δάκοι δάκινα. "A field-flower, which Pliny (xx. 8) calls *beta silvestris*." (Grimm)——who compares our *daisy* and the Germ. *tag*. But in Arm., '*beta rubra*' is *gakndet*. Subtracting *det*, which signifies 'medicine, herb, colour,' there remains *gakn* to compare with δάκινα. The word *gakhin*, 'a marsh,' is very probably not allied to *gakn*. In Rhæt.-Rom., *giaccun* is '*plantago*, waybread,' which "hath great large leaves, almost like to a beet-leaf." (Dodoens). Now *giaccun*, phonetically, = *gakn*.[1]

15. Ξυρίς. 'Ρωμαῖοι γλαδίολουμ, οἱ δὲ ἰριμ ἀγρέστεμ, Δάκοι ἄπρους. In Arm., *prisk* is 'Thapsia, a kind of dill;' but ἄπρους is more nearly the Arm. *aprovst*, 'salus,' the literal meaning of ἀλθαία or *salvia*. In Pers., *ipár* is 'thyme.'

16. Ἄγρωστις. 'Ρωμαῖοι γράμεν, οἱ δὲ ἀσιφόλιουμ, οἱ δὲ σαγγουινάλεμ, οἱ δὲ οὐνίολαμ, Ἱσπανοὶ ἀπαρία, Δάκοι κοτίατα. This seems decidedly Arm., as *khot* signifies in Arm., 'herb, grass, hay, forage,' = ἄγρωστις, = *gramen*. Many of the plants previously noticed are unnamed in Arm., but merely described as certain 'herbs' (*khotch*). The last member of κοτ-ίατα may have defined the particular 'herb' (*khot*), or it may be regarded as a termination like the Arm. -*avêt*. Cf. Arm. *kot*, 'perfume ;' *kotavêt*, 'odoriferous.'

The Spanish name for *gramen*, it appears, was ἀπαρία. May it be connected with ἄπρους and κερκερ-αφρών, and referred to the Arm. *apr-il*, 'to live, to escape ;' *apr-ovst*, 'safety,

---

[1] The plant is also called in Rhæt.-Rom. *plantagien* and *luoza*. The Esth. is *te leht* or *te lehked*, 'way-leaf.'—Cf. 34.

nourishment, provision'? See *ante*, in Lyd., s. v. πανδούριον; and *inf.*, 'on the possible extension of the Thracians to the west of Etruria.'

17. Βάτος. Ῥωμαῖοι σίντις, οἱ δὲ ῥούβουμ, οἱ δὲ μόρα βατικάνα, Δάκοι μαντεῖα. "I hold this for the Gr. μαντεία." (Grimm).

18. Πεντάφυλλον. Ῥωμαῖοι κιγκεφόλιουμ, Γάλλοι πεμπέδουλα, Δάκοι προπεδουλά. The Celtic word is evidently genuine, as Grimm notices. Bret. *pemp*, 'five;' Gael. *duille*, 'a leaf.' The Dacian is more doubtful. If we divide into προ-πεδουλά, we may compare the last part with the Dacian φθεθελά (*inf.* 27), the Gr. πέταλον, and the Arm. *thitheïn*, 'lamina,' or *ptort*, 'fructus.' Yet προ- cannot mean 'five:' the Arm. is *hing*, which would require ἰγγοπεδουλά. But 'cinquefoil' was also called ξυλοπέταλον (Diosc.) Now 'wood' is in Arm. *pr-ak*, 'a stick' is *bir*, and 'a rush' is *priov*. In Alb., *phrē* is 'a pole.' These may explain προ-, as well as προ-δίορνα (28), and πρι-αδήλα (32).

19. Τράγιον, τραγόκερως. Ῥωμαῖοι κορνουλάκα, οἱ δὲ βιτουένσα, Δάκοι σαλία. *Sélk* is Kurd. for 'beet.' The Arm. has nothing nearer than *selkh*, 'a melon;' *zalik*, 'a flower;' *zil, zlot*, 'a stalk, a stem;' *zalk*, 'a stalk, a rod;' *salarth*, 'a leaf, a hair.' In Esth., *salk* or *sallo* is 'a small bush.' Gr. θαλλός. See *ante*, in Phryg., s. v. ζέλκια.

20. Ὑοςκύαμος. Ῥωμαῖοι ἰνσάνα, δεντάρια, Γάλλοι βιλινουντία, Δάκοι διέλεια. Henbane has no name given in Arm.; but διέλεια is readily derived from the Arm. *del*, 'medicamen, venenum,' χόρτος, βοτάνη, unguentum, color.' Cf. Arm. *mkndel* (*m(on)kn*, 'mouse, rat'), 'arsenic,' *i. e.*, 'ratsbane.' In *del dalar* (*dalar*, 'green, θαλερός'), 'herbs,' *del* appears to mean simply 'herb.' In *gakndel*, 'beta rubra,' we have perhaps the Hellenised Dacian, δάκινα διέλεια. See *ante*, 14.

21. Στρύχνον ἁλικάκαβον. Ῥωμαῖοι βισσικάλις, οἱ δὲ ἀπολλινάρις μίνωρ, οἱ δὲ ὀψάγινεμ, Δάκοι κυκωλίδα. Grimm suggests *cuculus*, in Arm., *kkov*. In Persian *kôk* is 'lettuce.'

Cuckoo's meat is *wood-sorrel.* Κυκωλίς is *winter-cherry.* The nearest Arm. word is *kakovi,* 'soft.' But see *Appendix.*

22. 'Ακαλύφη, οἱ δὲ κνίδη, 'Ρωμαῖοι οὐρτίκα, Δάκοι δύν. Welsh *danad,* 'nettles.' Gael. *deanntag,* 'a nettle.' Arm. *danak,* 'a knife,' which compare with κνίδη.

23. Ποταμογείτων. 'Ρωμαῖοι βῆναι φόλιουμ, οἱ δὲ ἐρβάγω, οἱ δὲ γλαδιατώριαμ, Δάκοι κοαδάμα, Γάλλοι ταυρούκ. Κοαδάμα nearly resembles the Arm. *kotem,* 'cress, nasturtium,' one kind of which is ποταμογείτων. In Georg., *kuda* is 'privet.'

24. 'Αστὴρ ἀττικὸς, οἱ δὲ ὑόφθαλμον, 'Ρωμαῖοι Ιγγυράλις, Δάκοι ῥαθίβιδα. Grimm refers to the Old Norse *rádhibidh,* 'tempus consultandi,' and instances the 'forget-me-not.' From the Arm. we should get *khrat-avet,* 'monition-announcer.' *Avetel,* 'to announce,' has a favourable sense : *avetaran* is 'Gospel.'

25. Βούγλωσσον. 'Ρωμαῖοι λογγαίβουμ, οἱ δὲ λίγγονα βόβουμ, Δάκοι βουδάλλα. It does not appear that δάλλα signifies 'tongue' in any language. Grimm cites the Swiss *läl* (in Stalder, *lälle*), 'tongue,' comparing *dingua* and *lingua.* In Arm., *lal* is 'lamentation.' Cf. Lat. *lallare.* The Arm. for 'tongue' is *lezov ;* for 'ox,' *ezn ;* and for 'bugloss,' *eznalezon.* The nearest approach to βουδάλλα is in the Gael. *buagkallan* or *buadk-ghallan,* 'groundsel' (lit. 'good-bough').

26. Κατανάγκη. 'Ρωμαῖοι ἔρβα φιλικλὰ, οἱ δὲ δατίσκα, οἱ δὲ 'Ιόβις μάδιους, Δάκοι καροπίθλα. For -πίθλα see 27. Karo- might be explained in many ways from the Arm.——*kar,* 'strength ;' *kar,* 'thread, string ;' *her,* 'hair ;' *char,* 'stone ;' *khar,* 'forage.' No name appears in Arm. for fern, though for ἀδίαντον we find *tarkhot,* i.e. 'mane-wort.'

27. 'Αδίαντον. 'Ρωμαῖοι κιγκινάλις, οἱ δὲ τέρραι καπίλλους, οἱ δὲ σουπερκίλιουμ τέρραι, Δάκοι φιθοφθεθελά. Divide with Grimm into φιθο-φθεθελά. Φιθο, πιθλα, and φθεθελα might all be derived from one root. Grimm instances, for the last two, πίταλου, supposed = π(τ)έταλου, and φύλλον, perhaps

= φ(θ)ύλλον. In Arm., we have *phthith*, 'the blowing of a flower,' *phththil*, 'to blow, to bud, to sprout, βλαστάνειν;' *phththot*, 'blowing;' *phththeal*, 'blown;' and, which may be a kindred term, *thithetn*, 'a blade, a leaf' (but only of metal). The final *n* in *thithetn* is a common superfluity in Arm. Compare—

phak, 'closing'. . *phakel*, 'to close'. . *phaket*, 'a bandage.' (*bat*), th. of . . . *batel*, 'to join' . . . *batetn*, 'ivy.'

phthith, 'blowing'. *phththil*, 'to blow'. $\begin{cases} φθεθελά, \text{qu. 'a blade.'} \\ thithetn, \text{'a blade.'} \end{cases}$

Compare also Arm. *thev*, 'a wing,' *thethev*, 'light, active,' *thel*, 'thread, fibre, stalk of grass,' and *theph*, 'bran,' with *filum*, *filix*, πτίλον, and the Dacian φιθ(o), πιθλα, and φθεθελα: also πτέρις with πτερόν, = Arm. *phetovr*, = Germ. *feder*, = Eng. *feather*. In Alb., *poupëlyë* is 'down.' One of the three Dacian expressions, and perhaps the second, πιθλα, may have signified 'fern;' and καροπίθλα, our *tree-fern* or *wall-fern*, may have meant 'stone-fern' (Arm. *char*, 'stone'). Φιθο-φθεθελά was perhaps *thethevathithetn*, 'light-bladed.' So we have in Arm., *thethevathev*, 'active, light' (lit. 'light-winged'); and *thethevatart*, 'light' (lit. 'lightly-moved'). The Arm. continually forms adjectives by the combination of two substantives without any inflexion. Grimm proposes to read for προπεδουλά, 'cinquefoil,' in 18, something like πιμπέτυλα or πιμφθίθελα, thus giving φθεθελά very nearly the sense of the Arm. *thithetn*. The Arm. for 'five-bladed' would be *hingathithetn*, ἱγγαθίθελα.' Πεδουλά is also like the Arm. *ptovi*, 'fruit,' which, as well as *pletn*, 'an elm,' may be allied to πίθλα, *phthith*, &c.

28. Ἐλλίβορος μέλας. Ῥωμαῖοι βεράτρουμ, οἱ δὲ σαράκα, Δάκοι προδίορνα. 'Hellebore,' is in Arm., *koǧ Wraži*, 'Georgian stalk;' *koǧ* being apparently = *koǧt*, 'stalk, stem.' Cf. κυκωλίδα (21). From the Arm. *prtov*, 'juncus,' and the suffix *-órén*, we might form for προδίορνα the word *prtovórén*, 'junceus.' See also 18.

29. Ἀκτή, οἱ δὲ δίνδρον ἄρκτου, οἱ δὲ ἥμερον, Ῥωμαῖοι σαμ-

βούκουμ, Γάλλοι σκοβιὴν, Δάκοι σίβα, καλαμοειδεῖς ἔχουσα κλάδους. "Old Norse *séf*, Swed. *säf*, 'juncus'—Serv. *zova*, 'sambucus nigra.'" (Grimm). Arm. *seav*, gen. *sevoy*, 'black' —cf. Georg. *savi*, 'black;' *savi*, 'populus nigra'—*sevni*, 'a dress woven with palm-leaves.' The Arm. for 'elder' is *thanthrmeni*. The Servian word may be originally Dacian.

30. Χαμαιάκτη, οἱ δὲ Ἕλειος ἀκτή, οἱ δὲ ἀγρία ἀκτή, Ῥωμαῖοι ἐβουλλουμ, Γάλλοι δουκωνὶ, Δάκοι ὄλμα. Phryg. ἔλυμος, 'αὐλός,' = Arm. *elégn*. Arm. *elevin*, 'a pine;' *eling*, a nettle.'

31. Κολοκυνθίς. Ῥωμαῖοι κουκούρβιτα σιλβάτικα, Δάκοι τουτάστρα. Arm. *tkovz*, 'a fig;' *thovth*, = Kurd. *thu*, 'a mulberry;' *ddovm*, i.e., *dedovm*, 'a gourd,' = Gipsy *dudum*.

32. Ἄμπιλος μέλαινα, οἱ δὲ βρυωνία μέλαινα, οἱ δὲ βουκράνιον, Ῥωμαῖοι ὑβλαμήνια, οἱ δὲ βατανούτα, οἱ δὲ βετισάλκα, Δάκοι πριαδήλα, οἱ δὲ πεγρίνα. No name is found for *briony* in Arm. Πριαδ-ήλα might possibly be compared with προδ-ίορνα (28), the Arm. suffix -*et* replacing the Arm. suffix -*órén* or -*ybrén*. See also 18. Πεγρ-ίνα, if by *metathesis* for περγ-ίνα, might be derived from the Arm. *prk-el*, 'to bind tightly.' Cf. *vitis*.

To these Dacian names Grimm adds one used by the Bessi in Thrace—

33. Βήχιον. Ῥωμαῖοι τουσιλάγω, οἱ δὲ φαρφάριαμ, οἱ δὲ πουστουλάγω, Βεσσοὶ ἀσᾶ. Arm. *kaz*, 'a cough, βήξ, *tussis*.'

One name seems to have been overlooked by Grimm—

34. Ἀνδράχνη ἀγρία. Ῥωμαῖοι ἐλλίκεβραμ, οἱ δὲ πορτουλάκα. Δάκοι λάξ. A kind of *sengreen* or *houseleek*. Germ. *lauch*. Eng. *leek*. Arm. *elég*, 'endive.' Gael. *lus*, 'herb.'

When we examine such of the above names as admit of clear explanation, we shall find that one (3) is Lithuanian, and one (22) Celtic. Five (16, 20, 23, 31, 33), of which one is Bessian, may be claimed, with scarcely any hesitation, as Armenian, and probably even more. Thus 1 would be either

Celtic or Armenian, but rather the former, and 27 appears to present a peculiar instance of Armenian affinity: 14 also, when compared with 20, coincides very accurately with the Armenian. A number of other names are readily derived and formed from the same language; as 2, 3, 6, 9, 12, 15, 24, and 26: and several more might possibly be deduced from Armenian roots. One thing is remarkable in the Dacian names, the terminations formed with λ. Thus there are—τουλβ-ηλά and πριαδ-ήλα, δοχ-ελᾶ and φιϑοφϑεϑ-ελά, καρο-πίϑ-λα, and μόζ-ουλα and προπιδ-ουλά. Such terminations are characteristic of Armenian, as will be exemplified in the examination of the Etruscan, where they are likewise continually found; and also in Albanian: e.g., *modh-oulë*, 'a pea;' *tsing-ouly*, 'a kind of fig;' *trang-oul*, 'a cucumber.'[1] At present it will be enough to refer to such Armenian words as have been already cited in the analysis of the Dacian names—*phthth-eal*, *phak-el* and *pt-eln* and *bal-eln* and *thith-eln*, *kog-l*, and *pt-ovt* and *kak-ovt*. There are also διλεια and σαλία on one side, and on the other *del* and *ził*, or else *zalik*, probably a diminutive of *zal*. Nor is it without importance that, in explaining the names of simples, so many Armenian names for vegetables and the parts of vegetables should suggest themselves.

The value of these coincidences cannot be better estimated than by Grimm himself, whose object is to prove the Dacians and Getæ to be Teutonic. 'It is,' says the great philologist, 'amply sufficient, if *six* or *eight* of my explanations be true, and the rest more or less probable: no further proof is requisite, that the Dacians and Getæ were Germans (*Deutsche*), nations of Teutonic race (*Deutschverwandte Völker*).' Would not this argument rather prove the Dacians to be Armenians? I cannot think that the German resemblances, which his complete mastery of *all* the Teutonic dialects at every period of their existence has enabled the author of the *Deutsche Gram-*

---

[1] Cf. Arm. *waroung*, 'a cucumber.'

matik to adduce, are so many or so plain as the Armenian language *singly* affords. If the English reader should not be acquainted with the *Geschichte der Deutschen Sprache*, yet he may apply a tolerably fair test to the question. Dacia is claimed on one side as Armenian, and on the other as Teutonic. The country lies midway between Armenia and England, and in England a Teutonic dialect is used. Can the relics of the Dacian language be explained as well from the English as from the Armenian? If the difference of age between the English and the Armenian should be urged, the Anglo-Saxon might be used in the place of the English. At all events, if the Dacian were Teutonic, some *one* Teutonic dialect ought to explain it as well as the Armenian does. If *all* the Teutonic dialects together cannot do this, there is a still greater reason for giving the preference to the Armenian.

If the Dacians and Thracians be ranked with the Armenians, there will be gained in Europe, for the Armenian language, a territory extending from the Ægean to the Carpathians, and from the Euxine to the frontiers of Pannonia and Illyria. In Scythia, to the east of Dacia, the Armenian seems to have died away; and to the north, beyond the Carpathians, it is not likely to have penetrated: indeed, one apparently Lithuanian word is found in Dacia itself. In Greece, as in Scythia, it may have been subordinate to another element, the Hellenic; and in Asia Minor it does not seem, as a language, to have passed over Taurus. We have now to examine whether it penetrated beyond the Thraco-Dacian area to the west, *i. e.*, into Illyricum. Here the language to be compared with the Armenian is the residuary element in Albanian, or that which remains after the elimination of all Turkish, Greek, Latin, and other intrusive words. These elements render the task rather difficult, as many Albanian words allied to the Armenian are borrowed from the Turkish and Greek, but especially from the Turkish, which has itself borrowed them elsewhere in its turn. For instance—

THE ARMENIAN ORIGIN OF THE ETRUSCANS. 81

Alb. *zaman*, 'time,' = Arm. *tam, tamanak*.
Alb. *simbile*, 'basket,' = Arm. *zambil*.
Alb. *zindan*, 'prison,' = Arm. *zëndan*.

All these Albanian words are borrowed from the Turkish, which has itself borrowed them from the Persian or Arabic. Whether I have entirely succeeded in keeping such words out of the following list, I cannot say: a Turkish scholar would probably detect some additional cases. My Albanian words are derived from Dr. Hahn's *Albanesische Studien*.

Albanian words allied to the Armenian.

1. *Ago*, 'God.' Arm. *ogi*, 'spirit.'
2. *Ai, ayn*, 'he, this (man).' Arm. *ays, ayd, ayn*, 'this, that.' The terminations, -*s*, -*d*, -*n*, are borrowed from the personal pronouns, *es, dov, inckn*, 'I, thou, he:' therefore the demonstrative pronoun is properly *ay*. Osset. *ay*, 'this.'
3. *Ala, ala*, 'quickly.' Arm. *walwal*, 'quickly.'
4. *Amëlyë*, 'sweet.' Arm. *hamel*, 'sweet.' Esth. *hämelelik*, 'agreeable.'
5. *Anë*, 'a shore.' Arm. *aphn*, 'a shore.'
6. *Arë*, 'a field.' Arm. *art, wayr*, 'field, land,' = Gael. *ar.* Gr. ἄρουρα.
7. *Ari*, 'a bear;' *aronike*, 'a female bear.' Arm. *arj*, 'a bear.' Gr. ἄρκτος.
8. *Arnoiį*, 'I mend.' Arm. *arnel*, 'to make.' Gr. ἄρω.
9. *Apher*, 'near.' Arm. *kovp, hpavor*, 'near.' Gr. ἄφαρ.
10. *Akhour*, 'a stable.' Arm. *akhor*, 'a stable,' = Pers. *åkhúr*.
11. *Vay*, 'woe;' *vai*, 'alas!' Arm. *way*, 'woe;' *wáy*, 'alas!' Gr. αἴ. Lat. *vœ*. Germ. *weh*.
12. *Vath*, 'a court.' Arm. *óth*, 'a lodging.'
13. *Valyë*, 'a wave.' Arm. *alich*, 'a wave.' Swed. *bölja*, 'a wave.'
14. *Vapë*, 'hot.' Arm. *eph*, 'cooking.' Gr. ἕψω.

G

15. *Vatrë,* 'a fire-place.' Arm. *atr,* 'fire.'
16. *Vëla,* 'a brother.' Lapp. *welja,* 'a brother.' Arm. *ełbayr,* 'a brother.'
17. *Vend,* 'land.' Arm. *and,* 'land.' Welsh *gwent,* 'a plain.'
18. *Vetš,* 'except, but.' Arm. *bayž,* 'except, but.' Pol. *bez,* 'except, but.'
19. *Vlyësge,* 'husk, shell.' Arm. *błžakn,* 'a covering.' Rhæt-Rom. *bleuscha,* 'husk, shell,' = Pied. *pleuja,* = Irish *blaosg,* = Welsh *blisg.*
20. *Vlyorës,* 'the name of Avlona and its district' (Acroceraunia). Arm. *blovr,* 'a hill.'
21. *Barth,* 'white.' Arm. *bovṛ,* 'chalk.'
22. *Bats,* 'a companion.' Arm. *matéil,* 'to join one's self to.'
23. *Bëiš, bañy,* 'I make, I do.' Arm. *bay, ban,* 'word, thing.'
24. *Bely,* 'a spade.' Arm. *petel,* 'to dig.' Gr. πέλεκυς.
25. *Boukë,* 'bread.' See *ante* in Phryg. (p. 15) s. v. βέκος.
26. *Boukhar,* 'a chimney. Arm. *bowch,* 'a furnace.'
27. *Yam,* 'I am.' Arm. *em,* 'I am.'
28. *Gaphorre,* 'a crab.' Arm. *khephor, kheżemorth,* 'shell, shell-fish ;' *khećaphaṛ,* 'a crab ;' th. *khež, khęgek,* 'shell, husk;' *morth, phaṛ,* ' skin ;' *phor,* 'a sea-scorpion.'
29. *Gëzoph,* 'a hide.' Arm. *kashi,* 'a hide ;' *kheż,* 'a shell.' Compare the previous word.
30. *Gëlër,* 'gain.' Arm. *yalthel,* 'to gain.'
31. *Genyeiš,* 'I deceive.' Arm. *nengel,* 'to deceive.' Gael. *gangaid,* 'deceit.'
32. *Goyë,* 'mouth ;' *gogesiš,* 'I gape;' *gyoukë,* 'tongue, language.' Arm. *gogel, khósil,* 'to speak ;' *gočel,* 'to cry out ;' *khósaran,* 'mouth.' Germ. *kosen.*
33. *Gorgë,* 'a cave.' Arm. *khoroć, khorš,* 'a cave.'
34. *Gyi,* 'breast ;' *gyiri,* 'relationship.' Arm. *girk,* 'breast.'
35. *Gyizë,* 'cheese.' Arm. *kathn, kith,* 'milk, milk-food' (*laitage*).

36. *Gyoumë*, 'sleep.' Arm. *chovn*, 'sleep.' Gr. ὕπνος. Lat. *somnus*. Gael. *suain*. Rhæt.-Rom. *chüna*, 'bed.'

37. *Gyus, gyusmë, gyumës*, 'half.' Arm. *kés, kisamasn*, 'half' (*masn*, 'a portion.')

38. *Dhalë, dhaltë*, 'butter-milk.' Arab. *dahl*, 'milk.' Arm. *dayl, dal*, 'a cow's first milk;' *daysak*, 'a nurse;' *daysakordi*, 'foster-brother, *frère-de-lait*' (lit. 'nurse-son'). Gael. *dalta*, 'a foster-child.' Irish *dairt*, 'a heifer.' Eng. *dairy*.[1]

39. *Dham, dhëmb*, 'tooth.' Arm. *atamn*, 'tooth.' Gr. ὀδούς. Lat. *dens*.

40. *Dhëmpës*, 'rushing.' Arm. *dimel*, 'to rush,' th. *dëm*; *-pés*, Arm. adverbial termination, signifying 'like,' and to be compared with Germ. *-lich*, Eng. *-ly*: e.g. Arm. *ays*, 'this,' *ayspés*, 'thus;' *phovth-al*, 'to haste,' *phovthapés*, 'hastily.'

41. *Dhsrë, derë*, 'bitter;' *tharëtö*, 'sour.' Arm. *darn*, 'bitter.'

42. *Dki*, 'a goat.' Arm. *tik*, 'a goatskin.' Georg. *tkkavi* = Pers. *takka* = Phryg. ἄττηγος = Germ. *siege*, 'a goat.'

43. *Deky*, 'deceit.' Arm. *dav*, 'deceit.'

44. *Derë, durë*, 'a door.' Arm. *dovrn, dovrch*, 'a door.' Gr. θύρα, &c.

45. *Des*, 'I die;' *dekouri*, 'dead.' Arm. *di, diakn, dígoyn*, 'dead, a corpse.' Sansk. *dí*, 'perire, evanescere.'

46. *Dzañ, zañ*, 'I learn.' Arm. *janaćel*, 'to know;' *zaseay*, 'I have known.'

47. *Dimën, dimör*, 'winter.' Arm. *zmern*, 'winter.' Pol. *zima*, 'winter.' Turk. *simistan*, 'winter.'

48. *Ditë*, 'day.' Arm. *tiv*, 'day.' Sansk. *dina*, 'day.' *Tina*, 'the Etruscan Jupiter or Diespiter.'

49. *Dorë*, 'a hand.' Arm. *zern*, 'a hand.' Gr. δῶρον, 'a hand or palm.' Gael. *dorn*, 'a fist.'

50. *Drouse*, 'perhaps.' Arm. *therevs*, 'perhaps.'

---

[1] Grimm remarks (*Gesch. der Deut. Spr.* p. 1015): 'die Engländer mit einem wort, das ich nirgends erklärt finde, nennen kuhweide und milcherei *dairy*.' May it not be a word of Celtic origin?

51. *Dšind*, 'a spirit.' Arm. *šovné*, 'a spirit;' *inéel* 'to breathe.' Lat. *genius*.

52. *E*, 'and.' Arm. *ev*, 'and.'

53. *Errë*, 'darkness;' *errētē*, 'in the evening.' Arm. *erek*, 'evening.' Gr. ἐρεμνός.

54. *Ers*, 'honour;' *erseli*, 'honourable.' Arm. *yarg*, 'dignity, esteem;' *yargel*, 'to honour;' *yargeli* (participle), 'to be honoured.' The Arm. termin. *-eli* = Lat. *-andus*. Germ. *ehre*.

55. *Zyarr, zyarem*, 'fever, heat in fever.' Arm. *ǰermn*, 'heat.' Turk. *gherm*, 'heat.' Gr. ϑερμός.

56. *Ze, zañ*, 'voice.' Arm. *žayn*, 'voice.'

57. *Zi*, 'black.' Arm. *sev*, 'black.' Turk. and Pers. *siyáh*, 'black.' Osset. *sau*, 'black.' Sansk. *çyáva*, 'black.'

58. *Zi*, 'grief.' Arm. *žav*, 'grief.' Turk. *sëzë*, 'grief.'

59. *Zi*, 'famine.' Arm. *sow*, 'famine.'

60. *Zipht*, 'pitch.' Arm. *živth*, 'pitch,' = Pers. *zift*.

61. *Zok, zogou*, 'a bird, a young bird.' Arm. *žag*, 'a young or small bird.' 'Sparrow' (Luke x. 6) is rendered in Arm. by *žag*, in Alb. by *zok*.

62. *Thagëmë*, 'a wonder.' Arm. *thagovn*, 'mysterious;' *thagovžanel*, 'to conceal, to bury,' = Lapp. *tjäket*.— Gr. ϑαῦμα.

63. *Thekërë*, 'rye.' Arm. *hagar*, 'rye.' Turk. *dakhl*, 'rye.' Lat. *secale*.

64. *Im, yem, yim*, 'my.' Arm. *im*, 'my.' Gr. ἐμός.

65. *Ka*, 'an ox.' Arm. *kow* = Swed. *ko* = Germ. *kuh* = Eng. *cow*. Sansk. *go* = Zend *gáo*, 'bos.'

66. *Kalli*, 'an ear of corn.' Arm. *kalin*, 'an acorn.'

67. *Kam*, 'I have, I am, I shall,' (aux. verb). Arm. *gom*, 'I am;' *kam*, 'I am, I continue, I subsist.'

68. *Kanëp*, 'hemp.' Arm. *kaneph*, 'hemp.'

69. *Karrë*, 'a carriage.' Arm. *karch*, 'a carriage.' Swed. *kärra* = Eng. *cart*.

70. *Kars*, 'coarse.' Arm. *garš*, 'coarse.'

71. *Katount*, 'territory, town, village.' Arm. *getin*, 'land, ground.'

72. *Këlëph*, 'case, cover.' Arm. *kelev*, 'skin, bark, shell.' Gr. καλύπτω.

73. *Këpoutsë*, 'a shoe.' Arm. *kósik* or *kavsik*, 'a shoe,' = Pers. *kafš*.

74. *Kikël*, 'a summit.' Arm. *gagathn*, 'a summit.' Lat. *cacumen*.

75. *Kodrë*, 'a hill.' Arm. *katar*, 'an eminence.'

76. *Kol*, 'a party, a band.' Arm. *kot*, 'part, side.'

77. *Koran*, 'a trout.' Arm. *karmrakhayt*, 'a trout:' th. *karmir*, 'red;' *khayt*, 'spotted.'

78. *Koritë*, 'a boat.' Arm. *kovr*, 'a boat.'

79. *Koskë*, 'a bone.' Arm. *oskr*, 'a bone.' Pol. *košć*, 'a bone.' Lat. *os*. Gr. ὀστίον.

80. *Kotse*, 'a girl.' Arm. *koys*, 'a girl.' Turk. *kiz*, 'a girl.'

81. *Kouth*, 'a pot.' Arm. *kovt*, 'a pot.' Gr. χύτρα.

82. *Krots*, 'an ass' colt' (*bourriquet*). Arm. *grast*, 'an ass' (*bourrique*).

83. *Kyendis*, 'I choke.' See *ante* in Lyd. (p. 40) s. v. κανδαύλης, 'σκυλλοπνίκτης.'

84. *Kyilis*, 'I roll.' Arm. *glel, glorel*, 'to roll;' *glan, glanak*, 'a cylinder.' Gr. κυλίω, κυλίνδω.

85. *Lap*, 'I lick.' Arm. *laph*, 'licking;' *laphel*, 'to lick.' Gr. λείχω.

86. *Lezouet*, 'a reader.' Arm. *lezov*, 'tongue, language.' Gr. λέγω. Lat. *lego*. *Lezouet* is declined as a substantive, not as a participle (Bopp *on the Alb.* p. 27). It may be compared with Arm. substantives which add *-ić* to the root; as *phrk-el*, 'to deliver,' *phrk-ić*, 'a deliverer;' *arar-ch*, 'creation,' *arar-ić*, 'a creator;' *tarr*, 'substance, nature,' *tarr-ić*, 'a maker, a creator;' *tović*, 'a giver.' So there might be formed from *lezov*, 'language,' an Arm. subst. *lezović*, 'a speaker,' which is nearly identical with the Alb. *lezouet*. The

declension of *lezouei* is—nom. and acc. *lezouei;* gen., dat., and abl. *lezoueji.* The declension of *ţović,* is—nom. *tović;* acc. (z)*tović;* gen. and dat. *tovéi;* instr. *tovćav.*

87. *Lidjĕ,* 'a warm-spring.' Arm. *lig,* 'a pond.' Lat. *liquor, lix.*

88. *Loi,* 'a club.' Arm. *lakht,* 'a club;' *tek,* 'an oar.' Eng. *log.* Lat. *lignum.*

89. *Lyargĕ,* 'far' (*weit*). Arm. *larel,* 'to stretch, to extend.' Lat. *largus.*

90. *Lyarĕ,* 'a bath.' Arm. *logaran,* 'a bath;' *lovanal,* 'to wash, to bathe.' Lat. *lavacrum, lavare.* Lapp. *laugo,* 'a bath.'

91. *Lyartĕ,* 'high;' also, 'an eminence.' Arm. *leaṛn,* 'a mountain;' *leṛnagin,* 'very high.'

92. *Lyĕ, lyañ,* 'I leave.' Arm. *lićh,* 'left;' *lchanel,* 'to leave.'

93. *Lyei,* 'a corpse.' Arm. *leikamaik, laikamaik,* 'skin' (*maik,* 'skin, tegument, membrane'); *laikar,* 'a body of men.' Kurd. *lesc,* 'corpse.' Germ. *leiche.*[1] In Pers. *laik* signifies 'a piece,' and *laikar,* as in Arm., 'a body of men, an army.'

94. *Lyith,* 'I fasten.' Arm. *lẓel,* 'to fasten.'

95. *Lyind,* 'I give birth to.' Arm. *linel,* 'to be, to become, to live;' *etanil,* 'to be made.'

96. *Mayĕ,* 'top.' Arm. *mak,* 'above.' Esth. *mäggi,* 'mountain.'

97. *Matḣ,* 'great.' Arm. *meẓ, ameth,* 'great.' Gr. μέγας.

98. *Maitounĕ, mayounĕ,* 'rich.' Arm. *meẓatovn,* 'rich.'

99. *Marr,* 'ich fasse.' Arm. *marzel,* 'to form.'

100. *Mbar,* 'I carry.' Arm. *berel,* 'to carry.' Gr. φέρω, &c.

101. *Mbaiǵ, mba,* 'I hold.' Arm. *pahel,* 'to retain.'

102. *Mbarĕ,* 'good.' Arm. *bari,* 'good.' Lapp. *pnore,* 'good.'

103. *Myekrĕ,* 'a beard.' Arm. *mbrouch,* 'a beard.'

---

[1] Or we might compare the Teutonic *fleisc, fläsk, flesk, flesh.*

104. *Myergoulë*, 'a mist.' Arm. *marakhovt, mrayl*, = 'a mist.' Lapp. *murko*, 'a mist.'

105. *Melingonë, merminh*, 'an ant.' Arm. *mrǰivn*, 'an ant,' = Osset. *mälzüg*, Gr. μύρμηξ, Swed. and Ang.-Sax. *myra*, Irish *moirb*, Pers. *mur, mīrūk*.

106. *Mèrgoiǰ*, 'I put away.' Arm. *mertel*, 'to put away.'

107. *Miš*, 'flesh, pulp.' Arm. *mis*, 'flesh, pulp.' Eng. *meat*.

108. *Mourë*, 'north wind.' Arm. *mrrik*, 'high wind, storm.' Sansk. *marut*, 'ventus.'

109. *Mourk*, 'dark, black.' Arm. *mrel*, 'to blacken.' Eng. *murky*.

110. *Mout*, 'dung.' Arm. *miš*, 'filth.' Germ. *mist*. Eng. *muck, mud*.

111. *Mukourë, mukounë*, 'grey.' Arm. *mokhragoyn*, 'grey.'

112. *Napht*, 'property, goods.' Arm. *nivth*, 'matter, substance.'

113. *Nge*, 'leisure.' Arm. *ninǰ*, 'repose.' Lapp. *najo*, 'laxamentum.' Rhæt.-Rom. *nanna*, 'cradle, bed.'

114. *Ngyir*, 'depth.' Arm. *nerekin*, 'low.' Gr. νέρθε.

115. *Ndë*, 'into, to.' Arm. *ënd*, 'into, to.' Gr. ἔνδον.

116. *Oborr*, 'a court.' Arm. *aparanch*, 'a court.'

117. *Ouyë, ouyëtë*, 'water.' Arm. *kivth, vivth*, 'water;' *wêt*, 'a wave;' *wtak*, 'a brook.' Lat. *udus*. Gr. ὕδωρ. Phryg. βέδυ, 'water.'

118. *Oulë, oudë*, 'a way, a road.' Arm. *ovli*, 'a way, a road,' = Turk. *yol*, = Lith. *ulyczia*. Gr. ὁδός. Cf. Ὀδυσσεύς and *Ulysses*.

119. *Ouñth*, 'a bowl, a pot.' Arm. *anóth*, 'a vessel, a pot.'

120. *Ourth*, 'ivy.' Arm. *orth*, 'a vine, a basket.' Gr. ὄρχος: th. εἴργω. See *inf.* in Etrusc. s. v. *atæsum*, and compare also Arm. *ovṛ*, 'a vine-branch,' *ovṛi*, 'willow, osier,' *ovṛkan*, 'a net;' and Lat. *vimen, vitex, vitis, vinea, vieo*, and *vincio*.

121. *Ousta*, 'skilful.' Arm. *ovšim, ovšaton*, 'wise, careful.'

122. *Oult,* 'invocation against the evil eye.' Arm. *ovkht,* 'vow, prayer.' Gr. τύχή.

123. *Pa,* ' un'- (privative prefix.) Arm. *ap-, apa-, api-,* 'un-.' Gr. ἀν-, ἀπο-.

124. *Pakē,* 'little.' Arm. *pakas,* 'deficient;' *phockr,* 'little.' Lat. *paucus.* Gr. παῦρος. Ital. *poco.*

125. *Patē,* 'a goose.' Arm. *bad,* 'a duck.' Arab. *wazz,* 'a goose, a duck.' Compare *anas* and *anser.*

126. *Pyesē,* 'a part, a share.' Arm. *bat, bazin,* 'part, contribution.' Lapp. *pekke,* 'a piece.'

127. *Pëgërē,* 'impurity, dirt.' Arm. *pagsot,* 'foul.' Lat. *fæx.* Lapp. *pádo,* 'sordes.'

128. *Pelyky,* 'I defile.' Arm. *ptzel,* 'to defile.' Eng. *filth.*

129. *Pengoiḡ,* 'I bind.' Arm. *pndel,* 'to bind.'

130. *Poungi,* 'a fist;' *poupē,* 'a bunch, a tuft.' Arm. *phovnḡ,* 'a bunch, a tuft.' Lat. *pugnus.*

131. *Prassē,* 'a leek.' Arm. *pras,* 'a leek.' Gr. πράσον.

132. *Psikyē,* 'a bladder.' Arm. *phćel,* 'to blow;' *phchal,* 'to be inflated;' *phovch,* 'wind, gust, swelling;' *phosi,* 'powder.' Gr. φυσάω, φύσιμα. Lapp. *pusset,* 'flare.'

133. *Pul,* 'a forest.' Arm. *povrak,* 'a forest.'

134. *Rouphē,* 'drinkable, soft, *schlürfbar*' (applied to an egg). Arm. *rovph,* 'syrup of grapes.'

135. *Samar,* 'a pack-saddle.' Arm. *thambel,* 'to saddle.'

136. *Siri,* 'sex, kind.' Arm. *ser,* 'sex, kind.'

137. *Skalis,* 'I lop, I carve.' Arm. *selb,* 'the blade of a knife.' Thrac. σκάλμη, 'a sword.'

138. *Skyurē,* 'a plate.' Arm. *skovtel,* 'a plate.' Lat. *scutra, scutella.*

139. *Soulyts,* 'a bolt, a bar.' Arm. *zalk,* 'a rod, a stick;' *sol,* 'a bar, a pole;' *solnak,* 'a bolt.'

140. *tus,* 'I dip.' Arm. *sovzanel,* 'to dip;' *sovzi,* 'I dipped.'

141. *tami,* 'a kerchief.' Arm. *wartamak, warsakal,* 'kerchief, fillet' (*warsch,* 'hair.')

142. *Selkyiñ*, 'a melon.' Arm. *setkh, sekh*, 'a melon.' Gr. σίκυς.

143. *Souatë, sout*, 'sad.' Arm. *sovg*, 'mourning, grief.'

144. *Sour*, 'sand, gravel.' Arm. *čor*, 'dry.'

145. *Sourrë*, 'water.' Arm. *govr*, 'water.'

146. *Tayö*, 'a wet-nurse.' Arm. *tazel*, 'to nourish.'

147. *Tokë*, 'land.' Arm. *yatak*, 'land.'

148. *Tserlë*, 'a blackbird.' Arm. *sarik*, 'blackbird, starling;' th. *sarel*, 'to cry.' Thessal. ἀστραλός, 'ψαρός.'

149. *Tsingouly*, 'a kind of small fig.' Arm. *thovz*, 'a fig;' *thzeni*, 'a fig-tree.'

150. *Tsinkërë*, 'ice.' Arm. *zivn*, 'snow.' Lapp. *tsewe*, 'nix durior, quæ subtus crustam habet glacialem.' Abas. *zeh*, 'snow.'

151. *Tsitsë, sisë*, 'breast.' Arm. *zoü*, 'breast.' Germ. *zitze*. Pol. *cyc*.

152. *Tsoulyë*, 'flute, pipe.' Arm. *sovlel*, 'to pipe.' Lat. *sibilare*.

153. *Tsokhë*, 'cloth.' Arm. *čovkhay*, 'cloth,' = Turk. *choha*, Pol. *chustka*, Germ. *tuch*.

154. *Tsap*, 'a step.' Arm. *čaph*, 'a measurement, an ell'
——Arm. *savil*, 'a step.'

155. *Tsark*, 'a circuit.' Arm. *sovrǰ*, 'around;' *srǰan*, 'a circuit.' Lat. *circus*.

156. *Tsikë*, 'a little, few.' Arm. *sakav*, 'a little, few.' Basque *chiquia*, = Span. *chico*, 'little.'

157. *Ul*, 'a star.' Arm. *sot*, 'a ray of light.' Lat. *sol*, = Welsh *sûl*, = Swed. *sol*.

158. *Uliber*, 'a rainbow;' *ap ultin*, 'I bend' (*ap*, 'I give,' or 'I give up'). Arm. *atetn*, 'a bow.'

159. *Phouphoupheikë*, 'an owl.' Arm. *bov*, 'an owl.' Lat. *bubo*.

160. *Phtoua*, 'a quince' (μῆλον Κυδώνιον). Arm. *ptovṭ*, 'fruit' (μῆλον).

161. *Cha*, 'I eat.' Arm. *ǰatel*, 'to eat;' *khah*, 'cooked meat.'

162. *Chapëtë,* 'bright in colour' (γλαυκός). Arm. *kapoyt;* Pers. *kabód;* Sansk. *kapota;* 'blue, azure' (γλαυκός).
163. *Chi, chiñ,* 'ashes.' Arm. *ajivn,* 'ashes.' Lat. *cinis.* Lapp. *kuna.*
164. *Choundë,* 'the nose.' "Root, *chouny* or *ouny* (?), 'to put down, to bend.'" Arm. *ovnéch,* 'the nose;' *ovnj,* 'the lowest part, the foot, the ground.' Osset. *fünz,* 'the nose.' Abas. *pintsa,* 'the nose.'

The Rhæto-Romansch language is the next in order. It is spoken, in two principal dialects, in the Swiss Canton of the Grisons, and is almost entirely derived from the Latin and German. My authority for these dialects is Carisch's *Taschen-Wörterbuch der Rhätoromanischen Sprache.*

Rhæto-Romansch words allied to the Armenian.

1. *Acola,* 'a farm (*gut*) with stabling (*stallung*) outside a village.' Arm. *akhor;* Pers. *ákhár;* 'a stable.'
2. *Adinna,* 'always.' Arm. *andén,* 'always, immediately.'
3. *Adom,* 'a fastening' (*befestigungsring an den schlitten-latten*). Arm. *yódel,* 'to fasten.'
4. *Aegla.* 'Boschg ('shrub') d'*ägla,*' 'holm-oak.' Arm. *katin,* 'an acorn,' = Lyd. ἄκυλον, Germ. *eichel.* Cf. also Lat. *galla,* Span. *agalla.*
5. *Aisel,* 'active.' Arm. *ays,* 'spirit.'
6. *Ancanuras,* 'sometimes.' Arm. *angam,* 'time, *fois, mal.*'
7. *Ancarna,* 'corner, angle.' Arm. *ankiun,* 'a corner.' Lyd. ἀγκών. Germ. *winkel.*
8. *Aneg,* 'suddenly.' Arm. *anaknkal,* 'sudden:' *an-,* privative; *akn,* 'an eye;' *kal,* 'to be;' *aknkalel,* 'to expect.' Goth. *anaks,* 'suddenly.'
9. *Anfis,* 'disagreeable.' Arm. *anpét,* 'useless, vile, detestable:' *an-* privative; *piti,* 'il faut.' Eng. *unfit.*
10. *Araig,* 'a king.' Arm. *archay,* 'a king.'——Gael. *righ* = Lat. *rex.*

11. *Arfüdar,* 'to reject.' Arm. *phoyth,* 'haste;' *phovthal,* 'to hasten.' Gael. *put,* 'to push, to throw.' Lyd. ἀρφύραινον, 'a quoit.' Piedm. *arfudè,* 'to reject.' Lat. *repudio.* Eng. *refuse, refute.*

12. *Argiavenna,* 'bear's-foot' (*acanthus*). Arm. *arj,* 'a bear;' *aph,* 'the palm of the hand' (?).

13. *Asienf,* 'usury.' Arm. *watch,* 'usury.'

14. *Asöl, asoula,* 'a kid' (*ziegenlamm*). Arm. *ayz,* 'a goat;' *ovl,* 'a kid.'

15. *Avdar, abitar,* 'to dwell.' Arm. *öth* or *avth,* 'a dwelling.' Lat. *habitare.*

16. *Aziever,* 'to fetch.' Arm. *azel,* 'to bring.'

17. *Baguord,* 'ugly.' Arm. *pagsot,* 'foul.'

18. *Bambesch,* 'cotton.' Arm. *bambak,* 'cotton.' Ital. *bambagia.*

19. *Bap,* 'father, grandfather.' Arm. *pap,* 'grandfather.'

20. *Bargalir,* 'to rise.' Arm. *larzr,* 'high.'

21. *Bassiar, bassegiar,* 'to make haste.' Arm. *wazel,* 'to hasten.' Lyd. βάσκε, 'ἐξεθόαζε.'

22. *Basta,* 'enough!' Ital. *basta!* Arm. *báv é,* 'enough!' The first element in *ba–sta* would = Arm. *bav, sta* being = Lat. *stat.* So also the Lat. *sat* = Arm. *sat,* as well as Gael. *sath.*

23. *Blada,* 'the consecrated wafer.' Arm. *blith,* 'bread, cake.' Gael. *bleath, bleith, bleth,* 'to grind.'

24. *Bletsch,* 'wet.' Arm. *blkhil,* 'to flow.'

25. *Boda,* 'pestilence.' Arm. *wat,* 'bad.' Lith. *béda,* 'calamity;' *bodus,* 'troublesome.'

26. *Brainta,* 'mist.' Arm. *bovrel,* 'to exhale, to smell;' *bovrovmn,* 'odour.' Lyd. βρίνθιον, 'μύρον.'

27. *Bröl,* 'an orchard.' Arm. *ber,* 'fruit;' *bovrastan,* 'an orchard.'

28. *Bural,* 'an orifice.' Arm. *beran,* 'orifice, mouth.' Lith. *burna,* 'mouth.'

29. *Büsen,* 'a reed;' *büschen,* 'water-pipes;' *buschun,*

'strong.' Arm. *bovsak*, 'a plant;' *bovsanil*, 'to grow, to rise.' Lapp. and Swed. *basun*, 'tuba.'

30. *Candarials.* See *ante*, in Lyd. (p. 40) s. v. κανδαύλης.

31. *Cattar*, 'to find.' Arm. *gtanel*, 'to find;' *givt*, 'invention.' Eng. *get*.

32. *Chuz*, 'destitute.' Arm. *échoti*, 'poor, abject.'

33. *Clech*, 'amiable, tender.' Arm. *ktkath*, 'loving, affectionate.'

34. *Crap*, 'a stone.' Arm. *char, kharak*, 'rock, stone.'

35. *Creppa*, 'a skull.' Arm. *kafaphn*, 'skull, head.' Ital. *greppa*, 'a mountain-top,' = Welsh *crib*. Gr. κάρα. Cf. *Carpates* Montes.

36. *Cuosp*, 'a wooden shoe.' Arm. *kósik*, 'a shoe.'

37. *Custer*, 'near.' Arm. *koys, kovst*, 'side.' Lat. *costa*.

38. *Cuzzantar*, 'to preserve.' Arm. *zgovsanal*, 'se garder.'

39. *Daja, tegen, degien*, 'a dagger.' Arm. *dasoyn, datnak*, 'a dagger;' *dakovr, dakr*, 'an axe;' *tég*, 'a spear.' Esth. *tägi*, 'pike, sword.' Gorm. *degen*. Lyd. τεγοῦν, 'λροτήν.'

40. *Disch*, 'length of time.' Arm. *tich*, 'age;' *tivch*, 'days.'

41. *Dischöl*, 'indigestion.' Arm. *dt-* = Gr. δυς-; *hal*, 'digestion.'

42. *Dondagiar*, 'to waver, to reel.' Arm. *dandatel*, 'to waver, to reel.'

43. *Evna*, 'a week.' Arm. *evthn*, 'seven.' Alb. *yavë*, 'a week.'

44. *Fadigna*, 'a bough.' Arm. *phayt*, 'wood, tree.' Gael. *fiodh*, 'timber, wood.'

45. *Falc*, 'hoary.' Arm. *bal*, 'paleness, obscurity.' Lat. *pallor*.

46. *Fassui*, 'a pickaxe.' Arm. *phosel, phaparel*, 'to dig.' Lat. *fossa*.

47. *Fecht*, 'desire.' Arm. *phaphach*, 'desire.'

48. *Fig, fich*, 'very;' *fig fig*, 'extremely.' Arm. *yoyt*, 'very;' *yoyt yoyt*, 'extremely.'

49. *Foppa*, 'a hollow, a ravine.' Arm. *phap, phapar,* 'a hollow, a cave, a hole.' Lapp. *fuoppe,* 'angustia.'

50. *Friank*, 'an asylum' (*freistätte*). Arm. *phrkel*, 'to free;' *phrkanch*, 'deliverance.' *Briges*, or *Phryges*, signified 'free' in Lydian.

51. *Ga, gada, giada,* 'time, *fois, mal*.' Pers. *gah,* 'time.' Arm. *gam,* 'time, *fois, mal;' gizak,* 'time, *temps, zeit,'* = Lith. *gadyne*.

52. *Giantar, jentar,* 'to dine.' Arm. *jaŝel,* 'to dine;' *jamb*, 'food.' Thrac. γίντα, 'meat.' Span. *yantar,* = Basque *jan,* 'to eat.' Lat. *jentaculum*.

53. *Giever,* 'at least.' Arm. *géth,* 'at least.'

54. *Gig,* 'long.' Arm. *gagathn,* 'height.' Gr. γίγας.

55. *Gitti,* 'avaricious.' Arm. *kẓẓi,* 'avaricious.' Germ. *geizig*.

56. *Glivrer,* 'to finish.' Arm. *glkhel, glkhavorel,* 'to finish.'

57. *Gniff,* 'muzzle.' Arm. *kngith,* 'muzzle.'

58. *Gniocc,* 'a ball of paste.' Arm. *gndak,* 'ball, pellet.'

59. *Guis,* 'a marten.' Arm. *kovz, kznachis,* 'a marten, a pole-cat.' Pol., Serv., and Bohem., *kuna,* Russ. *kuniza,* Lith. *kiaune,* 'a marten.' The Rhæt-Rom. *guis,* though partly allied to the Slavonian, can be derived, as far as I am aware, from no European language. The Lat. for 'marten' is *martes*; the Basque, *martea*; the Germ., *marder*; the Fr., *martre* or *fouine*; the Gr., γαλίη; the Gael., *taghan* or *neas*; the Lapp., *mart* or *neete*; and the Esth., *nuggis,* in which we find the termin. of the Arm. *kz-nachis.* See also *ante,* p. 11, in Cappad. s. v. νηεξίς. The Slavonic *ku-na* and *ku-niza* may not improbably be equivalent to the Arm. *kznachis,* = *kovz-nachis;* in which case, one of the two Arm. words would appear to have travelled westward with the Thracians into the Grisons, and the other to have been taken up by the Sarmatians. The root of the Arm. *kovz* and Rhæt-Rom. *guis* may perhaps be found in the Arm. *khovzel,* 'to seek, to *ferret* out (*fureter*).' Thus the origin of a word used at the source of the Rhine is found at the source of the Euphrates.

60. *Gutta,* 'a fir-cone;' *giutt,* 'a barleycorn.' Arm. *kovt, kovtak,* 'grain, berry, kernel, globe, ball.'

61. *Ieli,* 'oil.' Arm. *ivt, et,* 'oil.'

62. *Lävi,* 'grand, brilliant.' Arm *lav,* 'good, fine.' Lith. *lábas,* 'good.'

63. *Leih,* 'a lake.' Arm. *lij,* 'sea.'

64. *Maladera,* 'sheep-fold.' Arm. *machi,* 'an ewe;' *mayel,* 'to bleat.' Phryg. μᾶ, 'sheep.' Gr. μῆλον.—Arm. *hót, hóran,* 'a flock,' = Span. *hato.*

65. *Marangun, margun, bargun,* 'a hay-loft' (*fenil*). Arm. *marag,* 'a hay-loft.'

66. *Maschchar,* 'to chew.' Arm. *matel,* 'to bite, to eat.' Ital. *masticare.*

67. *Matt,* 'a child.' Arm. *matat,* 'young.' Ital. *mozzo.*

68. *Mazzar,* 'to kill.' Arm. *mah,* 'death;' *mahatan,* 'what kills;' *mahanal,* 'to die.' Ital. *ammazzare.* Span. *matar.* Lat. *macto.*

69. *Mott,* 'sense.' Arm. *mitch,* 'sense.' Germ. *muth.*

70. *Murtitsch,* 'parchment, white leather' (*weissleder*). Arm. *morth,* 'skin, leather.'

71. *Nausch, nosch,* 'bad, wicked.' Arm. *wnas,* 'evil, wickedness.' Lat. *noceo.*

72. *Nuir,* 'new.' Arm. *nor,* 'new.'

73. *Nuorsa,* 'a sheep.' Arm. *nokhaz,* 'he-goat, ram;' *oroj,* 'a lamb.' (?)

74. *Palusa,* 'a caterpillar.' Arm. *balting,* 'gad-fly, wasp.'

75. *Paratscha,* 'the husk or hull of a nut' (*hülse*). Arm. *parazazkel,* 'to envelop' (*küllen*).

76. *Pass,* 'dried up;' *pissun,* 'dry grass;' *paschantar,* 'to burn away by caustics.' Arm. *pasch,* 'excessive thirst.' Manx *paays,* 'thirst.'

77. *Pazzen,* 'a painted consecrated image' (*gemaltes heiligenbild*). Arm. *bagin,* 'an idol, a sacred image.'

78. *Peda, peida,* 'time.' Arm. *pateh,* 'time.' Lapp. *pádd,* 'tempus.'

79. *Pettla,* 'filth.' Arm. *pitɣ,* 'filth.'

80. *Piaun, painch,* 'butter;' *puonna,* 'newly made cheese or butter.' Arm. *panir,* 'cheese.' Lith. *pénas,* 'milk.' Pers. *pih,* 'grease.' Lat. *pinguis.*

81. *Pit,* 'pay.' Arm. *pitani, piloy, pitoych,* 'profitable, useful, necessary.' Thrac. πιτύγις, 'treasure.'

82. *Raschlir,* 'to burn.' Arm. *hranal,* 'to burn;' *hratek,* 'ardent.'

83. *Ravuigl,* 'bosom.' Arm. *orowayn,* 'bosom.'

84. *Sain, saign, senn,* 'a bell.' Arm. *zank;* Pers. *zang;* 'a bell.' Arm. *tayn,* 'voice, sound, tone, noise.'

85. *Salipp, sagliutt,* 'a locust.' Arm. *strid,* 'a cricket;' *salap,* 'gliding, quick.'

86. *Sava,* 'threshold.' Arm. *seam, seamch,* 'threshold.'

87. *Stuver,* 'to be obliged' (*müssen*). Arm. *stipel,* 'to constrain.'

88. *Talach,* 'a little bell.' Arm. *tal,* 'song.' Pers. *tálás,* 'voice.' Eng. *talk, tell, toll.*

89. *Tarlahar,* 'to mock.' Arm. *satrel,* 'to mock.'

90. *Tarmanigl,* '*zigerkübel;*' *tarmantucc-upp,* 'eine Alpspeise, brod und *ziger* in butter *geröstet;*' *tierm,* '*ziger,*' i.e., the solid part of milk, of which cheese is made; *chierm,* 'fodder.' Arm. *darman,* 'victuals.' Sansk. *dharma,* 'what supports all men.' But *tierm* is more nearly the Arab. *tirm,* 'butter;' cf. τυρός. In *tarmantucc-upp,* compare *tucc* with Arm. *thkh(el),* 'to bake,' and *upp* with Arm. *eph,* 'cooking.'

91. *Tarna,* 'a moth;' *fafarinna,* 'a butterfly.' Arm. *thithern,* 'a butterfly.' Ital. *farfalla.* Lat. *papilio.*

92. *Tev-(d'puerch),* 'side (of bacon).' Arm. *deh;* Irish *taobh;* 'a side.'

93. *Theu,* 'a pine-tree.' Arm. *thi,* 'an oar;' *thelót,* 'a pine-tree;' *elevin,* 'a pine-tree, a cedar;' *elat,* 'a cedar;' Georg. *urtheli,* 'a pine-tree.' *Theu* and *thi* probably meant originally 'a tree;' and *theu* would have come to signify '*the* tree of the Alps, i.e., 'a pine-tree.' In *th-el(ós)* = *el(evin)* = ἐλ(άτη), the

last member would signify 'pine,' and *th-*, 'a tree,' would be found in *thi*, 'an oar.'

94. *Tutta*, 'a kind of reed, of which children make squirts.' Arm. *thathar̄*, 'a siphon, a spout.'

95. *Uettar*, 'to anoint.' Arm. *ōzanel*, 'to anoint;' th. *ōz*.

96. *Umblauna*, 'ptarmigan, (*schneehuhn*). Arm. *amayi*, 'desert;' *ameyi*, 'wild' (?): *alavni*, 'a pigeon,' = Osset. *balón*. Lat. *palumbes*. Another word for 'ptarmigan' is *arblauna* (*weiss-huhn*). It does not appear whether we should divide into *ar-blauna* and *um-blauna*, or into *arb-launa* and *umb-launa*.

97. *Verr*, 'a wild boar.' Arm. *waraz*, 'a wild boar,' = Russ. *wehr*, = Sansk. *vardha*. Lat. *verres*.

98. *Verscha*, *uerscha*, 'the crown of the head.' Arm. *wer*, 'above;' *werǵ*, 'end.' Lat. *vertex*.

99. *Zaina*, 'a drinking-glass.' Arm. *san*, 'urn, kettle.' Pied. *sana*, 'a drinking-cup.' Lapp. *saja*, *saun*, 'situla.' O. Pers. σαννάκρα, 'a cup.' Thrac. σανάται, 'drunk.'

100. *Zapp*, 'a step;' *zaplida*, 'a sledge-road little used.' Arm. *tavit*; Arab. *sabīl*; 'path, footstep' (τρίβος, Mark i. 3.)

101. *Zezna*, 'dung.' Arm. *zazir*, 'foul;' .*zazrovthivn*, 'ordure;' *zaz̄az̄*, 'vile.'

102. *Zottla*, 'a wagtail.' Arm. *z̄it*, 'a sparrow;' *z̄iz̄arn*, 'a swallow;' *z̄iz̄arnovk*, 'a nightingale'——or perhaps better from *z̄et*, *tovin*, 'a tail,' and *dotal*, 'to wag.' Pers. *sisdlak*, 'a wagtail.'

103. *Zuncla, juncla*, 'leather thong, latchet;' *sua, suga*, 'cord.' Arm. *covan*, 'cord, string.'

The last, and most important, of the languages to be considered, is the Etruscan. Its relics consist of: (1) words of which the meaning has been given; and (2) inscriptions. The interpreted words will claim the first notice: I am indebted for them to the collection of Etruscan words in Dr. Donaldson's *Varronianus*.

Etruscan Words.

1. *Æsar,* 'Deus:' αἰσοί, 'Ξεοί.' Gael. *aos,* 'fire, the sun, God;' *Aosar* (= *Aos-fear*), 'God.' Irish *Aosar, Aesar,* 'God.' O. Norse *ás,* 'deus.' Arm. *ays,* 'spirit, demon;' *nesar,* 'demon.'

2. *Agalletor,* 'παῖς.' Gael. *og, ogail,* 'youthful;' *oglach,* 'lad;' *ogalachd,* 'youth.' Welsh *og, ogl,* 'full of motion or life, young' (cf. ὠκύς, *agilis*); *ogledd,* 'fulness of life or motion.' Arm. *ogi,* 'spirit;' *ogeliž,* 'full of spirit.' Lith. *waikas, waikélis,* 'a child.' Georg. *akhali,* 'young.' Turk. *oghul,* 'son;' *oghlan,* 'boy.' Alb. *dyallyë,* 'child;' *dyallythi,* 'lad.' *Agalletor* seems = Gael. *ogalachd* with the Gael. termination *-or*, and to the Welsh *ogledd* with the Welsh termination *-wr*.

3. *Antar,* 'ἀετός.' Arab. and Pers. *nasr,* 'vulture, eagle.' Arm. *angt,* 'vulture;' *anzet,* 'jay.'

4. *Antæ,* 'ἄνεμοι:' *Andas,* 'Boreas.' Arm. *aniu* (in compos. *aniž*), = O. Norse *ande,* = Gael. *anam,* = Lat. *anima.* Lat. *ventus.* Germ. *wind.* Gr. ἄνεμος. *Antar,* 'an eagle,' may be allied to *andas,* as *aquila* is to *aquilo.*

5. *Aracus,* 'ἴἑραξ.' Arm. *arag, erag,* 'swift,'[1] = Gr. ἀργής, = Sansk. *ara,* = Lapp. *arwok;* *aragil,* 'a stork or heron (ciconia seu erodius);' *arsin,* 'stork, falcon;' *arziv,* 'an eagle,' = O. Pers. ἄρξιφος, = Goth. *ara,* = Lapp. *arts,* = Lith. *arélis; ori,* 'a sparrow-hawk;' *ovrour,* 'a kite.' *Aracus* is the name of an Armenian in the Behistun inscription.

It appears rather probable that *aragil,* which signifies 'stork' in Armenian, or some word very like *aragil,* signified 'falcon' in Lydian. For, in that language, βαθ-υρρηγάλη signified 'ἰκτῖνος' (*ante,* p. 39). Bötticher compares βαθ- with the Arm. *bad,* 'anas,' and adduces the German name of a bird of prey, *entenstösser.* We have a kind of hawk called a

---

[1] ἴρηκι ἐοικὼς
ὠκέϊ, φασσοφόνῳ, ὅστ' ὤκιστος πετεηνῶν.—*Il.* xv. 237.

ken-driver, as well as a *sparrow-hawk*. Βαθυρρηγάλη may be equivalent to *duck-hawk*.

6. *Arimus*, 'πίθηκος.' Arm. *ayr*, 'vir, homo;' *ari*, 'virile, bold,' *i. e.* 'resembling man.'——Heb. *charum*, 'simus.'

7. 8. *Arse verso*, 'averte ignem.' Lat. *arceo*. Gr. ἀρκέω. Arm. *argel*, 'hindrance, obstacle, opposition.'——Arm. *herchel*, 'to repel.' Alb. *err*, 'to keep off.'——Irish *fursan*, 'flame.' Gael. *buirseach*, 'flame.' Arm. *hovr, war, borboch*, 'fire.' Germ. *feuer*. Gr. πῦρ.

9. *Atæsum*, 'ἀναδίνδρας.' Pied. *autin*, 'a vine.' Arm. *yódel*, 'to bind.' Gael. *iadh*, 'to bind.' This would give the first syllable of *at-æsum*; while *-æsum* may perhaps be explained from the Arm. *aygi*, 'a vine;' Pers. *ázakh*, 'a cutting of a vine;' Pehlvi *as, asia*, 'wine;' *asiav*, 'a vine.'[1] Compare Fr. *lier* and *lierre*; Arm. *batel*, 'to bind,' *bateln*, 'ivy;' and Gael. *iadh*, 'to bind,' *eidheann*, 'ivy.' These instances may illustrate the derivation of *vitis* from *vieo*, and of *autin* and *atæsum* from *yódel* or *yavdel*. So also the Germ. *rebe* is connected with the Ang.-Sax. *ræpen*, 'to bind' (Diefenbach, *Lex. Comp.* v. ii. p. 163).

10. *Balteus*, 'the military girdle.' Eng. *belt, baldric,* = Iceland. *belti*, = Gael. *balt*. Gael. *bolt*, 'lacinia, ora, margo.' Arm. *bolor*, 'garland, circle;' *bolorel*, 'to gird;' *batcl*, 'to join.'

11. *Burrus*, 'κάνθαρος.' Arm. *bor, borel*, 'a gad-fly;' *bzéz, bziz*, 'a beetle;' *bzzel* or *bëzzel*, 'to buzz' (= Fr. *bourdonner*). Thus the primitive meaning of *burrus* would be 'the buzzer,' 'the beetle' that 'wheels his droning flight,' 'the shard-borne beetle with his drowsy hums.' Alb. *vousë*, 'a dung-beetle;' *bourkth*, 'a cricket.' Pers. *buzk*, 'a kind of *cantharides*, a cricket, a rose-worm.' Turk. *bujik*, 'a beetle, any creeping thing.' Gael. *burruis*, 'a caterpillar.' Rhæt-Rom. *bau*, 'a small beetle or insect.' Georg. *buzi*, 'a fly.'

---

[1] *His* is the name of the vine in Imeretia and Mingrelia, the ancient Colchis. Parrot, p. 274. The vine climbs there to the summits of high trees, and then hangs down to the ground.

12. *Capra,* 'αἴξ.' Welsh *gafyr;* Bret. *gavr;* Gael. *gabhar;* O. Norse *hafr;* 'a goat.' Lapp. *habra;* Arm. *chôsh* or *chavsh;* 'hircus.'

13. *Capys,* 'falco.' Arm. *gavaz,* 'a small sparrow-hawk.' Gael. *cabhar;* Lapp. *hapak, hapke, hauka;* Germ. *habicht;* Welsh *hebog;* 'a hawk.'

14. *Cassis,* 'helmet or *casque*,' properly *capsis.* Gael. *cap, ceap;* Bret. *kab;* Welsh *cop;* 'head.' Lat. *caput.* Gr. κεφαλή. Germ. *kopf, haupt.* Lapp. *kaip;* Esth. *kapo;* 'a hat.' Eng. *cap.* Germ. *haube.* Fr. *casquette.*

15. *Celer,* 'swift:' *celeres,* 'equites.' Pers. *gelak,* 'valde agilis.' Arm. *khatal,* 'to go, to leap;' *chaylel,* 'to walk.' ——Gr. κέλης, κέλλω. Alb. *kaly,* 'a horse;' *kalyëri, kalyori,* 'riding;' *kalyores,* 'a rider.' Carian ἄλα, 'equus,' = Gael. *al.*

16. *Damnus,* 'ἵππος.' Lapp. *támp,* 'equus.' Fin. *tamma;* Arm. *zambik;* 'equa' (*jument*). Basque *zamaria,* 'jumentum vectorium, *caballeria.*' Arm. *thambel,* 'to saddle;' *hamberel,* 'to bear.' Cf. *onus* and ὄνος. Alb. *samaros,* 'jumentum.' Pehlvi *djemna,* 'a camel.' Mantschu *temen,* 'a camel.' Old Mexican *tamanes,* 'carriers.' Gael. *damh,* 'an ox, a stag.'

17. *Druna,* 'ἀρχή.' Irish *dron,* 'right;' *dronadh,* 'direction;' *dronain,* 'throne.' Gr. Θρόνος.——Arm. *tér,* 'sovereign;' *térovni,* 'belonging to the Lord.'

18. *Falandum,* 'cœlum.' Lat. *palatum, palam.* Gr. φαλαρός, = Arm. *phaylovn.*——Pers. *buland,* 'high;' *buland o pusht,* 'high and low, heaven and earth.' Pehlvi *beland,* 'high.'—— Arab. *falak,* 'the sky.'—— Lapp. *palwa,* 'nubes.'——Gael. *failbhe,* 'the aerial void.'

19. *Februum,* 'inferum.' (Also Sabine). O. H. Germ. *furbjan,* 'purgare.' Eng. *furbish.* Fr. *fourbir.* Ital. *forbire.* Ang.-Sax. *feormian,* 'purgare.' Gael. *foirfe,* 'without fault;' *fior,* 'pure;' *feabh,* 'good;' *feabhas,* 'beauty, goodness, improvement.'

20. *Gapus,* 'ὄχημα.' Gael. *cap,* 'a cart.' Lat. *capsus.* Gr. κάψα, καπάνη.

21. *Ginis*, '*γέρανος*.' Bötticher considers that Lat. *auca* = Sansk. *vaka*, 'grus,' *a clangore*. So *ginis* may be considered = χήν and *gans*, and be compared with O. Norse *gína*, = Germ. *gähnen*, = Gr. χαίνω, and Lat. *cano*. In Arm. we have *ganćel*, 'to cry;' *kanćel*, 'to call;' and *khanćel*, 'to yelp,' = Lat. *gannire*.

The names of the crane seem generally to be derived *a clangore*. Thus γέρανος and *grus* may be referred to γηρύω, Lat. *garrio*, = Sansk. *krus*; the Germ. *kranich* to *krähen*; the Gael. *garan* to *gair*, 'a shrill cry;' and the Arm. *khord* and *krnkan*, to *khordal*, 'râler,' and *krnćel*, 'crier.'

22. *Hister*, 'ludio.' Arm. *hest*, 'easy, light, pleasant;' *hestali*, 'agreeable, diverting;' *hestalovr*, 'supple;' *hestanal*, 'to amuse one's self.'

23. *Itus*, 'idus.' Irish *itir* or *idir*, 'between.' Alb. *ith*, 'through.'

24. *Læna*, 'a double cloak.' Gael. *leine*, 'a shirt, a shroud, a kind of dress.' Lat. *lana*. Pers. *layn*, 'indusium breve angustis manicis.' Gr. χλαῖνα, χλάνις. Arm. *khlay*, *lódik*, 'a cloak.' Lat. *lòdix*. Swed. *kläde*. Germ. *kleid*. Eng. *cloth*, *clothe*.

25. *Lanista*, 'gladiator.' Irish *lann*, 'a sword.' Welsh *llafyn*, 'a blade.' Lat. *lanio*, *lamina*.

26. *Nanus*, 'πλανήτης.' Arm. *neng*, 'craft, deceit;' *nengel*, 'to deceive' (πλανάω); *nanir*, 'vain, futile.'

27. *Nepos*, 'luxurious.' Pers. *nefsani*, 'luxuriosus, carnalis.' Arab. and Turk. *nefs*, 'delicatus.' The th. is the Arab. *nefs*, = Heb. *nefes*, 'breath, soul, animal, body, flesh.' Pol. *napaiać*, 'to inspire, to give to drink;' *napasé*, 'to glut.' Alb. *nepës*, 'a glutton.' Arm. *nivth*, 'body, matter.'

28. *Subulo*, 'tibicen.' Goth. *svilja*, 'pfeifer, αὐλητής.' Upper Germ. *schwibeln*, 'pfeifen.' Welsh *çwib*, 'a pipe.' Lat. *sibilare*, = Pers. *siflidan*, = Arm. *sovlel*. Alb. *tsoulyë*, 'a flute.' Rhæt-Rom. *schiblot*, 'a flute.'

29. *Vorsus*, 'a measure of land one hundred feet square.'

THE ARMENIAN ORIGIN OF THE ETRUSCANS. 101

(Also Umbrian). Pers. *warg̀*, 'a digging, an area round a house;' *warz*, 'agriculture, a field having a raised border round it.' Arm. *wayr*, 'space, extent, piece of ground;' *warel*, 'to cultivate, to prepare;' *wartel*, 'to prepare.' Compare *acre, acker*, and *ackern*.

For the explanation of the words contained in this Etruscan vocabulary, two languages are indispensable, the Armenian and the Celtic. Now the Etruscan nation in Italy was in all probability made up of two elements, the Tyrrhenian and the Umbrian. To the latter of these we may attribute the Celtic element in the Etruscan language, and to the former the Armenian element. The structure of the language we should expect to be Armenian, as the Umbrian would be the intrusive element in Etruscan. Accordingly, when we come to examine the Etruscan inscriptions, we shall find this to be the case.

Etruscan Inscriptions.

Etruscan inscriptions are mainly of two kinds, sepulchral and votive. By the recurrence of the same words and forms in these inscriptions, and by comparing them, in addition, with similar inscriptions in Latin, we are enabled, not merely to deduce with great probability the meaning of single Etruscan words, but also to proceed step by step to the interpretation of some complete Etruscan sentences, and thus to become sufficiently acquainted with the signification of Etruscan expressions, and the grammatical forms and mechanism of the language, to pronounce with increased confidence upon its affinities. The result of such a process appears to be in accordance with the inferences already drawn, that the Etruscan is a Thracian dialect, which has taken up some Celtic words, but is still represented in substance by the Armenian. And here it may be well to notice the degree of affinity between the Armenian and Etruscan which it is required to prove. It is such a degree of affinity as exists between the English and German, or between the Greek and Latin; not such a degree as exists between the English and Anglo-Saxon, or between the Italian and Latin. The Etruscan is to be regarded as the sister, not the daughter, of the Armenian; and as the sister, not of the oldest Armenian now existing, but of an Armenian language still more ancient by several centuries. For the Armenian, dating from about 400 A.D., may be a thousand years younger than some Etruscan inscriptions. If, therefore, we can make such progress towards the interpretation of the Etruscan by the Armenian, as an Englishman ignorant of German, or a Latin ignorant of Greek, could make in similar circumstances towards the interpretation of German or Greek, we shall then have advanced as far as we ought to advance by the aid of philology towards the establishment of the Armenian origin of the Etruscans. Such a point, I think, we shall succeed in gaining, even if, in the inscription of Cervetri, we do not go beyond it.

The first Etruscan inscriptions to be noticed are sepulchral.[1]

---

[1] The commonest forms of Etruscan sepulchres are the chambers in the rock where there are cliffs or hills, and the *tumuli* or conical barrows, with internal chambers, on more level ground. Some of the tombs in the rocks, as in the case of the Casuccini tomb at Chiusi, consist of a hall, with the entrance from without on one side, and openings into smaller chambers on the three other sides. A very similar arrangement will be observed in the rock-tomb of Van in Armenia, of which a plan and description is given by Layard (*Nineveh and Babylon*, p. 390). With respect to Etruscan *tumuli*, the writer best acquainted with them says: 'If the tumular form of sepulture were not one of natural suggestion, and which has therefore been employed by almost every nation from China to Peru, it might be supposed that the Lydians, who employed it extensively (see vol. i. p. 353) had copied the subterranean huts of their neighbours the Phrygians, and introduced the fashion into Etruria. *The conical pit-houses of the ancient Armenians might in the same way be regarded as the types of the tombs of that form which abound in southern Etruria*, and which are also found south of the Tiber, as well as in Sicily; for the description given of them (Xenophon, *Anab.* iv. 5, 25; cf. Diodor. xiv. pp. 258-9) closely corresponds. The interiors of these subterranean huts of Armenia presented scenes very

Etruscan Epitaphs.

Several words are repeatedly found in Etruscan epitaphs, in conjunction with proper names, so that their meaning may be

---

like those in an Italian *capanna* (Dennis, *Cities and Cemeteries of Etruria*, p. 61, note).

The dwellings of the Armenian peasantry are scarcely altered at the present day. A modern traveller says of them: 'The houses, however, are not properly subterraneous, in the common sense of the term. They are generally made by excavating the earth and raising a wall of loose stones to the required height. Trunks of trees are then laid across for rafters and covered with branches. Then the earth is piled on until the whole is covered, and the fabric attains a semi-globular shape. Sometimes the whole is built upon the surface, but, in both cases, the external appearance is that of a bare mound of earth. As the traveller approaches one of these villages, he discerns nothing at first but an apparent unevenness in the ground. Soon the rounded tops become distinguished.'—(Southgate, *Travels in Armenia, &c.* vol. i. p. 203). Again, (p. 305), the author observes: 'In the neighbourhood of the city (Ourmiah) there are several mounds, which the missionaries conjecture to be the hills of the ancient fire-worshippers. There are strong appearances of their being, at least, artificial. Some have been excavated, and large walls or masses of stone, regularly laid, have been found within. Human bones have also been discovered.'—Compare Micali, *Monumenti Inediti*, Tav. lv, lvi.; also Fergusson's *Handbook of Architecture*, Asia Minor and Etruria. In Sir C. Fellows' *Lycia*, c. vi., it is shown how the forms of the Lycian tombs are derived from those of domestic buildings. This illustrates the present question, and also explains the difference between the Etruscan and Lycian forms of sepulchres.

The form of Etruscan tombs thus favours, as far as such evidence can, the theory of the Armenian affinities of the Etruscans. But there are also tombs in Etruria of a third construction, and probably the work of an earlier race. Mr. Dennis gives a representation of one at Saturnia (v. ii. p. 305). There are a great many at the same place. The author writes (p. 316): 'Here the eye is startled by the striking resemblance to the cromlechs of our own country. Not that one such monument is actually standing above ground in an entire state; but remove the earth from any one of those with a single cover-stone, and in the three upright slabs, with their shelving, overlapping lid, you have the exact counterpart of Kit's Cotty House, and other like familiar antiquities of Britain; and the resemblance is not only in the form, and in the unhewn masses, but even in the dimensions of the structures. We know, also, that many of the cromlechs or kistvaens of the British Isles have been found inclosed in barrows, sometimes with a circle of small upright slabs around them; and from analogy we may infer that all (?) were originally so buried. Here is a further point of resemblance to these tombs of

very probably deduced. They may be divided into three classes: (1) words implying age; (2) words apparently implying relationship; (3) words probably referring to the tomb or urn itself. There are also (4) a few bilingual inscriptions, where proper names are given in Etruscan and Latin. The epitaphs which I shall quote are all taken from Lanzi, and indicated by his numbers. What are proper names I have indicated by capital initials. They are sometimes contracted in form.

Words implying Age.

The first seven of the following epitaphs are consecutive in Lanzi, and are numbered 450—456:

  Rav. Velan Ar. *ril* xlii. *leine.*
  L... Ste. La... *ril* xiiii. *leine.*
  Nevile Papa *aivil* xxii.
  Tha. Leivai Ma. Krake *avil* xxxiii.
  S. Svetiu L. *avil ril* lxv.
  A. Pekni *ril* liii. *leine.*
  Thana Kainei *ril leine* lv.
  Av. Leku *ril* ixx. (10).

Comparing these with the expressions, *vixit annos, annos, anno ætatis,* and *ætatis,* and observing that *leine* is joined with *ril,* and not with *avil,* the following interpretations are deduced—

  avil, 'ætas.' *ril,* 'annus.' *leine,* 'vixit.'
avil, 'ætus'.. Arm. *aveli, yavét, ar-avel,* 'more, excessive;'
    yavit-ean, 'an age;' *hav* = Lat. *avus; avag,*
    'elder;' *ót* or *avt,* 'a ring' (annulus). Lapp.
    jape, 'annus.' Goth. *aivs,* 'time.' Germ.

Saturnia. In some of the cromlechs, moreover, which are inclosed in tumuli, long passages, lined with upright slabs, and roofed in with others laid horizontally, have been found; whether the similar passages in these tombs of Saturnia were also covered in, cannot be determined.' Though cromlechs are not peculiar to the Celts, yet this close resemblance is valuable as subsidiary evidence in support of the position, that the predecessors of the Etruscans in Etruria were of Celtic origin.

ewig. Eng. *ever.* Lat. *ævum* = Gr. αἰών = O. Norse *æfi* = Arab. *abad.* Osset. *afon*, 'time;' *afey*, 'a year.'

Av-il seems to consist of the root *av*, which is Arm., and of the termination *-il*, which is also Arm. Thus we have *tes-il*, 'appearance,' from *tes*, 'sight;' *arag-il*, 'a stork,' from *arag*, 'swift.' So also *kath* and *kath-il* both signify 'a drop,' and *kath-il*, likewise, 'to drop.' All Arm. infinitives, which partake of the nature of nouns and are declined as such, terminate in *el, al, ovl*, or *il*.[1] The Arm. present participle, again, terminates in *avi, ói* or *ol*, and the past participle in *eal:* so that the terminations *l* and *t*, which are common in Arm., imply the state of being or having been what the root indicates. As forms ending in *l* are so frequent in Etruscan, it may be well to illustrate the character of the Arm. in this respect by noticing some of the derivatives from a single root, *tes*, and explaining what parts of speech they properly are.

tes, 'sight.'

tesanel, 'to see,' a form in *-anel* analogous to λαμβ-άνω.

tesanel, 'aspect,' the preceding verb used as a noun.

tesanol, 'one who sees, a seer, a prophet,' pres. part. of *tesanel*.

tesaneli, 'visible,' fut. part. of *tesanel*.

tesanelich, 'sight, the eyes,' the plural form of *tesaneli*.

---

[1] *Gol*, 'to be,' is anomalous.

tesol, 'one who sees, a prophet,' pres. part. of a non-existent verb, *tesel.*

tesil, 'aspect,' a non-existent verb, *tesil,* the pass. of *tesel,* 'to see.'

ril, 'annus'.. Arab. *rigl;* Heb. *regel,* 'time, an age.' The primitive sense is 'foot,' from the root *rag,* 'to move' (Gesen.) = Arm. ṛaḥ, as appears from the Arm. ṛaḥel, 'to go forward' (= Gael. *rack*), ṛaḥ, 'a way.' The termination of *r-il* may be explained like that of *av-il.* Compare also ṛaḥ-il and *r-il* with *niḥ-il* and *n-il.*

Arm. *aṛal-ót,* 'time.'

Georg. *roloi,* 'a clock;' *rli,* 'to run.'

Welsh *rhi,* 'what intervenes;' *rhif,* 'what divides, a number;' *rhil,* 'an interstice,' *i.e.,* 'an interval (of space):' 'a year' is 'an interval (of time).'

Leine, 'vixit'. Arm. *linel,* 'to be, to become, to exist, to live.' Hung. *lenni,*' to be;' *lény,* 'existence.' Lapp. *lei,* 'erat,' = Arm. *linér.* Germ. *leben.* Gael. *linn,* 'an age, a period.' Alb. *lyeiġ,* 'I am born;' *lyind,* 'I give birth to.' *Leine,* from its form, would rather be compared with the Arm. present, *lini,* 'he is,' than with the imperf. *linér,* 'he was.' *Linel* has no perfect.

Words apparently implying Relationship.

Klas (passim).

klan ... Gael. *clann,* 'offspring, descendants.' Welsh *plan,* 'a scion;' *plant,* 'a son.' Gr. κλάς, κλάδος, κλών, κλάω, φλάω, τλάω. Lat. *planta.* Manx *cleiḥ,* 'people;' *clein,* 'a clan;' *cleuin,* 'a son-in-law;' *cleuinys,* 'affinity;' *cloan,* 'children;' *cluight,* 'offspring.'

A more recondite and perhaps a better interpretation of *klan* is given by Müller (*Etrusker*, v. i. p. 446). He compares the two inscriptions on the same monument—

    La. Venete La. Lethial[1] *etera*
    Se. Venete La. Lethial *klan*

and observes: 'If *etera* be taken to mean 'other, second,' *klan* must be 'first, firstborn.' *Etera* is thus compared with the Gr. ἔτερος, Umbr. *etre*, Arm. *őtar*. Dr. Donaldson argues in the same manner (*Varronianus*, p. 171): 'If then *etera* means, as is most probable, the *second* of a family' (just as Arm. *mivs*, 'other,' does signify the *second* son of five—St. Martin, *Mémoires*, v. ii. p. 174), '*klan* must mean the *first* or *head* of the family.' This might bring us to the Arm.—
klan .. Arm. *glovkh*, 'head, summit, the first rank;' *glkhan tovkn* (lit. 'head-fish'), 'a chub;' *glkhani*, 'the chief persons in a city, the nobility.'

Glkhan would become *klkhan* in Etruscan; or, omitting the aspirate, *klan*.

    mi Kalairu *fuius* (191).
    Lth. Marikane *via* (315).
    Larthi Vetus Klaukes *pnia* (310).
    Arnth Vipis Serturis *pniak* Sutat...i (311).
    Anes Kaes *puil* hui...(123).

fuius
via
pnia   } Gael. *fuil*, 'blood, family, tribe, kindred.' Lat. *filius*.
pniak   Gr. υἱός, φυλή. Hung. *fin*, 'son.' Syriänic *pi*,
puil   'son.'[2] Esth. *poia*, 'son,' *pois*, 'boy.'

    Larthia Kaia Huzetnas Arnthalisa Kafatl *sak* (68).
    Titi Velimnias Akril *sek* (37).
    Ramthn Matulnei *sech* . . . . . . (471).

sak   { Arm. *zavak*, 'blood, son, child;' *zag-il*, 'to be born
sek   or derived;' *zag-el*, 'to produce young;' *zag*, 'a
sech   young bird (νεοσσός).' Gr. τέκος.

---

[1] *Lethus* is given as a Pelasgian name. (*Il.* ii. 843.)
[2] The Syriänians are a Finnish tribe in the Russian provinces of Arkhangel, Vologda, and Perm.

The exact meanings of *klan*, *fuius*, and *sak*, are not perfectly clear. *Klan* and *sak* might possibly define the *familia* or the *gens* of the deceased; and *fuius* imply youth, as parentage is indicated in Etruscan without any word signifying 'son' or 'child.' The following epitaphs, 87 and 124, shew the distinction between *klan* and such words as *fuius* or *puia*:—

    Tlatisal *puiia* Larthias Rutenei .. aural *klan* line.
    klan puiak Arnth Kaes Anes Ka . . . . .

With respect to the termination of *puiak* it may be observed that the termination -*ak* forms Arm. diminutives.

Words probably referring to the tomb or urn, or to the deceased.

Suthi. This term is frequently found. There is the following inscription at the entrance of the tomb of the Volumnii, described by Vermiglioli, near Perugia:—

    Arnth Larth Velimnas
    Arvneal Thusiur
    suthi akil theke.

The Italian antiquaries, as cited by Vermiglioli, seem to agree in regarding *suthi* as a sepulchral term. Orioli says that 'the nature of the localities on which it is found inscribed does not permit a doubt on the subject.' Migliarini interprets *eka suthi*, 'hic situs est,' or 'questa è la tomba.' Vermiglioli himself, also regarding *suthi* as a sepulchral term, seems inclined to follow Lanzi in Hellenising the Etruscan, and in referring *suthi* to σωρηρία. But the most obvious meaning is certainly 'tomb,' or 'is buried.'[1]

---

[1] There may be some slight objections to these interpretations. We find *suthina* on a statue (Micali, *Mon.* Tav. xxxv.), and on a *patera* or mirror (Tav. xlviii:). *Suthil* is also found on a kind of bronze disk of uncertain use (Lanzi, v. ii. p. 412). *Suthina* might possibly, though it does not appear probable, be etymologically unconnected with *suthi*. Its termination -*uthin(a)* resembles the Arm. termination -*ovthivn*, and the root might be the Arm. *zoh*, 'hostia;' *zoh-el*, 'θύω;' whence we might form *zohovthivn*, 'θῦμα.'

THE ARMENIAN ORIGIN OF THE ETRUSCANS.   109

suthi { Welsh *swth*, 'a heap.' Gael. *suidh*, 'a seat.' Carian σοῦα, 'a tomb.' Arm. *sovzanel*, perf. *sovzi*, th. *sovz*, 'to thrust in, to cover, to hide.'

In the previous epitaph, *theke*, found elsewhere under the form, *teke*, resembles the Gr. ἔθηκε, as Lanzi notices. It will be found that *theke* or *teke* can hardly signify anything but 'makes' or 'brings.' The Arm. words which most nearly resemble it are—*dizé*, 'erigit;' th. *déz*, 'acervus,' = Gr. θίς, θίν: *agé*, 'ducit, fert:' *çagé*, 'τίκτει, τίκει.' Cf. τίκτων: also Lapp. *takket*, Fin. *tekä*, Esth. *teggema*, 'facere.' *Akil* may be a proper name, *Acilius*, the nom. to *theke*.

Instead of *eka suthi* ('ecce sepulcrum,' or 'hic jacet'—*suthi* might be either a noun, or a verb in the 3 pers. sing., in Arm.), we sometimes meet with *eka suthi nesl*, followed by a proper name.[1] Now the word *nesl*, being found on tombs, readily leads us to the Arm. *nas*, 'a bier, a coffin;' *nekh*, 'putror;' *nekhel*, 'putrefacere;' *nekhot*, 'putrefaciens;' *nekheal*, 'putrefactus,' *i.e.* 'mortuus, cadaver, νεκρός, νέκυς.' The Arm. *sovzanel*, 'condere, mergere,' and the passive, or in this case the reflective form, *sovzanil*, 'sese condere, mergere,' are verbs like ἁμαρτάνω, which insert -*an*- between the root and the final inflexion. It would be more common to derive from a root like *sovz* the active and passive forms, *sovzel*, 'condere,' and *sovzil*, 'condi.' However, the Arm., as it is, will give us—

     ahá   sovzani   nekheal . . . . .
     ecce sese condit putrefactus . . . . .

from which we may explain the Etruscan—

     eka   suthi   nesl . . . . .

     hic conditur { mortuus / cadaver } . . . . .

     here lies { the deceased / the body of } . . . .

The Etruscan root, *nes*, would be intermediate in ortho-

---

[1] See the plate of the Campanari Museum in Dennis, v. i. p. 442. The proper name is lost.

graphy, and also in meaning, to the Arm. *nekh* and *nal*. We shall subsequently meet with another Etruscan word, *sansl*, resembling *nesl* in form, and which may be also interpreted as a participle, and identified with the Arm. *ënzavl* or *ënzol*. We have already discerned this last Arm. participial form in the Lyd. κανδαύλ-ης, = Arm. *kheldavl*, 'πυίγων.' *Ante*, p. 40.

Thutnei *thui* (76).
Laris Vete *thui* (80).
Larth Vete Arnthalisa *thui* Larth Vete line (86).
thui Larth Petrni Larthalisa (313).

Lanzi ranks *thui* with *fuius* and *puia*, and interprets it 'filius,' or 'filia.' This does not appear to me very probable. We find the root *thu* (*thov*) in the following Arm. words:—

thiv (gen. *thovoy*), 'numerus.'
thov-el, 'numerare.'
thov-é, 'numerat.'
thov-i, 'videtur, numeratur.'
thov-ich, 'sententia,' the plural form of *thovi*.

By extending a little the meaning of *thovel*, we might make it signify 'numerare, nominare, memorare,' and obtain for *thovi* the meaning, 'memoratur,' corresponding in an epitaph to 'in memoriam.' We might then interpret (86)—

Larth Vete Arnthalisa   thui.   Larth Vete   line.

Lartia Vettia Arnthalisa memoratur. Lartia Vettia $\begin{cases} \text{fuit}^1 \\ \text{vixit} \end{cases}$.

---

¹ Cf. Fr. *feu*, Ital. *fù*, 'deceased,'= Lat. *fuit*. In the beginning of the inscription of the *Torre di San Manno* (Lanzi, ii. p. 438) there occurs, in conjunction with *suthi*, 'is buried,' the word *thues*, which, if *thui* signifies 'memoratur,' ought, as *thues* has the form of a genitive, to signify 'memoriæ.' The inscription begins thus:—

Kehen   suthi   hinthiu   thues   sains   Etve   Thaure
Hic   conditur   memoriæ   Etvus   Thauru
Lautne . . . . . .
Lautnus . . . .

These meanings of *suthi* and *thues* seem not unlikely to be correct. If we should attempt to complete the translation of these few words, the Arm. would supply, for *hinthiu*, the prep. *enth*, which, with the sense of 'for,' governs a gen. *Sains* appears to agree with *thues:* we have in

Thovi, being implied in *thovich*, is both a noun and verb in Arm.

    tular Rasnal (457).
    tular Hilar .. s Serv (458).
    tular Svuriu Au. Papsinasl A. Kursnis 1 (460).
    Tetrnter*tular* (461).
tular. Arm. *thatar*, 'an earthen vessel;' *thatel*, 'to bury' (*enterrer*); th. *that*, 'tellus.' Gael. *tula*, 'a hillock.' Gr. τύλη, τύλαρος. Phryg. *telat(os)*. *Ante*, p. 32.
    Lth. Velkialu Vipinal *lupu* (465).
    L. I(n)eni Ramthai *lupu* avil xxiii (463).
    Arni Thanie *lupu* avils xvii (464).
lupu. Irish *lubha*, 'a corpse;' *lu*, 'a heap.' Gael. *lobh*, 'to putrefy.'

Bilingual Epitaphs.

    C. Licini C. f. *Nigri*.
    V. Lekne V. *Hapirnal*. } (5)

The root in *Hapirnal* is *Hapir:* it appears = *Niger*. Cf. Arm. *khavar*, 'darkness;' *khavarin*, 'dark;' *khavaranal*, 'to become dark;' *khaphtik*, 'a negro.'

    Aelie Fulni Aelies *Kiarthialisa*.
    Q. Folnius A. f. Pom. *Fuscus*. } (7)

The root in *Kiarthialisa* is *kiarth* or *kiar*. Gael. *ciar* means '*fuscus*.'

In the first of these epitaphs, as in many others, Etrusc. *Vele* = Lat. *Caius*. Compare Arm. *el*, 'height,' Gael. *aill*, 'noble, a cliff,' with Gael. *caid*, 'summit' and *caidh*, 'noble.'

Arm. *hin*, 'old,' = Welsh *hên*, = Gael. *sean*, = Lat. *sen(ex)*. These would give—

Kehen	suthi	hinthiu	thues	sains	Etve	Thaure
Hic	conditur	causâ	memoriæ	veteris	Etvus	Thaurus
Lautne						
Lautnus . . .						

The interpretations of *hinthiu* and *sains* are not to be relied on; but those of *suthi* and *thui*, given in the text, may acquire some additional probability from this inscription.

From the short epitaphs examined above, a tolerably complete vocabulary of Etruscan sepulchral expressions may be derived. We may now proceed to notice an epitaph of greater length, the longest, indeed, which is given by Lanzi (Ep. 471). It is copied by him, but not accurately, from Maffei (*Oss. Lit.* tom. v. p. 310), and is also found in the *Mus. Etrusc.* tom. iii. tav. vii. p. 108. This epitaph was discovered, written in black, more than a century ago, in a grotto at Corneto, the ancient Tarquinii. It seems to run thus, in four lines, with some *lacunæ*, when the proper names are indicated by capital initials :—

Ramthn Matulnei sech Markes Matulm—
puiam Amke Sethres Keis–ies kisum tame–u
Laf— nask Matulnask klalum ke–s– kiklenar–m–
a-avenke lupum avils—achs mealchlsk Eitvapia me—

Here we meet with the words, *sech*, *puia*(m), *lupu*(m), and *avil*(s), already noticed. It remains to be seen what assistance can be derived from the Armenian towards an interpretation of the whole. Such an interpretation must necessarily be in some degree empirical, but still it will show what can be done by a particular language, even though the accuracy of the interpretation must frequently remain doubtful. I shall take the words in their order.

Ramthn . . . A proper name, acc. of *Ramtha*. The nom. *Ramtha* and the gen. *Ramthai* are found in Lanzi's epitaphs, 232 and 463.

Matulnei . . In the original, *Matulnvi*. The Etrusc. *V* is a digamma or *F*, so that *E* and *V* are easily confounded. *Matulnei*, 'of Matulna.'

sech . . . . . 'belonging to the *gens* or *familia*,' already explained.

Markes . . . In the original, *Markve*. *Markes*, 'of Marcus' or 'Marca.'

Matulm— . Read *Matulnei*, supposing $M = N I$, and the *I* to form the beginning of an *E*, the rest being

THE ARMENIAN ORIGIN OF THE ETRUSCANS. 113

              obliterated. In the original there is no break between *Markvs* and *Matulm*—.

puiam . . . 'daughter,' already explained.

Amke . . . . A proper name, perhaps the same as *Amycus*, a reputed Bebrycian, and therefore Thracian name.

Sethres . . . A proper name, gen. of *Sethra* or *Sethre*, the former of which is found three times among Lanzi's epitaphs, as well as *Sethres* and *Sethresa*.

Keis—ies . . Read *Keisinies*. We have *Keisinis* in an epitaph in the same grotto; and Cicero, as Lanzi observes, mentions *Cæsennia* as possessing a *fundus* at Tarquinii.

kisum . . . Arm. *géš*, gen. *giši*, 'a corpse.' We find *kizi* on another tomb in the same grotto. Heb. *gešem*, 'a body.'

tame—u . . 'buries,' or 'buries here.' Arm. *damban*, *dambaran*, 'tomb, sepulchre, vault, catacomb,' = Lat. *tumulus*, Gr. τύμβος, Gael. *tuam*.

Laf—nask } 'The *gentes* or *familiæ* of Laf—na and Ma-
Matulnask } tulna.' Arm. *azg*, 'sort, race, family,' forming also a suffix, as in *aylazg*, 'different' (lit. 'other-sort'); *luvazgi*, 'noble' (lit. 'good-race').

klalum . . . 'funera.' Gr. κλαίω. Arm. *lal*, 'to mourn,' *lal, lalivn, lalovmn, lalich, lalovnch, lalovthivn*, 'mourning.'

ke—s . . . . Perhaps *kechas* or *kechase*. We find in Etrusc., *kecha, kechase,* and *kechasi*. Arm. *chakeaš*, 'solvit' (perf.); *chakeaš*, 'expiavit;' *kaheaš*, 'paravit.'

kiklenar-m- Read *kiklena Ramtha*. Arm. *kaktanal*, 'to become tender.' *Kiklena*, 'dulcissima,' an epithet occurring *passim* on children's graves. Or *kiklena* might be explained 'mortua,' from

I

the Arm. root *sig*, 'extinction, death,' and the suffix *-etén*, 'compositus:' e. g. *marmnetén*, 'corporeal' (*marmin* 'corpus').

a-avenke . . Read *apavenke*, 'se confugit ad,' or 'deponit.' Arm. *avandel*, 'to consign, to give up;' *avandé* (*z*)*kogin*, 'he gives up the ghost' (*kogi*), 'he dies;' *apavén*, 'security, refuge, retreat;' *apavinil*, 'to commit one's self to.' *Ap*-, in Arm., = Gr. ἀπ-, Lat. *ab*-. The termination *-il*, in *apavinil*, marks the passive or reflective voice. The active would be *apavinel*.

lupum . . . . Already explained. Either 'tomb,' or 'body.'

avils . . . . 'ætatis,' already explained. In the *lacuna* after *avils* would have been the number of years lived.

achs . . . . Doubtful. Cornish *ach*, 'soboles:' Welsh *ach*, 'stem, lineage.' Sansk. *vaks* 'growth,' = Arm. *ag*. *Achs*, 'adolescens, infans' (?).

mealchlsk . Also extremely doubtful. Guided by mere assonance, we might derive from the Arm., *metk*, 'μαλακός,' and *lask* or *lesk*, 'σῶμα.' See *ante*, in Alb. s. v. *lyes*. *Mealchlsk*, 'μαλακόσαρκος.' Similarly, from *phaphovk*, 'tender,' *marmin*, 'flesh, body, corpse,' and *mortk*, 'skin,' the Armenian forms the adjectives, *phaphkamarmin*, 'tender-bodied,' and *phaphkamorth*, 'tender-skinned;' so that it might also form the adj. *metkalesk*, 'μαλακόσαρκος.'

Eitvapia . . Apparently a proper name. Other readings are *Πτvapia* and *Eitvapla*. If *apia* or *vapia* could be connected with ἀπία, 'γῆ,' *eit vapia*, or *eite apia*, would suggest 'sit terra.' Arm. *izé*, 'sit;' Irish *ibh*, 'terra.'

me—— . . Uncertain. Perhaps 'me (facit);' or 'mitis,' = Arm. *melm*, Gael. *malda*. 'Sit terra levis' is a common valediction at the conclusion of Latin epitaphs.

The Armenian would thus enable us to arrive at the following interpretation for the epitaph :—

Ramtha, Matulnei sech,   Markes Matulnei
Ramtham, Matulnæ prolem, Marcæ Matulnæ
puiam, Amke   Sethres   Keis(in)ies kisum   tame-u.
filiam, Amycus a Sethre Cæsennia cadaver sepelit.
Laf—nask,   Matulnask,   klalum   ke(cha)s.
Laf—nia gens, Matulnia gens, funera { solvit. }
{ paravit. }

Kiklena   R(a)m(tha)   a(p)avenke   lupum,
{ Dulcissima } Ramtha { se confugit ad tumulum, }
{ Mortua }   { deponit   corpus, }
avils —,   achs   mealchlsk. Eitvapia me—
ætatis —, { infans } tenera. ——————[1]
          { adolescens }

I alluded above to an epitaph in the same grotto, containing the words *Keisinis* and *kizi*. It is this—

*Larth Keisinis Velus klan kizi zilachnke
meani munikleth methlm nuphzi*[2] *kanthke kalus—lupu.*

Here we meet with *kizi*, as we do with *kisum* in the previous epitaph; also with *meani*, which may be compared with the

---

[1] Compare the following epitaph in Muratori (p. MCLXXI):—
Herennie Nice
V. A. III. M. VIII. D. XVI.
Anicetus Pater Fec.
Condita Sum Nice Quæ Jam
Dulcissima Patri Ducens
Aetatis Tenera Quat
tuor Annos Abrepta Su
peris *Flentes* Jam Liqui
Parentes.
The resemblance of the first and third sentences of the Etruscan epitaph to the first two sentences of the Phrygian epitaph (*ante*, p. 84) is rather remarkable. The Phrygian, unlike the Etruscan, requires no Celtic for its explanation.

[2] Or *nupthzi*.

Arm. *mahanal,* 'to die.' *Munikleth* might be explained as a 'sepulchral monument,' from the Gael. *muin,* = Lat. *mon(eo),* and the Gael. *claidhe,* 'burial;' *cladh,* 'a sepulchre.' *Klan* and *lupu* are familiar expressions. As *Methlna* and *Methlnal* are found in Lanzi (v. ii. p. 295) as proper names, *methlm* ought to = *Metellum.* A nominative, *Methlna, Methls,* or *Methlis,* would rather be expected. The verbs appear to be *zilachnke* and *kanthke,* of which the last resembles the Arm. *chandaké,* ' he engraves or cuts.' *Zilach-nke* might be an Arm. verb in *-anakel.* Compare *phok-é* and *phokh-anaké,* 'he changes.' *Zilach-* might contain the Arm. *elag* 'fossa,' *z* being prefixed, as in *teli,* 'place,' *zetelel,* ' to place;' *akn,* ' eye,' *zakanel,* ' to eye.' Cf. Gael. adh*laic,* 'sepeli,' and Phryg. *lachit* (*ante,* p. 30). *Kizi* might be the dat. plur., = Arm. '*i géts,* the dat. sing. being *gili* or '*i gét.* The change of the *s* of *kisum* into the *z* of *kizi* might be thus explained; for the Etrusc. *z* sometimes = *ss,* as in the case of *Utuze,* = 'Οδυσσεύς. *Kizi,* ' with the dead.'

The word *zilachnke* appears twice on an urn found at Bomarzo (*Giorn. Arcad.* v. cxix. p. 325) in the connexion—*zilachnke avil SI*—which Orioli renders conjecturally (*Giorn. Arcad.* v. cxx. p. 232), ' obiit, depositus est, sepultus est (o simile) ætatis—.' Thus the Arm. would give for *kizi zilachnke* a sense which is probable, ' mortuis infoditur.'

The interpretation of the second line cannot be surmised with any confidence, but its tenour may not improbably be, that the grave and entombment were due to the care of a person named Metellus, perhaps ' with' or ' for' *nupthzi,* ' nepotibus' or ' nepoti.'

We meet with *kis* again in another epitaph, one of those contributed by Campanari to the *Giornale Arcadico,* v. cxix. It is found, p. 322 ——

Vipinans Sethre Velthur . . . Meklasial Thanchvilu *avils kis keal XS.*

The last word is a number: $X = L$ (50) in Etruscan numeration. The Arm. for 50 is *yisovn*, a modification of *hing*, 'five,' and the termination *-sovn*, in which we recognize the Gr. -κοντα, the Lat. *-ginta*, and the Goth. *-hund*. Campanari interprets *XS, LV*, though *S* does not usually signify *V* in Etruscan. Let, however, *XS* = *LV*, as it will not affect the question of affinity. We have now to explain *avils kis keal*.

avils .. 'ætatis.'

kis .... 'corpus,' if its meaning has been rightly conjectured.

keal .. Arm. *keal*, 'vivere.' The pres. part., being formed in Arm. by adding *-ol* to the root, would be *keol*, instead of which the adj. *kendan* or *kendani*, 'vivus,' is employed. The perf. part., being formed by adding *-eal* to the root, or else to the perf. *keł(i)*, 'vixi,' would be *keal* or *kełeal*, of which forms the latter is in use. But *keal* would be a genuine Arm. form for 'having lived,' which may probably be the meaning of the Etrusc. *keal*. (Compare the perf. parts. in the Armenian epitaph, *ante*, p. 28, note). So also the two forms of the perf. part. of the Arm. *kal*, 'to be, to abide, to live,' would be *keal* and *kałeal*. The four words, *avils kis keal LV*, might then be interpreted, 'having lived as to the body 55 (years) of age,' or, 'having become a corpse at 55 (years) of age.'

The following epitaph is also given by Campanari (*Giorn. Arcad.* v. cxix. p. 534). It is on a sarcophagus—

Atnas Vel. Larthal klan stalke avil LXIII.
. . . th Marutra Tarils kenaphe lupu.

We have here to explain *stalke* and *kenaphe*, both probably verbs. The Arm. suggests no root for *stalke*, but from the Gael. we get the verb *stalc*, 'become stiff.' Taking this root into the Arm., we form *stalkel*, 'rigescere, torpescere, i.e., mori,' and *stalké*, 'moritur.'

For *kenaphe* the Gael. gives *cean*, 'a debt;' *ceannach*, 'a reward;' *ceannaich*, 'to buy'(= Heb. *kanak*): and the Arm.

gin, 'a price;' *gnel, i.e., gënel,* 'to buy;' and *gné, i.e., gënê,* 'he buys.' *Gënê* becomes in Etruscan orthography *kene*. For the difference between *kene* and *kenaphe* compare the two Arm. synonyms—

khovsé,
khovsaphé, } 'he flies.'

This point will be more fully illustrated in dealing with the inscription of Cervetri. *Stalke avil LXIII.* would thus appear to mean, 'dies at the age of 63,' and *kenaphe lupu,* 'pays for the sepulchre' or 'entombment,' or something similar.

I now proceed from sepulchral to votive Etruscan inscriptions—

Words on votive offerings, statues, &c.

Kana. Lanzi interprets this word, 'ἄγαλμα.' It is found on sculptures, perhaps (dubbiamente) on an altar (v. ii. p. 407). It appears in the two following inscriptions, both on statues—

mi *kana* Larthial Numthrul Laukin.... (p. 465).
mi *kana* Larthias Vanl Velchinei Sai .. ke (p. 466).
kana .. Gael. *caon,* 'resemblance' (εἰκών, *simulacrum,* both
votive expressions). Arm. *khan,* 'a table.'

Turke and *fleres.*
On a candelabrum (Lanzi, v. ii. p. 421):
Au. Velskus thuplthas alpan *turke.*
On a round plate of bronze, apparently a cover (p. 422):
mi suthil Velthura thura *turke* Au Velthuri Fniskial.
On a statue (p. 446):
Thuker Hermenas *turuke.*
On a statue of Apollo (p. 448):
mi *fleres* Epul .fe Aritimi
Fasti R. fr. a *turke* klen kecha.[1]

---

[1] In the text, *keka;* on the plate of the statue itself, *kecha.* In another inscription we find *kecha.* The missing letter in *fe* appears from Maffei, *Oss. Lit.,* to be *a*.

On a statue (p. 449):
   Larke   Lekne   *turke fleres.*
On a statue (p. 455):
   fleres zek sansl kver.
On a picture upon a vase (Dennis, v. ii. frontispiece):
   eka crske nak achrum *flerthrke.*

From these examples it will be seen that *turke* and *fleres* imply 'giving' or 'dedicating.' Lanzi interprets *turke,* 'donavit,' or 'donum dedit.' I believe it signifies 'dat.' *Fleres* would be a corresponding substantive. Dr. Donaldson says (*Varron.* p. 173): '*fleres* clearly means *donarium* or something of the kind,' and compares it with *fleo* and *ploro.* The Arm. will supply the following explanations—

turke . Arm. *tovrck,* 'gift,' the plural form of *tovr.* Gael. *thoir,* 'da.' Gr. δῶρον.

fleres . Arm. *ovlerż, óterż,* 'gift, homage;' *ovlerżel, ëterżel, otorżel,* 'to offer.'
   Arm. *alers,* 'a prayer, a supplication.'
   Arm. *eter,* 'lamentation.' Gael. *blaor,* 'a cry.'

The initial vowels in these Arm. words are probably due to the circumstance, that scarcely any Arm. word is allowed to begin with *l* = χλ. In this case, 'a gift' would be *lerż* (χλερζ); 'a prayer,' *lers,* (χλερς); and 'lamentation,' *ler* (χλερ). The *f* in *fleres* probably represents this χ : indeed we may almost perceive it does by comparing (*e*)*ter* with *fleo.* So *Fl*uellen = *Ll*ewellyn, the Welsh *ll* being = Arm. *l,* or χλ.

In the last of the above inscriptions, *fler*(*es*) and *turke* seem combined into *flerthrke,* which may be rendered 'donum datum,' *i.e.*, 'a votive offering.' For the omission of the *u* in -*thrke,* compare Arm. *troż* and *trowch,* the gen. and instr. cases of *tovrch* (*turch*). The whole of this inscription may be interpreted, as we know the subject of the picture on which it is written. It represents the parting of Admetus and Alcestis. In the centre of the picture, Admetus (*Atmite*) and Alcestis

(*Alksti*) are taking the farewell embrace. Behind Alcestis is Charon, the minister of Hades, with his mallet uplifted against her. Running down between him and Alcestis, and commencing above the name *Alksti*, is the inscription—

eka erske nak achrum flerthrke.

As the last word signifies 'a votive offering,' and the inscription would relate to Alcestis, it can hardly describe anything but her self-devotion to death for her husband. Mr. Birch, in his *Ancient Pottery*, regards it as the speech of Charon relative to the parting. *Achrum*, therefore, probably means 'Acheron,' and *nak*, 'to.' These interpretations will give the following analogies—

nak . . . Arm. *nakh*, ' first, before,' adj. and adv.; in compos. 'towards' or 'against,' as in *nakh-anż*, 'zeal, envy,' *i.e.*, '*animus* towards or against.' Germ. *nach*. Welsh *naç*, 'opposition.' Heb. *neged*, 'before' (coram); *nekhah*, 'opposite.' Kurd. *nek*, 'near, by.' Alb. *nga*, *ngakha*, 'to.'

achrum . Arm. *okh*, 'hatred;' *okherim*, 'malevolent.' Cf. Στύξ and στυγέω. We might also suppose *achrum* = *okherim*, 'the malevolent,' to apply to Charon, the messenger of death, who seems about to strike Alcestis.

The first word, *eka*, often begins Etruscan inscriptions. It would either signify 'here' or 'behold.' I take it = Lat. *ecce*, = Arm. *ahá*, = Gael. *aca;* Span. *acá*, 'here.' The inscription then becomes—

Eka   erske   nak   Achrum   flerthrke.
Behold!   to   Hades   a votive offering.

For the remaining word, *erske*, the Arm. again comes to our aid, and supplies the exact word that is required—

erske . . Arm. *eresé*, 'she offers' or 'presents herself:' th. *eres*, *eresch*, 'front, face.'[1]

---

[1] Mr. Dennis (v. i. p. xc) is inclined to give *erske* the meaning, 'she saves,' connecting it with the Etrurian *arse*, 'averte.' He interprets the

If we write the Armenian, according to Etruscan orthography, under the original inscription, we should have—

Etrusc. *Eka erske nak achrum fler-thrke.*

Arm. Aha erese nach ucherim $\begin{cases} \text{ulerz-turch} \\ \text{alerz-turch} \\ \text{eler-turch.} \end{cases}$

Another of the previous inscriptions, on the statue of a boy, runs thus—

fleres zek sansl kver

This Dr. Donaldson compares (*Varron.* p. 176) with—

fleres tlen-asies sver

and observes that *kver* and *sver* are probably different forms of the same word. They would meet in the Welsh *çwaer,* 'sister,' which is almost identical with the Pers. *khwáhar,* or *khwáher (khwáhr).* The Irish for 'sister' is *siur.* The Arm. is *choyr,* gen. *cheṛ.* The interpretation of the first inscription now becomes—

fleres zek sansl kver.
votum   soror.[1]

This leads us to consider auother formal expression, *sansl*. It is found a second time in the inscription on the base of the statue of 'the Orator,' shortly to be noticed. The termination *-l* would induce us to suppose, from Armenian analogy, that *sansl* is a participle. Now from observing Latin votive inscriptions it may be inferred that there is one participle, and only one, which must occur in such dedications. This is the word *libens,* which would identify *sansl* with the Arm. *źnzol,* 'rejoicing' (gaudens, libens), the participle of *źnzal,* 'gaudere.'

The meaning of the remaining word, *zek,* can only be doubtfully conjectured. The most obvious Armenian analogies are furnished by *źgel,* 'to bring,' and *źevak,* 'form, figure.' Adopting this last, we should obtain the interpretation—

---

whole inscription: 'Lo, she saves him from Acheron, and makes a votive offering of herself.' To interpret *nak,* 'from,' seems objectionable.

[1] Compare the two following inscriptions in Gruter (p. mccexlviii):—
D. M. C. Egnatio Epicteto et C. Egnatio Floro modesta *soror.*
Fortunato fratri pientissimo fecerunt *sorores.*

fleres zek sansl kver.
votum statuam libens soror (dat).

Klen kecha. This form occurs in the inscription, already given, on the figure of Apollo:

mi fleres Epul afe Aritimi
me votum Apollini et[1] Artemidi
Fasti Rufrua turke klen kecha
Fausta Rufria dat

Klen kecha also occurs on another inscription afterwards to be analysed. The most probable meaning for *kecha*, judging from Latin votive inscriptions, would be either 'consecrat' or 'solvit.' The Arm. has both *chaké*, 'he expiates,' and *chaké*, 'he dissolves:' also *chahansy*, 'a priest.' The meaning of *klen* is less clear; but it may be connected with the Gael. *glan*, 'clean, pure, sincere, righteous,' and be nearly identical in meaning with *pius* or *pia, pie, rite.* Cf. Arm. *sovrb*, 'clean, pure, sacred,' from which is derived *srbel*, 'to purify, sanctify, consecrate, dedicate.' This exemplifies the appropriateness of the combination, *klen kecha*, 'sacer sacrat,' '*sovrb srbé.*' He who consecrates, *kecha*, ought to be holy, *klen*. We have a similar reduplication in *sacrosanctus* and in *donum dedit*. The Hebrew, again, prefixes the participle to the verb to make the sense more emphatic. The complete interpretation of the inscription would thus be—

Me votum Apollini et Artemidi
Fausta Rufria dat, { pia } { consecrat. }
                   { rite } { solvit.   }

Thupltlas alpan. This form occurs in the first of the group of inscriptions given above (p. 118) for the determination of *turke* and *fleres*—

Au. Velskus thuplthas alpan turke.
Aulus Veliscus   dat.

We also find *thuf lthas alpan* in another inscription presently to be noticed. *Thup* or *thuf* suggests the analogies of τύπος

---

[1] Arm. *ev*, 'and.'

and τύπτω, = Arm. *tip* and *tophem*, which may give for the Etruscan word the meaning, 'signum.' *Lthas* seems well connected by Lanzi with λιτή, = Arm. *alóthch*, the plural form of *alóth*. The Arm. has also *ilt*, 'desire,' gen. *ëlzi; ëlzal*, 'to desire, to wish for;' in which the root of λιτή, λίσσομαι, and λίττω, again appears. There remains *alpan*, which may be explained from the Arm. *olbal*, 'to lament, to groan.' For the termination, compare *iskhel*, 'to rule,' with *iskhan*, 'a ruler.' The explanation of the inscription would therefore be—

  Au. Velskus thuplthas alpan turke.
  Aulus Veliscus signum-precis supplex dat.

Signum precis, 'the sign' or 'memorial of a prayer,' would correspond to *votum* and *ex voto*, or to εὖχος, εὖχή, and εὖχῆς ἕνεκα.

Tinskvil. "A solemn form of consecration or presentation, already found on three other monuments discovered in this neighbourhood (Cortona), and which may reasonably be considered sacred offerings: *i.e.*, the Chimæra of the Royal Gallery of Florence found at Arezzo in the year 1554; the Griffin found at Cortona in 1720; and a small pedestal of bronze in the Museum of Cortona, on which a statue would have stood."—Micali, *Mon. Ined.* p. 80.

In the beginning of *tinskvil*, which is to be compared with *Thana* and *Than-kvil* (Tanaquil), the name of *Tina*, the Etruscan Jupiter, has long been recognised. *Kvil*, therefore, remains to be explained.

kvil . . Arm. *khilay*, 'a gift.'
  Arm. *chavel, chahel*, 'to expiate.' Cf. Arm. *ṛahel*, and
  Etrusc. *ril*.

On the celebrated candelabrum of Cortona, the masterpiece of Etruscan toreutic art, is the following inscription:

  thapna lusni.
  inskvil athli.
  salthn

Owing to a fracture, part of a letter, apparently an *i*, is lost after *athli*, and probably a whole letter after *lusni*. This last letter Micali considers with great probability to be the *t* wanting to complete the word (*t*)*inskvil;* an opinion in which Mr. Dennis is also inclined to concur.[1] The inscription would thus appear to be—

> *thapna lusni tinskvil athlii salthn.*

thapna . . Arm. *tap,* 'fire;' *thaph,* 'ardour;' *tapanal,* 'to burn.' The Arm. has also *tapan,* 'an urn, a box, a tomb.'

lusni . . . Arm. *loys,* 'light;' *lovsin,* gen. *lovsni,* 'the moon;' *lovsn-thag* ('light-crown'), 'the planet Jupiter.' *lorźanel,* 'to light.'

tinskvil . . 'offered to Tina.'

athlii . . . A proper name. We have both *Ath* and *Athl* in sepulchral inscriptions: *e.g., Ath Sekune Athl* (Lanzi, v. ii. p. 363).

---

[1] *Cities and Cemeteries of Etruria,* note, p. 443. In a note, p. 444, Mr. Dennis observes of this candelabrum: 'It is a lychnus, such as were hung from the ceilings of palaces or temples, and as have been found also suspended in sepulchres—even in Etruscan ones, as in the tomb of the Volumnii, at Perugia. Micali thinks it a sepulchral monument—a funeral offering to the great god of the infernal regions, consecrated by some lady of illustrious race, as the inscription seems to show.' (Micali considers *thapna* a proper name, and compares it with *thapia,* which he conjectures to be = *Apia* or *Appia.*) 'He suggests that it may have hung in the chamber, where the funeral feast was wont to be celebrated, as well as the annual *inferiæ* or *parentalia.* The use of sepulchral lamps by the ancients is well known, and gave rise, in the middle ages, to strange notions of perpetual fire; for it was asserted that some were found still burning in the tombs, though fifteen or twenty centuries had elapsed since they were lighted. It seems, however, that lamps were sometimes kept burning in sepulchres long after the interment. Micali cites an extract from Modestinus, which shows that a certain Roman gave freedom to his slaves at his death, on condition of their keeping a *light burning* in his sepulchre: 'Saccus servus meus et Entychia et Hiene ancillæ meæ omnes sub hac conditione liberi sunto, ut monumento meo alternis mensibus *lucernam accendant,* et solemnia mortis peragant.'' Cf. Grævius, *Ant. Rom.* p. 1451, and pp. 901-1020. It will be seen how this bears on my interpretation of *thapna lusni.*

salthn .. *sal-el,* 'to mix, to mould (*pétrir*), to envelop.'
sal-il, 'a carcase.'
sal-ovmn, 'an envelope.'
sal-mn, 'an embryo.'

Compare these terminations with the Etruscan names, Volt-*umna,* Tol-*umnius* (Arm. *dolvtmn,* 'horror').

archay, 'a king.'
archay-ovthivn, 'a kingdom.'

charoz, 'a herald' (κῆρυξ).
charoz-el, 'to proclaim' (κηρύσσειν).
charoz-ovthivn, 'a proclamation' (κήρυγμα).

So we may form from the root *sal*—
salovthivn, or, omitting the last two vowels, *ov* and *iv, salthn,* 'a moulded work' (τόρευμα), or simply, 'a work' (opus).

Salthn might also be compared in form with the Arm. *sovrthn,* = Pers. *súrákh,* 'an orifice.'

And the inscription would mean—

'A burner of light, offered to Tina, the work of Atilius.'[1]

---

[1] Compare the following inscription (Gruter, p. mcxlviii):—
Have Septima sit tibi
terra levis quisq.
huic tumulo posuit
ardente(m) *lucernam*
illius cineres aurea
terra tegat.
and the formal expression—
O. F. N. D., '*opus* fecit *numini devotus.*'
Cf. also Gr. λυχνοκαΐα, and see Herod. ii. 62, 130.
Another interpretation may be suggested. *Lovsin,* gen. and dat. *lovsni (lusni),* is the Armenian name for the moon; and we find on a *patera* or *mirror* (Lanzi, plate xii. No. 6) Diana called *Losna.* Now *thapna* may be interpreted as meaning by itself 'a lamp;' and *tinskvil* might be taken in the general sense of *deo-datus* or *numini-devotus.* The inscription would then be thus interpreted:—
thapna,   lusni   tinskvil,   Athlii   salthn.
lampas,   Dianæ   numini devota,   Atilii   opus.
Cf. Pausan. lib. ii. c. 22. 'Ἀφιᾶσι δὲ καὶ νῦν ἔτι ἐς τὸν βόθρον καιομένας λαμπάδας Κόρῃ τῇ Δήμητρος; i.e. to Hecate, the Infernal Diana. Pausa-

Tlen-asies. This is found in the inscription previously cited—

      fleres   tlenasies   sver.
      votum   soror.

Another form is *tlenacheis. Asies,* or *acheis,* may be referred to the Arm. *atéch,* acc. *atés,* 'pretium,' a plural form; while *tlen* may be explained from the Gael. *dleas,* 'duty;' *dligh,* 'to owe;' which would give for *tlen* the meaning 'debitus,' supposing *-en* to be an adjectival termination engrafted on the root *dl-,* in Etrusc. *tl-.* Cf. Arm. *tap,* 'heat;' *tapean,* 'hot.' This reduces the inscription to—

      fleres   tlenasies   sver.
      votum debitum-pretium soror (dat).

The votive offering (*votum*) was the due acknowledgment (*debitum pretium*) of a mercy received. *Tlen-asies* would nearly correspond to the Latin expressions, *dignæ grates, merita gratia, debiti honores, merita dona.*

We may now interpret the inscription on the statue of 'the Orator.' (Lanzi, v. ii. p. 468. Micali, *Mon.* Tav. xliv):—

    Aulesi Metelis Ve Vesial klensi
    ken fleres teks sansl tenine
    tuthines chiseliks.[1]

The words requiring explanation here are *klensi, ken, tenine, tuthines,* and *chiseliks—Klensi* I take to be nearly identical in sense with *klen,* which has already been interpreted '*pius.*' For the suffix *-si,* compare Arm. *layn* and *laynsi,* 'broad;' *bolor,* 'a circle,' *bolorsi,* 'round'—*Ken* seems nearly the same as *kehen,* which we sometimes find in sepulchral inscriptions taking the place of *eka,* 'ecce.' It may thus be compared with the Gael. *cheana,* 'certe, sane, *en,* ita,' = Heb. *hen.* But

---

nias is here speaking of a tomb or monument near Corinth, said to be the grave of Tantalus. This monument was supported by three figures of Diana, Jupiter, and Minerva. Near it was the tomb of Pelasgus, the son of Triopas, and the temple of Demeter Pelasgis.

[1] In the original, *chiseliks.* I have before noticed the resemblance between the Etruscan *V(F)* and *E.*

kén is also found in Arm., though only in composition. From the relative *or*, 'who, which,' are formed the adverbs *or-kén*, *or-bar*, and *or-pés*, 'as, for instance:' and we find also, *hi-kén*, *hi-bar*, and *hi-pés*, signifying likewise 'as,' (*or-kén* probably = 'which-like,' and *hi-kén* = 'this-like'). From this it is plain that *kén*, *bar*, and *pés*, are very nearly synonyms; and *pés* (= Sansk. *peça*, 'forma') signifies 'like, such,' and also 'so that, as, when;' and therefore *kén* might have the force of *ut*, *quum*, or *ita*——For *tenine*, the best Armenian analogies are: *tani*, 'he brings,' or 'renders;' *dné*, 'he places;' *tóné*, 'he solemnises;' *tóné*, 'he presents, dedicates, consecrates'—— *Tuthines* appears to be the gen. of *tuthin*, *tuthina*, or *tuthine*. If we resolve the nom. into *t-uthin*, we get the common Arm. termination *-outhivn*, corresponding to the Lat. *-atio;* and for the root the Arm. verb *t(al)*, '*d(are)*:' whence we form *touthivn*, 'datio, δωτίνη.' The actual Arm. form is rather different. The root of 'giving,' *t-* or *tov*, is first taken: then the suffix *-ić* is added to form *tovié*, gen. *tovéi*, 'dator;' and then again the suffix *-outhivn*, to form *tovéouthivn*, 'datio.' *Tuthines* may be interpreted 'gratiæ, χάριτος,' and might signify either 'thanks' or 'a mercy received.' I shall take the latter signification.—The last word, *chiseliks*, may be explained from the Arm. *yitelich*, 'a memorial.'—The following interpretation for the inscription is thus obtained:—

Auleśi	Metelis	Ve	Veśial	klenśi
Aulus	Metellus,	Veli filius,	Vesia natus,	pientissimus

ken	fleres	teke	sansl	tenine
ut	votum	ponit,	libens	reddit

tuthines   chiseliks.
gratiæ   monumentum.

'Aulus Metellus, the son of Velus and of Vesia, as he devoutly presents (this) votive offering, gladly brings a memorial of mercy received.'[1]

---

[1] Or 'a memorial of gratitude.' Compare *tenine tuthines chiseliks* with the Gr. votive expressions, ἀνέθηκεν χαριστήριον (Gruter, p. lxxv), or χαριστήρια ἀνέθηκεν (Muratori, p. lxxxix).

In this last inscription, *tenine* has been considered identical with the Arm. *tani*. Now there are four conjugations in Armenian, distinguished by the terminations of the infinitive, *-el*, *-al*, *-oul* (*ul*), and *-il*, the last having usually a passive sense. *Tenine* might belong to the first, as *tani* does to the fourth of these. The *-in-* in *ten-in-e* may be analogous to the Arm. *-an-*, which frequently occurs in verbs: e.g. *liz-an-é* = *liz-é* = *liz-ov* = *lez-ov*, 'he licks,' *gol-an-ay* = *gol-é*, 'he steals;' *kheṛ-an-ay* = *kheṛ-i*, 'he insults.' There is also *kam-en-ay* = *kam-i*, 'he wishes.' We meet with a similar form to *tenine* in an inscription cut in the rock at Vulci (Micali, *Mon. Ined.* Tav. lix.). This form is *kerinu*. The inscription runs thus, surrounding the sculptured figure of a man:—

  eka suthik Velus Evpus klensi kerinu.

Here *suthik* appears like an Arm. diminutive in *-ik* of *suth*, or *suthi*, 'a tomb.' Cf. Arm. *loys*, gen. *lovsoy*, 'light;' *lovsik*, 'little light.' *Kerinu* probably means 'excavates' or 'carves,' and would be allied to the Arm. *cherel*, 'to scrape;' *grel*, 'to write,' i.e. 'to engrave;' *gir*, 'γράμμα, χαρακτήρ;' *kṛel*, 'to hammer, to carve.' Cf. γράφω, *graben*, and *grave*. Thus the meaning of the whole inscription would be—

  'Here Velus Evpus devoutly excavates a tomb.'

Kerinu may be most completely illustrated by comparing the Arm.—*kovṛ*, 'carved, hammered;' *kovṛck* (plural form of *kovṛ*), 'image, statue;' *kṛé*, 'he hammers, he carves;' *kṛan*, 'a hammer, a pickaxe;' *kṛané* 'he hammers, he forges.'

The last inscription required for the exemplification of votive terms is on a statue (Lanzi, ii. p. 455. Micali, *Mon.* Tav. xliii.)——

Velias Fanaknal thuf lthas[1] *alpan lenache klen kecha tuthines tlenacheis.*

Lenache is the only word here uninterpreted. Now when we compare—

---

[1] In his text, but not in his plate, Lanzi erroneously gives this word as *lethas*.

with
and
thuf lthas alpan lenache klen kecha
thuplthas alpan turke
fleres . . . turke klen kecha
which are found in the first and fourth of the group of votive inscriptions in p. 118, we may see that *lenache* is probably a verb and may be substituted for *turke*, 'gives.' If we resort to the Arm., we get—

linel, 'esse, fieri, existere.'
elanil, 'fieri.'
elanak, 'modus, forma.'
elanakel, 'modulari.'
elanaké, 'modulatur.'

These analogies suggest for *lenache* the sense, 'facessit,' and make it closely correspond to the Lat. *faciendum curavit* and the Oscan *upsannam deded*. Compare also the Arm. suffix *elén*, 'made of:' e.g. *oskelén*, 'made of gold' (*oski*) ; *arzathelén*, 'made of silver' (*arzath*); and *erkathelén*, 'made of iron' (*erkatk*).[1] The inscription would then be rendered—

Velias Fanaknal thuf lthas alpan lenache klen
Veliæ Fannacia-natæ signum precis supplex facessit pia
kecha tuthines tlenacheis.
consecrat gratiæ debitum-pretium.

'(This) memorial of the prayer of Velia, the daughter of Fannacia, she suppliantly produces (and) devoutly consecrates (as) the due price of a mercy received.'[2]

It may be instructive to collect together here, in conclusion, the various forms of dedication above considered, so as to present a full list of Etruscan votive expressions. Each form would be completed by the name or designation of the

---

[1] When we compare these names of metals with the Lat. *aurum, argentum*, and *ferrum*, and the Celtic *or, aur, aour; airgiod, arian, argan; iarunn, haiarn, houarn;* we may perceive the respective degrees of affinity, as far as these words are concerned, between the Celtic, Latin, and Armenian. The Celtic is very near the Latin, the Armenian considerably more remote.

[2] Or 'devoutly pays a due acknowledgment of gratitude.'

donor. In four cases (2, 3, 7, 8) I have been obliged, for the sake of comparison, to reverse the order in which two words occur.

1. *klensi fleres   teke   sansl tenine tuthines chiseliks.*
2. *alpan thuf lthas lenache klen keeha tuthines tlen-acheis.*
3. *alpan thup lthas turke.*
4.   *fleres* . . . . *tlen-aries.*
5.   *fleres   turke   klen   kecha.*
6.   *fleres-zek* . . . *sansl.*
7.   *fler-thrke erske.*
8.   *fleres   turke.*
9.   *turuke.*

The following would be the vocabulary of votive words:—

Alpan 'supplex,' = Germ. *flehend*. . .} Arm. *olò,* 'fletus:' *-an, -ean,* Arm. adjectival terminations. The Etruscan possesses neither *o* nor *b*.

Chiseliks or *Chisvliks,* 'monumentum.'} Arm. *yiselich,* 'a memorial,' the plural form of *yiseli,* of which the dimin. would be *yiselik,* and its plural form *yiselikch,* in the acc. *yiseliks*. The root here is *yis,* whence is formed the infinitive *yisel,* 'to remember,' and the future participle *yiseli,* which appears in the plural form in the noun *yiselich*. In a similar manner we have, from the root *t-, tal,* 'to give,' and *talich,* 'a gift;' also *lsel,* 'to listen,' and *lselich,* 'ear, hearing, audience;' *ëmpel,* 'to drink,' *ëmpelich,* 'beverage.' But the Arm. forms derived from the root *khal* will most clearly illustrate the supposed formation of *chiseliks* from a root *chis,* = Arm. *yis*.

THE ARMENIAN ORIGIN OF THE ETRUSCANS. 131

     Arm.   *Etrusc.*
    khal, 'ludus.' . . . . *chis.*
    khalal, 'ludere.'
   . *khalali,* 'ludendus.'
    khalalich, 'ludus,' prop.
       'ludenda.'
    khalalik, 'ludus,' dimin.
       noun.
    khalaliks, 'ludos.' . . *chiseliks.*

    For the affinity between *chis* and *yis,* compare the Arm. *khovzel, yovzel,* 'to seek.' The Arm. *y* is aspirated.

Erske, 'sese offert' . . Arm. *eresé,* 'sese offert:' th. *eres, eresch,* 'facies.'
Fleres, 'votum, do- { Arm. *ovlerz,* 'donum;' *alers,* 'precis;'
num' . . . . { *eler,* 'fletus.'
Kana, 'simulacrum'. . Gael. *caon,* 'simulacrum.'
Kecha, 'expiat, conse- } Arm. *chalé,* 'expiat;' *chalé,* 'solvit.'
 crat, solvit' . . . . }
        ⎧ Gael. *glan;* Welsh *glan, glain;* Manx
Klen } 'purus, pius, ⎨ *glen;* 'pure, sincere, holy, righte-
Klensi } pientissimus' ⎨ ous.' Arm. *gelani,* 'fair, decent,
        ⎩ good.'——Arm. layn, *laynsi,* 'broad.'
Lenache, 'facessit' . . Arm. *elanaké,* 'modulatur;' *elanak,* 'modus, forma;' *elanil,* 'fieri;' *linel,* 'esse, fieri, existere.'
Lthas, 'precis, λιτής'. Arm. *alóthch,* 'preces;' *alóthel,* 'precari;' *itz,* 'desiderium;' *ëtzal,* 'desiderare.' The Armenian, as I have before observed, avoids the letter *t* as an initial; but we have *tzali* as well as *ëtzali,* 'desiderandus.'
Sansl, 'libens' . . . . Arm. *znzol,* 'gaudens, libens.'

K 2

Teke, 'ponit, fert'. . . . Arm. *ągé,* 'ducit, fert,' = Germ. *zieht; ząģé,* 'τίκτει, τίκει,' = Germ. *zeugt.*

Tenine, 'fert, reddit' . Arm. *tani,* 'fert, reddit, tenet.'

Thrke, 'donum'. . . . . Arm. *tovrch,.*'donum,' the plural form of *tovr.*

$\left. \begin{array}{l} Thuf \\ Thup \end{array} \right\}$ $\left. \begin{array}{l} \text{'signum,} \\ \text{τύπος'} \end{array} \right\}$ . . $\left\{ \begin{array}{l} \text{Arm. } tip, \text{ 'typus;' } tophel, dophel, \\ thopel, \text{ 'τύπτειν.' } Tip \text{ may be a} \\ \text{borrowed word, as } typus \text{ is in Latin;} \\ \text{but the root of τύπος appears plainly} \\ \text{in Armenian.} \end{array} \right.$

$\left\{ \begin{array}{l} Tlen\text{-, 'debitum'.} \\ \\ \\ \\ \text{-}aries \\ \text{-}acheis \end{array} \right\}$
Tlen-, 'debitum'. . Gael. *dligh,* 'debe;' *dlighe,* 'lex, debitum;' *dleas,* 'officium :' th. *dl-,* in Etrusc. *tl-*: *-ean,* Arm. adjectival termination.

-aries } 'pretium, Arm. *atéch,* 'pretium,' a plural noun :
-acheis } ἀξία.' in the acc. the final *-ch* becomes *-s.* Osset. *chas, chäs, ichas, achos,* 'a sum due;' *achza,* 'money.' Lapp. *áses,* 'merx.' Gael. *fiach,* 'value, worth, debt.' Another form of *atéch* is *artéch.* The th., as appears from *artel,* 'valere, mereri,' is *at* or *art,* = Gr. ἄξ(ιος).

Turke, 'dat, δωρεῖ.' . . Arm. *tovrch,* 'donum.' For the formation of the verb from the noun, see above, s. v. *erske.* It may have been observed, how many Etruscan verbs terminate in *-ke.* In seeking the root, the *k* must frequently, perhaps usually, be rejected, as well as the *e.* The Lydian seems here to resemble the Etruscan. Cf. Lyd. βάσκε, 'ἐξεθόαζε,' with Arm. *waz-el,* 'to hasten, to run.' *Ante,* p. 39.

THE ARMENIAN ORIGIN OF THE ETRUSCANS. 133

Tuthines, 'gratiæ,
χάριτος.' . . . } Arm. *t*(*al*), 'd(are);' *-ovthivn*, '-atio;' whence may be formed *tovthivn*, 'datio.' The actual Arm. form is *tovéovthivn*, similarly formed from *tovié*, gen. *tovéi*, 'dator.' The Arm. termination, *-ovthivn*, in Modern Arm., *-ovthin*, is so common as to occur no less than three times in the Lord's Prayer—in *archayovthivn*, 'kingdom;' in *phorzovthivn*, 'temptation;' and in *zórovthivn*, 'power.' To give another instance —the words *é* and *éak*, 'essence,' and *éakan*, 'essential,' all take this termination, and produce the three forms, *éovthivn*, *éakovthivn*, *éakanovthivn*, 'existence, substance.' *Ovthivn* may be compared with our termination, *-ation*, by which we recognise words of Lat. origin. *Suthina* and *salthn*, already noticed, may be similar forms to *tuthines*, but in the nom., not the gen.

Zek, 'signum, statua,
εἰκών' (?) . . . . } Arm. *zev*, *zevak*, 'forma, figura.'

The substantial correctness of the previous interpretations may in great measure be confirmed by a comparison with Latin votive forms. I have therefore selected a number of those which most usually occur, from Gruter and Muratori. By endeavouring to explain them from the Greek, a language confessedly akin to the Latin, the degree of affinity between the Armenian and Etruscan may at the same time be tested. It would be extremely difficult, if not impossible, to interpret the following forms by the aid of the Greek language alone, if the Latin had been lost.

Ex Voto P(*osuit*) V(*otum*) S(*olvit*) L(*ibens*) M(*erito*)
Ex Voto Posuit . . . . L(*ibens*) M(*erito*) *Dedicavit*
Voto } . . . D(*onum*) D(*edit*) L(*ibens*) M(*erito*)
Suscepto
                 Vot(*um*) Sol(*vit*) L(*ibens*) M(*erito*)
                 V(*otum*) S(*olvit*) L(*ibens*) M(*erito*)
Donum Posui . . . . *Libens Merito*
D(*onum*) P(*osuit*) . . . . L(*ibens*) M(*erito*)
D(*onum*) D(*edit*) . . . . L(*ibens*) M(*erito*)
               Votum Solvit Lib(*ero*) *Mun*(*ere*)
               Votum Dat Lubens Merito
V(*otum*) S(*olvit*) D(*onum*) D(*edit*)
               V(*otum*) S(*olvit*)
               Votum . . . . . *Libens* . . . . . . *Solvit*
Munus D(*edit*)
Donum Dedit
D(*onum*) P(*osuit*)
               Votum Retulit
Ex Voto Fecit . . . . *Dedicavit*
Ex Voto Posuit
Ex Voto Fecit
Ex Voto
Donum
        Posuit et . . . . *D.D.*
        Fecit et . . . . *D.D.*
        Fecit . . . . *Consacravit*
        Dedicavit et . . . . *Consecravit*
        Fecit
                     Gratias Agentes Posuerunt

The Etruscan forms, as I have interpreted them from the Armenian, with a slight assistance from the Celtic, correspond, it will be seen, closely to the Latin. Disregarding the difference of tense, *teke = posuit; kecha = solvit*, or else *consecravit; lenache = fecit; turke = dedit* or *dedicavit;* and *tenine = retulit. Sansl = libens; fleres = votum* or *donum; thuf lthas* corresponds to *ex voto;* and what the Latin expresses concisely by *merito,* the Etruscan explains more at length by *tlen-asies, tuthines tlen-acheis,* or *tuthines chiseliks; tlen* being = *merito* or *meritus,* and *asies* = *meritum.* If we take the two fullest Etruscan forms, and compare *fleres teke sansl tezine tuthines chiseliks* with *donum posuit libens merito,* the seventh of the Latin forms given above, or *thuf lthas alpan lenache klen kecha tuthines tlenacheis* with *ex voto posuit libens merito dedicavit,* the second of those forms, the close resemblance in sense will be at once apparent. Nor is it merely the roots of the Etruscan words which are Armenian: all the forms, with the exception of the genitives in *-as* and *-es,* belong to the Armenian language. Some words, indeed, as *sansl, chiseliks,* and *tuthin(es),* if rightly interpreted, exhibit in their construction very peculiar Armenian affinities.

The following inscription (Gruter, p. xlvii.) may still further illustrate the subject of votive expressions—

To *precor*[1] Alcide sacris invicte peractis
Rite[2] tuis *lætus dona ferens meritis*[3]
Hæc tibi nostra potest tennis perferre camina
Nam *grates dignas*[4] tu potes efficere
Sume libens *simulacra*[5] tuis quæ *munera*[6] cilo
Aris Urbanus *dedicat*[7] ipse sacris.

The inscription of Cervetri.

The following inscription was found on a small pot, made of antique black ware, at Cervetri, the site of the Pelasgian town of Agylla, which was said to have been afterwards taken by the Etruscans, and called by them Cære. The pot or cup, which appears to hold rather less than a pint, may be seen in the *Mus. Etrusc. Vatic.* pl. xcix. n. 7. The inscription would

---

[1] *Alpan.* [2] *Klen.*
[3] *Sansl tenine tuthines chiseliks, klen kecha tuthines tlenacheis.*
[4] *Tlenasies.* [5] *Kana, zek.* [6] *Fleres.* [7] *Turke, kecha.*

compose two hexameters, but the words are run together, so as to take the following form—

*minikethumamimathumaramlisiaithipurenai
etheeraisieepanaminethunastavhelephu*

This inscription derives a peculiar interest from its being considered by eminent philologists as a relic of the language of the ancient Pelasgians, the nation whose name has had so great an influence on the study of ethnology. There is little difference among the learned as to the division of the lines into words. Dr. Donaldson (*Varron.* p. 167) reads the inscription—

mi ni kethuma *mi mathu maram lisiai thipurenai
ethe erai sie epana* mi nethu *nastav helephu.*

and Lepsius—

mi ni ketha ma *mi mathu maram lisiai thipurenai
ethe erai sie epana* minethu *nastav helephu.*

If we take the first line according to this latter reading, dividing also *maram* into *mar-am*; and the second line according to Dr. Donaldson's reading; we shall obtain this couplet—

*mi ni kethu ma mi mathu mar am lisiai thipurenai
ethe erai sie epana* mi *nethu nastav helephu.*

Every word and form may here be considered as Armenian, as will appear from the following analysis:

Etruscan.   *Armenian.*
mi .... Nom. *es*, 'I.' .... *mech*, 'we.'
         Acc. (*z*)*is*, 'me.' .... (*z*)*mez*, 'us.'
         The forms, *mech*, 'we,' and (*z*)*mez*, 'us,' would be, according to analogy, the plural of *me*, 'I,' and *me*, 'me,' which thus exist implicitly in Arm. *Dov*, 'thou,' still makes *dovch*, 'ye.' So also we have—
         é, 'existence, he is' .. *e-m*, 'I am' ... *e-mch*, 'we are.'
         Kurd. *az, men*, 'I;' *me*, 'me.'

THE ARMENIAN ORIGIN OF THE ETRUSCANS. 137

Etruscan.   *Armenian.*
     Osset. *äz*, 'I;' *män, mä*, 'me.'[1]
     Georg. *me*, 'I.'
     Welsh and Gael. *mi*, 'I, me.'
ni . . . . . *mi* = Gr. μή = Lat. *ne*.
     Welsh and Gael. *ni*, 'not.' Pers. *mah, nah*. Lith.
     ne. Osset. *ne, ma*.
kethu . . . Nom. *get*, 'a river' . . *kath* and *tith*, 'a drop.'
     Gen. *getoy*.   *kathi*. *tthi*.
     Dat. *getoy*.   *kathi*. *tthi*.
     Abl. *getoy*.   *kathé*. *tthé*.
     Instr. *getow*.   *kathiv*. *tthiv*.
     Nom. *kathn*, 'milk' . . *kith*, 'milking.'
     Gen. *kathin*.   *kthoy*.
     Dat. *kathin*.   *kthoy*.
     Abl. *kathiné*.   *kthoy*.
     Instr. *kathamb*. *kthow*.
     I take *kethu* to be most probably a gen. or instr.
     case, and to signify 'of,' or 'with water.'
     Both *getoy* (*geto*) and *getow* (*getó*) would be-
     come in Etruscan orthography *ketu*, as the
     Etruscans had no medials and no vowel *o*.
     Kthoy and *kthow* would in like manner become
     kethu: *kathiv* (*kathü*) would become *kathu* or
     kathi: and *tthiv* would become *sethu* or *sethi*, or
     else *chethu* or *chethi*.
     Gael. *cith, gith*, 'imber.' Sansk. *tut*, 'stillare,
     fundere, effundere,' = Alb. *cheth*. Lat. *gutta*.
ma . . . . *na*, 'but, however, rather, in fact.'
     Arab. *ammá*, 'but.' Pers. *magar*, 'but, unless,
     moreover' (*gar*, 'if'). Osset. *ämä, ama*, 'and.'
mi . . . . . (As before, 'I').

---

[1] Among the European languages, the Lithuanian family exhibits the closest affinity to the Armenian, Kurdish, and Ossetic, in the form of the pronoun *I*.

138   THE ARMENIAN ORIGIN OF THE ETRUSCANS.

Etruscan.   *Armenian.*
mathu . . . Nom. *math,* 'syrup of grapes,
   raisiné, defrutum.' . . . . *melr,* 'honey.'
Gen. ⎫
Dat. ⎬ *mathoy.*   ⎫ *melov.*
Abl. ⎭   ⎬
Instr. *mathow.*   ⎭

Mathoy and *mathow* become, in Etruscan orthography, *mathu.*
mathovz, 'the fruit of the arbutus.' The termination resembles *thovz,* 'a fig.' Gr. μίθυ. Germ. *meth.* Eng. *mead.* Welsh *medd.* Osset. *müd,* 'honey.' Sansk. *madhu,* 'honey, wine, intoxicating drink;' *mad,* 'to be intoxicated, to rejoice;' *mada,* 'intoxication, madness.' Pers. *may, mul,* 'wine.' Gipsy *mol,* 'wine.' Lyd. μῶλαξ, 'εἶδος οἴνου.' Arm. *moli,* 'mad, intoxicated.'[1]

Cf. Heb. *debaš,* 'honey, honey of grapes, i. e., must, or new wine boiled down to a third or half' (Gr. ἕψημα, Lat. *sapa, defrutum,* Ital. *musto cotto*). Gesen. *s. v.*

mar . . . . Arm. *mar,* 'a measure of liquids'—'μετρητής, firkin, (John ii. 6), 'βάρος, i. e., בַּת, a measure' (Luke xvi. 6).

Pers. *mar,* 'measure, number.'

Gr. μάρις, 'a measure containing six κοτύλαι' (about three pints).

---

[1] The connexion of ideas here may be still further illustrated. Compare *bacca, Bacchus, bacchor,* and the Gael. *bach,* 'to intoxicate,' *bachar,* 'an acorn,' *backla,* 'a drinking cup;' also *uveo, uva,* and *uvidus,* and the Gael. *subh,* 'a berry,' *subhag,* 'a raspberry,' *subhach,* 'merry;' and ἄμπελος with the Rhæt-Rom. *ampa,* 'a raspberry,' and the Arm. *ovmp, impelich,* 'beverage.' With *bacca* and *bachar* we might also compare the Arm. *baklay,* 'a bean.' Similarly we find the Lat. *faba* in the Gael. *faob,* 'an acorn.'

| *Etruscan.* | *Armenian.* |

Alb. *merē*, 'every liquid and dry measure.'
Lith. *méra,* ⎫
Russ. *mjera,* ⎬ 'measure.'
Germ. *mass*, 'measure, pot, quart.'
Alb. *marr*, 'to hold, to contain.'
Georg. *marani*, 'a wine-cellar,' = Arm. *maṛan*.
I interpret *mar*, in a general sense, 'measure, pot, vas, κοτύλη.' The Gr. μάρις may be borrowed from the Thracians, as may also perhaps the Lat. *dolium*, which appears the same as the Arm. *doyl*, Pers. *dúl*, 'a bucket.'

am .... Arm. *em* ⎫
   Pers. *am* ⎬ 'I am.'
   Alb. *yam* ⎭

lisiai ... Arm. *lezov* ⎫
   Lith. *léžuwis* ⎬
   Arab. *lisán* ⎬ 'a tongue.'
   Heb. *lašon* ⎭

   Arm. ⎧ *lezovl* ⎫
      ⎨ *lizovl* ⎬ 'to lick.'
      ⎩ *lizel* ⎭
   Lith. *léžu*
   Pers. *lisídan*

Pers. *lís*, 'licking.'
Lisiai seems to be the dat. of *lisia*, 'a tongue,' i. e., 'a licker;' the root being found in the Pers. *lís*, or in the Arm. *liz* or *lez*. The declension of *lisiai* would resemble that of the Arm. *archæy*, 'a king,' which makes *archayi* in the gen. and dat.; or of *margaré*, 'a prophet,' which makes *margeréi*. But the best parallels are perhaps found in the declension of proper names: as—

	Etruscan.	Armenian.	

    Nom. *Anania,* 'Ananias.' *Anglia,* 'England.'
    Gen. }
    Dat. } *Ananiay.*   *Angliay.*
    Instr. *Ananiav.*   *Angliav.*
    Nom. *Achayia,* 'Achaia.' *Hermés,* 'Hermes.'
    Gen. }
    Dat. } *Achayiay.*   *Hermeay.*
    Instr. *Achayiav.*   *Hermeav.*

   The gen. and dat. of *lezov* (*lezu*) are *lezovi.*

thipurenai. *thaph,* 'ardour.' }
    tap, 'heat.' }
   tapean, 'burning, heated.'

   Either of the first two words may give the root, and the last word may give the meaning, of *thip-urenai;* but its termination must be explained from such Arm. words as the following:—

   { *hayr,* 'father.'
   { *hayr-órén,* 'paternally.'
   { *archay,* 'king.'
   { *archay-órén,* 'royally.'
   { *hamak,* 'entire, entirely' (th. *ham, hom,* = ὁμ(ός)).
   { *ham-órén,* 'entire, entirely.'
   { *ham-órini,* gen. and dat. of *ham-órén.*
   { *get,* 'beauty.'
   { *get-a-yórén,* 'pretty.'
   { *órén,* 'a law, a rule.'
   { *órinak,* 'example, type, form' (dimin. of *órén*).
   { *yórin-el,* 'to form, to shape.'
   { *órin-akel,* 'to form, to represent.'

   From these instances it may be seen, that the Arm. suffix *-orén* or *-yórén,* when adjectival, which is rarely the case, as it usually forms an adverb, has the force of the Lat. *-factus.* We may thus form from the Arm. *tap,* 'heat,' the adj.—

THE ARMENIAN ORIGIN OF THE ETRUSCANS. 141

Etruscan.   *Armenian.*
           Nom. *tapórén,* ' tepefactus -a -um.'
           Dat. *tapórini,* ' tepefacto -æ -o.'
           Tapórini becomes, in Etruscan orthography, *tapurini.*
           Compare also *tesaran,* 'a theatre;' th. *tes;* *Hayerén,* 'Armenian;' th. *Hay; phokharén,* ' payment;' th. *phokh.*
           Thipurenai would probably be a fem. adj. agreeing with *lisiai.* The Arm. has no indication of genders; but in proper names, such as *Athenas,* 'Minerva,' gen. and dat. *Athenay; Yowhanna,* ' Joanna,' gen. and dat. *Yowhannay;* we meet with words declined like *thipurenai.*

ethe . . . . *ethé,* 'if.' Zend *ethe,* 'when.'
erai . . . *erah*
           khrakh } 'joyous, gay.' *Ovrakh linel,* 'to be merry, εὐφραίνεσθαι' (Luke xv. 24).
           ovrakh
           erakhan
           rakhgan } 'a banquet, a feast.' Cf. Gr. ἔρανος.
           khrakhgan
           Kurd. *iarii,* 'a game, a sport.'

           If *erai* be an oblique case like *lisiai,* it may be interpreted 'of' or 'for joy.' *Erah* is indeclinable. But we might read, *eth(e) era isie epana,* regarding the termination of *ethe* as short, and here elided, and the terminations of *era* and *isie* as long, but shortened before vowels.

sie . . . . . *ise,* 'it may be;' *é,* 'it is.' Osset. *sua* or *isua,* ' it becomes.' Germ. *sei.* Goth. *siyai.* Sansk. *syât.* Lat. *sit.*
epana . . .   *eph,* 'cooking.'
                  ephel, 'to cook.'
           Nom. *ephovmn,* 'cooking.'

Etruscan.	Armenian.

Gen.⎫
Dat.⎭ *ephman.*

Abl. *ephmané.*

Instr. *ephmamb.*

But, for the termination of *epan(a)*, compare *kap*, 'a bond,' *kap-el*, 'to contract,' *kap-an*, 'a strait;' *gl-el*, 'to roll,' *gl-an*, 'a cylinder;' and see just above, s. v. *erai*. Compare also *chah-el*, 'to expiate,' *chah-anay*, 'a priest.' The Arm. prefers to terminate words with -*ay*, instead of -*a* simply. We meet, again, with such equivalent terms as *tarphovmn* and *tarphanch* (the plural form of *tarphan*), 'cupido.'[1]

Heb. *aphah*, 'to cook.' Gr. ὀπτάω, ἕψω, ὄψον. Lat. *epulum*, probably identical in meaning with *epana*.

mi . . . . . (As before; but here it seems to mean 'me,' not 'I').

nethu . . . Nom. *nivth*, 'substance.'. . . *helanivth*, 'fluid substance, liquor.'

Gen.⎫
Dat. ⎬ *nivthoy*   *helanivthoy.*
Abl. ⎭

I suppose *nethu* to be a gen. or abl., and to signify 'of' or 'from liquor.' *Nethuns* is the Etruscan form of *Neptunus*. *Nivthoy* (*nütho*) would be written in Etruscan, *nuthu* or *nithu*; although, as we have in Arm., *givl* and *gel*, 'a village,' and *ivl* and *el*, 'oil,' *nivth* would be very nearly *neth*.

nastav . . . Arm. *nsdeh* or *nideh*,[2] 'stranger, foreigner, emigrant' (ξένος).

---

[1] These words might be allied to *Turan*, the Etruscan name of Venus.
[2] *Nastes* was one of the two Carian leaders, *Il.* ii. 867, and C. Calidius *Nasta* appears as a proper name in a Neapolitan inscription.—*Donati*, p. 4.

Etruscan.   *Armenian.*

        Pers.   *naitá,* . . . . . 'stranger, foreigner.'

        Arab. $\begin{cases} \textit{názi,} \ldots \ldots \text{'stranger, foreigner.'} \\ \textit{naséil,} \ldots \ldots \text{'stranger, foreigner, visitor, } \textit{guest,} \text{ banquet.'} \end{cases}$

        Heb. *nasa,* 'to migrate, to remove;' *nasa,* 'to err.'

        In Armenian poetry, *nsdeh* would be written *nëdeh,* the vowel *ë* not being then, as usual, merely understood.[1]

helephu . . *helovl,* 'to pour out, ἐξεχέω' (Rev. xvi. 2). *zelovl,* 'to pour;' *zeikh,* 'drunken, dissolute.'[2] *helov,* 'he pours out, he empties.'

        The th. is *hel,* 'pouring, flowing,' found above in *helanivth. Nethu,* being qualified by *helephu,* would acquire the meaning of *helanivth* instead of *nivth.* The formation of *helephu* from a root *hel* may be thus illustrated from the Arm.—

$\begin{cases} \textit{sós,} \text{ 'causing tremor,' from which are derived—} \\ \textit{sós-aph-il,} \text{ 'to tremble.'} \\ \textit{thóth-aph-el,} \text{ 'to shake' (act.).} \\ \textit{ded-ev-el,} \text{ 'to reel.'} \end{cases}$

$\begin{cases} \textit{khovs-el} \\ \textit{khovs-aph-el} \end{cases}$ 'to fly.'

$\begin{cases} \textit{sars} \\ \textit{sarsaph} \end{cases}$ 'a trembling.'

$\begin{cases} \textit{sarsil} \\ \textit{sarsil} \\ \textit{sarsaphil} \end{cases}$ 'to tremble.'

        Similar forms are—*sósaphel,* 'to touch,' and *kachavel,* 'to dance.'

---

[1] The same peculiarity seems to distinguish the inscription of Cervetri from other inscriptions in Etruria. At least the customary deficiency of vowels is not apparent.

[2] Cf. Thrac. ζεῖλα, 'οἶνος,' and Gr. ἀσελγέω.

144   THE ARMENIAN ORIGIN OF THE ETRUSCANS.

Etruscan.   *Armenian.*
These examples show how *-aph-*, *-av-*, or *-ev-*, may be inserted in Arm. between the root and the verbal inflexion. Applying this principle to *ketovl*, we should obtain—

helaphov
helavov   } 'he empties,' or 'pours out.'
helevov

With regard to the construction of *helephu* with *nethu*, if the last word be taken as an ablative, it may be noticed that *ketovl* is used with an ablative as well as an accusative. In Rev. xvi. 2, 3, 4, ἐξέχεε τὴν φιάλην αὐτοῦ is rendered in the Arm. version by *ehel (z)skavaṛak ivr* (acc.), and in 8, 10, 12, 17, by *ehel 'i skavaṛaké ivrmé* (abl.). Again, in Acts ii. 17, ἐκχεῶ ἀπὸ τοῦ πνεύματός μου, is rendered by, *heliž yogvoy immé* (abl.).

We should perhaps read the last two words of the inscription, *nasta Fhelephu*, instead of *nastav helephu;* the digamma being introduced to avoid the hiatus, or the elision of the short vowel.

From the Arm. words which I have cited, we obtain, in grammatical syntax, though in a foreign idiom, the following Armenian couplet. The orthography is Etruscan.

es mi ketu na es mathu mar em lezui tapean
ethe erah ize ephuma zis nithu nesteh helu.

Or, adopting such modifications as I have shown to be warranted by the Armenian language, *i.e.*, writing *me* for *es*, 'I,' and *zis*, 'mes' *tapurini*, 'tepefactæ,' for *tapean*, (indecl.), 'tepidæ;' and inserting *-aph-* between the root and termination of *hel-u*—

(*me*) *mi ketu na* (*me*) *mathu mar em lezui tap(urini)*
ethe erah ize ephumn (*me*) *nithu nesteh hel(aph)u.*

Here then is an Armenian couplet, which scarcely differs at all from the inscription of Cervetri. Even the metre is but little impaired. Yet such a resemblance would hardly be possible, unless the Armenian and Etruscan were dialects of the same language, at least if the Armenian will give an appropriate sense for the Etruscan. But this is the case; for the Armenian would lead to the following interpretation of the inscription on the pot, which the recurrence of the word *mi* shows to be speaking of itself, and which, as it belonged to a Bacchanalian people, may be expected to speak in accordance with the national character—

Arm. Me mi kelu, na me mathu mar em   lezui tapurini:
Etrusc. Mi ni kethu, ma mi mathu mar am   lisiai thipurenai:
Eng. I not of water, but I of wine a pot am for the tongue thirsty:
Arm. Ethe erak ize ephumn, me   nithu   nestek helaphu.
Etrusc. Ethe erai sie epana,[1] *mi nethu   nastav helephu.*
Eng. If joyous be the feast, me of liquor the guest empties.

Wine for dry tongues, not water, I contain:
At joyous feasts the guests my liquor drain.[2]

Me vini haud lymphæ plenum sitit arida lingua:
Cum fervent epulæ me totum combibit hospes.

In order to obtain this interpretation, the meaning of some of the Arm. words has been slightly modified. The case would be analogous in Germ. and Eng. Let us, for instance, take the supposed meaning of the inscription in Germ., and compare the words with their kindred terms in Eng.—

Ich bin nicht ein Wasser-becher, aber ein Wein-becher für die durstige zunge:

I be not an water-beaker, (but) an wine-beaker for the thirsty tongue:

---

[1] If we read *ethe era isie epana*, the resemblance to the Armenian will be still closer.
[2] So Göthe sings of the King of Thule and his goblet—
Er leert ihn jeden Schmaus.

Wenn lustig ist das Fest, so säuft der Gast meinen Saft.
When lusty is the feast, so sups the guest mine sap.

I may add two independent examples from Schiller's elegiac couplets, in order to show that the Etruscan of Cervetri is as near to the Armenian as the German is to the English.

Jupiter to Hercules.

Nicht aus meinem Nektar hast du dir Gottheit getrunken:
Not out (of) mine nectar hast thou thee Godhead (y)drunken:
Deine Götterkraft war's, die   dir den Nektar errang.
Thine God-craft was't, that (to) thee the Nectar wrung.

Votive Tablets.

Was der Gott mich gelehrt, was mir durchs Leben
What the God me (y)learned,[1] what me through[2]-the life
geholfen,
(y)holpen,
Häng' ich, dankbar und fromm, hier in dem Heiligthum auf.
Hang I, thank(ful) and (devout), here in the halidom up.

The termin. of *dankbar* is found in *neighbour* (*nachbar*). Thus *dankbar* is English nearly in the same manner as *thipurenai* is Armenian, but not so obviously: as the corresponding English termin. is not so common as the Armenian.

Some modifications, which would not, however, affect the question of affinity, might be suggested in the interpretation of the inscription. Thus the Arm. would allow *kethu* to be rendered ' milk,' though the sense, ' water,' seems to suit the inscription better. If, again, we compare *kethu*, *mathu*, and *nethu* with the forms of the Phryg. βίδυ, 'water,' the Macedon. βίθυ, 'air,' the Sansk. *madhu*, or the Gr. μέθυ, we might be inclined to consider those Etruscan words as in the nom. or acc. case. If they be in the acc., then we should have to regard *maram* as a transitive verb, of the second Arm. conjugation, like *nitam*, ' I contrive, I form,' and signifying ' I con-

---
[1] Chaucer has *lered* for ' taught,' and we have still *lore*.
[2] Chaucer writes *thurgh*.

tain' or 'I dispense.' Cf. Alb. *marr*, 'I contain,' and Germ. *fass* and *fassen*. We should also have to interpret *mi nethu* as 'my liquor' or 'my contents,' considering *mi* as equivalent to 'my' or 'of me,' both rendered in Arm. by *im*. The Gael. for 'my' is *mo;* the Welsh, *my;* the Osset., *mä;* the Alb., *im, yim,* or *yem.* If *mi nethu* be a nom., then *helephu* would have a passive signification—the Arm. *zelov* is both active and neuter—and *nastav* would be in the instr. case, and = Arm. *nidehiv*, 'by the stranger,' *i.e.*, 'guest.' *Lisiai thipurenai* might also be connected, perhaps to the improvement of the sense, with the second line instead of the first; and the inscription be thus given and translated—

Mi ni kethu, ma mi mathu maram: lisiai thipurenai,
Ethe erai tie epana, mi nethu nastav helephu.

I do not contain water, but wine: on (his) thirsty tongue,
When there is a joyous feast, my liquor { the guest pours out.
                                          is poured out by the
                                          guest.

Vinum non lympham teneo: me fervida lingua
Haurit ubi dapibus lætis interfuit hospes.

The inscription of Cervetri lends itself to the Armenian, the representative of the Thracian family of languages, with more completeness and facility than any other inscription in Etruria. Now this inscription, as I noticed before, has been regarded by eminent scholars as Pelasgian rather than Etruscan. Were then the Pelasgians purer Thracians than the Etruscans? It seems not improbable that they might have been so. The Pelasgian name of Cervetri was *Agylla*, in which we may readily recognize the Arm. *givł*, *i.e., gyl*, 'a village.' When the Etruscans conquered it, they changed the name to *Cære*, which looks like the Welsh *caer*, though *char* signifies 'rock' in Arm. What then would the Etruscan conquest of the Pelasgian Agylla imply? Were the Etruscans, according to one conjecture, the previously subdued Celtic Umbrians recovering their land? Many reasons seem to render this supposition inadmissible. The *Etruscans*, for instance, are said to have conquered three hundred towns from the *Umbrians*; and the *Pelasgian* Ravenna is said to have submitted to the *Umbrians* for protection against the *Etruscans*. Had then the Etruscans so combined with the conquered Umbrians before the capture of Agylla as partly to Celticise their own speech? This may have been the case; though it would rather be expected that the Celtic element found in Etruscan, and mainly, it is probable, derived from the Umbrians, would have been due to a gradual infusion of later date after the complete conquest of Etruria had been effected. But, even if the Etruscan language had been thus partly Celticised at the time of the capture of Agylla, we have still to explain the distinction which was made between the Etruscans and Pelasgians at that particular time, and also the fact, due probably to the presence of Pelasgians at Agylla, and evinced by the inscription of Cervetri, that a dialect apparently not completely identical with the Etruscan,[1] but of a purer Thracian character, existed at that place. The solution may perhaps be this. It has been seen that a Celtic element seems to constitute the difference between the Scythian and Proper Thracian languages, the Celts having, as appears probable, passed into Europe to the north of the Thracians. Among the northern Thracians, those of Dacia, Pannonia, Noricum, and Rhætia, Celtic elements would also have penetrated. Of these northern Thracians the Etruscans may have been a branch. The Pelasgians, on the other hand, may have been southern or pure Thracians, who passed into Italy at an earlier period than the northern Thracians or Etruscans.

---

[1] Yet I cannot assent to the opinion, that the language of the inscription of Cervetri belongs to the same family as the Greek and Latin, and to a different family from the Etruscan. Would not these be the characteristics of Oscan and Umbrian, instead of Pelasgian—of the language of the Bantine and Eugubine tables, not of the inscription of Cervetri? This last, again, is written like Etruscan: it has no medial letters, and only the vowels, *a, e, i, u*.

Another mark of distinction may be discerned between the language of the inscription of Cervetri, and that of the Etruscan vocabulary. At Cervetri we find the word *neth*, which is the Arm. *nivth (nyth)*. But in the vocabulary, the same word takes the form *nepos*, which is the Alb. *nepës*. Does this indicate a difference of dialect among the Thracians; such, for instance, as obtains among the Kymry and Gael, or among the High and Low Germans? Did the Armenians and Pelasgians belong to one class, and the Etruscans and Illyrians to the other? I have before called attention to the fact, which may favour this last supposition, that a great part of the Albanians are still called *Toscans*. A similar distinction might also have helped to discriminate the Illyrians from the Proper Thracians.

These distinctions would, however, be superficial, and the language, or the dialects, of Etruria would be Thracian, or, when defined by language, Armenian. And this seems to render it difficult to accede to Mr. Rawlinson's conclusion, that the Etruscan language was 'decidedly not even Indo-Germanic' (v. iii. p. 541), especially when we perceive that the Etruscan possesses Aryan forms of declension which are deficient in Armenian. It is true that Mr. Rawlinson does not consider the Armenian language as perfectly Indo-Germanic (v. i. p. 652), regarding it, and probably with truth, as containing some Turanian elements. Yet this does not, and rightly does not, prevent him from considering the Armenians as Indo-Germans, though he does not admit them to be either Phrygians or Thracians. Indeed the different members of, as I conceive, one race, the Thracian, are by Mr. Rawlinson mostly separated from each other, and distributed into very different families. The (later) Armenians are attached by him to the Medo-Persian race (v. i. p. 676), which the further addition of the Cappadocians causes to extend from the Jaxartes and the Indian frontier to the Halys. The Phrygians, Mysians, Lydians, and Carians are united with the Greeks (ib.), and thus, it would appear, with the Latins also, so as to form a second great race between the Halys and the Tiber. The Thracians form a third branch of the Indo-Germanic stock (ib): and the Etruscans are not only unconnected with the Thracians, or Lydians, or Phrygians, or Armenians, but also with all the members of the Indo-Germanic stock, in Europe and Asia. And this exclusion is the more remarkable, as Mr. Rawlinson admits the Lycians, whose claim seems much weaker, into the Indo-Germanic family, considering that the Lycian language 'presents on the whole characteristics decidedly Indo-European' (v. i. p. 668), while the Etruscan language is 'decidedly not even Indo-Germanic.' Mr. Rawlinson's reasons for this last conclusion seem to be (v. iii. p. 541) 'that it is impossible, even from the copious inscriptions which remain (in Etruscan), to form a conjecture as to its grammar, or do more than guess at the meaning of some half-dozen words.' This may be doubted; and, even if it were the case, that is, if we knew substantially nothing of the Etruscan, would it not be rather hasty to say that a language of which we were almost entirely ignorant was decidedly not even Indo-Germanic? Suppose an Englishman were to draw a similar conclusion with respect to Polish or Russian, in which, if unacquainted with Slavonian, and possessed of only some inscriptions, he would very probably make out no more than Mr. Rawlinson decides to be possible in the case of the Etruscan. In either of these instances, or in any other, does the inability of an Indo-German to interpret a particular language prove that language beyond question not to be Indo-Germanic?

Some of Mr. Rawlinson's positions with respect to the Armenians seem also open to objection. The earlier Armenians, he considers, were Turanians, who were succeeded by the later Armenians, a tribe of Medo-Persian origin; and although the ethnic change by which an Indo-European thus succeeded a Tâtar preponderance in Armenia was prior, as he believes, to the time of Herodotus, yet the Indo-Germanic movement which effected the change was probably no earlier than the close of the seventh century B.C.—(v. i. pp. 652, 653). But is this comparatively late Indo-European movement, which must have influenced Armenia from the east, consistent with the fact of an Armenian and Indo-European dialect being spoken, and probably *then* spoken, far away to the west of Armenia, by the side of the Tiber? At all events, the Aryanising of Armenia could hardly have been effected by a Medo-Persian tribe. For the Armenian language is more nearly allied to the Etruscan and the Phrygian than it is to the ancient Persian, either as represented by the inscriptions of Behistun and elsewhere, or the Old Persian words collected by Bötticher in his *Arica*. Nor, on the other hand, does it appear probable, as reported by Herodotus, that the Armenians were colonists from Phrygia. It is in Etruria, not in Phrygia, that we find the language which most closely resembles the Armenian. The difference between the Phrygian and Armenian languages, and the distance between Armenia and Etruria, are reasons for throwing back to a time before the memory of man the separation of the three peoples from one another. The story of the Phrygian colony in Armenia cannot therefore be received as historic, but must be considered as an inference derived from the fact of the proximity of the two kindred nations. Neither should I be inclined to consider Armenia as a late Thracian conquest at all, but rather as the original seat of the whole Thracian race.

The Perugian inscription.

To complete a survey of the Etruscan language, it may be requisite to take some notice of the great Perugian inscription, the only Etruscan inscription extant of any great length. It is engraved on two contiguous sides of a block of stone, and the words are, as will be seen, to a great extent run together. Micali gives it thus:—

152   THE ARMENIAN ORIGIN OF THE ETRUSCANS.

1. eulat. tanna. *larezul*
2. amevachr*lautn*. *velthinase*
3. st*laafunas* slelethk*aru*
4. *tezanfusleri tesnsteis*
5. *rasnesipa*amahen*naper*
6. xii*velthina*thurasaraspe
7. raskemulmleskulz*ukien*
8. *eskiepltularu*
9. aulesi. *velthinas*arznal*kl*
10. *ensi*. thii. thilskuna. kenu. e
11. plk. feliklarthals*afunes*
12.   klen*thunchulthe*
13. falas chiem*fusle. velthina*
14. *hinthakap*muniklet *masu*
15. *naper* srankzlthiifalstiv
16. *elthina. hut. naper. penezs*
17. *masu*. aknina. klel. *afunavel*
18. *thinas*lerzinia. intemame
19. r. knl. *velthina*. zia satene
20. *tesne*. eka. *velthina*thurasth
21. aurahelu*tesnerasn*ekei
22. *tesnsteis rasnes*chimth*sp*
23. *el*thutaskuna*afunas*ena
24. hen. *naper*. kiknlhareutuse

velthinas . . . 25
atena*zuk* 26
ieneski ip . . . 27
a spelane . . . 28
thi fulumch . . 29
va*spel*thi . . . 30
renethiest . . . 31
ak*velthina* . . . 32
akilune 33
turunesk. . . . 34
nuezea*zuk* . . . 35
i. eneski. ath . 36
umiks. *afu* . . 37
nas. penthn . . 38
a. ama*velth* . . 39
ina. afun . . . 40
thuruni. ein . . 41
zeriunakch . . 42
a. thil*thunch* . 43
ulthl. ichka . . 44
*kechazi*chuch . 45
e 46

It will be readily seen that this inscription is of little use for philological purposes. Not merely are the words run together, but they are also frequently divided at the ends of the lines. Different readings of the inscription have consequently been adopted, and whole or partial interpretations have been suggested by the Italian antiquaries, by Campanari and Vermiglioli. Few such suggestions, however, seem very probable, and many are inadmissible. I shall merely notice some particular points, availing myself of Dr. Donaldson's opinion, that the monument is a *cippus* conveying some land for funereal purposes. One thing it seems allowable to take for granted, that the inscription must contain several verbs, and those in the third person.[1]

The beginning is full of proper names. *La* (1, 3), an abbreviation of *Lars*, and also *Lautn* (2) and *Afuna* (3), we know from other sources to be such. *Velthina*, as the inscription shows, would be another proper name. *Est*, which divides *Lautn Velthinas* and *La. Afunas* (2, 3), may be compared with the Arm. *ēst*, 'according to, for.' *Karutezan* (3, 4) is rendered conjecturally by Vermiglioli, 'proclamavit;' by Campanari, 'indixerunt.' The persons, or some of them, previously mentioned in the inscription, may very probably 'have declared' something by it. Compare Arm. *charozel*, 'to declare;' *charozeëin*, 'they have declared;' *charozeźan*, 'they have been declared.' *Karutezan* might also be connected with the Arm. *kaṛoyž*, 'fixing, establishing,' from which is formed *kaṛovž-anel*, 'to fix.' A regular verb, *kaṛovž-el*,

---

[1] That the Perugian inscription cannot be interpreted from the Armenian would be no argument against the theory of a common origin for the Etruscans and Armenians, even if the Etruscan had not taken up some Celtic elements. A knowledge of Latin would not render probable, or even possible, the interpretation of a page of Greek. There would be a similar improbability in the case of English and German. Take, for instance, the first paragraph in Schiller's *Thirty Years' War*—

'Seit dem Anfang des Religionskriegs in Deutschland bis zum Münsterischen Frieden ist in der politischen Welt Europens kaum etwas Grosses und Merkwürdiges geschehen, woran die Reformation nicht den vornehmsten Antheil gehabt hätte. Alle Weltbegebenheiten, welche sich in diesem Zeitraum ereignen, schliessen sich an die Glaubensverbesserung an, wo sie nicht ursprünglich daraus erflossen, und jeder noch so grosse und noch so kleine Staat hat mehr oder weniger, mittelbarer oder unmittelbarer, den Einfluss derselben empfunden.'

This passage is substantially English; but, if we take away the words which are originally neither English nor German, such as *Religion, politisch, Europen, Reformation, Staat*, there is not very much that an Englishman would recognise, unless he were acquainted with German. Though such a word as *Zeitraum* is genuine English, and=*tide-room*, yet he could hardly divine that it meant 'period;' nor would he be likely to succeed much better with *daraus, Weltbegebenheit, Anfang*, and several other words, which really exist, at least in their elements, in his own language.

would give *karovžežan*, 'they (the dimensions of the ground) have been fixed.' Compare also with *karut-ezan*—— Gr. ἔτυψαν, i.e., ἔτυπ-σαν; and Welsh *car-asant*, Irish *rochar-sat*, 'amaverunt' (Zeuss, *Gram. Celt.* pp. 429, 497).

The next expression which deserves notice is *tesnsteis rasnes* (4, 5). We find below, *tesne* (20), *tesnerasne* (21), and, again, *tesnsteis rasnes* (22). Campanari conjectures here, *tesne* (or, as he reads it, *tephne*), 'ten.' The Arm. is *tasn:* the Sansk. and Zend, *daçan*. If *tesns = decem*, then *teis*, it seems probable, = *duo*, and *tesnsteis = duodecim*. It is remarkable that we find xii. almost directly afterwards (6). *Rasnes* might be explained from the Pers. *rai*, 'a cubit,' or from the Pers. *rasan*, Arm. *arasan*, 'a cord;' Alb. *arśiñ*, 'a measure containing three ells.' Cf. Germ. *klafter*, 'a cord, a fathom.' The dimensions of the burying ground in length and breadth may be fixed by the words—

karutezan fusleri tesnsteis rasnes   ipa   ama hen naper xii.
                 duodenos cubitos, deinde   simul xii.

Thus, in a sepulchral inscription in Gruter (p. DCCCXL), we meet with the expression—

    In Fronte Pedes xii.   In Agro Pedes xii.
and in another (p. DCCCCXLVIII)—
    In F. P. xxxvi.   Retro P. xx.

I have just interpreted *ipa* (5, 27), 'deinde,' supposing it to be = Arm. *apa*, 'then, afterwards, in the second place.' I have also rendered *naper*, 'simul.' It occurs four times (5, 15, 16, 24), preceded twice by *hen* (5, 24), and once by *hut* (16). *Naper* may signify something like 'thus, moreover, likewise,' and be explained by combining the Arm. words, *na-ibr* or *na-bar*. We have in Arm.—

sa	}	*pés* } 'as.'	*sapés*, 'thus.'	
da	} 'this.'	*ibr* }	*hipés*[1] } 'as.'	
na	}	*bar*, 'manner.'[2]	*hibar* }	
			nayapés, 'like him.'	

---
[1] *Hi* seems here = Lat. *hi-c*.
[2] Preserved in the plural form, *barcħ*, 'manner.'

Na-ibr or *na-bar* might = *na-per*, just as we have previously formed the Arm. *na-imn* = Phryg. ναὶ μήν. So, again, in Arm., *naev* (*na*, 'this;' *ev*, 'and') signifies 'moreover;' and *ovremn* or *na ovremn*, 'accordingly.'

As we meet with *hut naper* in the Perugian inscription (16), so we also meet with *huth naper* in an inscription lately found at Volterra. This inscription is engraved, like the Perugian, on two contiguous faces of a block of stone; but each line must be read completely across from face to face. I write in capitals what are evidently proper names. One of them, *Mestles*, resembles Μισθλης, the name of one of the leaders of the Mæonians in the *Iliad* (ii. 864). The inscription runs thus, as I copied it in 1857—

Titesi Kale	si
kina Ks Mes	tles
huth naper	leskan
letm thui	
arasa then	ma
selaei tre	ks
.thenst me	natha

It may be worth while to analyse the first of these two parts or sentences. *Kina* seems = Arm. *kin*, Gr. γυνή, and may be compared with the *kuna* of the Perugian inscription (10, 23). *Thui* seems to show the inscription to be sepulchral, as the word is often found in epitaphs. I have explained it conjecturally (ante, p. 110), 'memoratur,' from the Arm. *thovi*, 'it appears, is counted.' *Letm* reminds us of *lethum*, and also of the Arm. *leth-il*, 'to languish;' as well as of the Arm. *atêtch* (plural form of *atêt*), 'misfortune, calamity,' *atêtali*, 'fatal, funereal, sad' (cf. *lethalis*). As the inscription is sepulchral, *leskan* may be compared with the Arm. *lesk*, 'a body' (in composition), Kurd. *lesc*, Alb. *lyes*, Germ. *leiche*, 'a corpse.' We find *leskul* in the Perugian inscription (7) near another word, *tularu* (8), which we may conclude from *tular* (ante, p. 111) to be a sepulchral term. An Arm. verb, *leskal*, formed from *lesk*, would give *leškan* for the 3 pers. plur. pres. ind., *leškol* for the pres. participle, and *leškeal* for the past participle. *Leškan* might also be an Arm. adjective formed from *lešk*, like *iškhan*, 'a ruler,' from *iškh-el*, 'to rule.' *Huth*, in the Perugian inscription *hut*, may be explained from the Arm. *het, yet, yetoy,* 'after, then, subsequently.' Cf. *Iri, yet,* and Heb. *od.*

It does not appear difficult to perceive the probable construction of the inscription on the sepulchral *cippus* of Volterra, or even to interpret its general meaning. It seems to be of this nature—

Titesi Kalesi,   *kina*   *Ks Mestles*
Titus Calesius, (his) wife (the daughter of) Caia Mestles

huth   *naper,*   *leskan.*   *Letm*
afterwards likewise, are buried (here). (Their) death
                              are dead.
thui.
is commemorated.

    Arasa thenma,   *selaei treks,*
  (A nominative),   (A genitive, defining *arasa thenma*),

.thenst   *me*   *natha.*
?   me (the *cippus*) provides. Cf. Arm. *nitay,* 'contrives;' *nivthé,* 'forms,' *nŏthģé,* 'procures.'

Compare the following epitaphs in Gruter, pp. DCCXLI. and DCLXXVII.—

                     Filii
                 Posuerunt Memoriam
            Saturniano Potio *Obito*
               Cum Compare Sua
               Valentiana Volusia.
Corpus Hic Situm Est L. Clodii L. F. Rufini Fil.
Clodii Pompeii Q. V. A. ix. M. vii. D. v.
     Sempronia C. F. Rufina Mater *Fec.*
(*Corpus hic situm est* = Etrusc. *eka suthi nesl,* p. 109).

To return to the Perugian inscription. *Zuki eneski* occurs

three times (7, 8; 26, 27; 35, 36). It may be a form of comprehension. Cf. Arm. *zoyg* 'equally, together;' *zoyg*, gen., dat., and abl., *zorgi*, 'equal, alike, united, similar.' The first section of the inscription, the eight lines terminating with *tularu*, seems to contain the names of the parties to the transaction commemorated by the *cippus*, the quantity of land conveyed, and a statement of the purpose to which the ground was to be devoted.

If we make *epl* (8) a participle like *nesl* and *sansl*, and connect it with the Arm. *wép*, 'ἴπος,' then *zuki eneski epl tularu* might signify something like, 'including the ..... of the said tomb.'

In 9, 10, we perceive the word *klensi*, and in 12, *klen*, terms with which we are already familiar (see *ante*, p. 131). The same may be said of *muniklet* (14), which we have seen before (p. 115) under the form *munikleth*. In 13, *Velthina* is a nom., to which *kape* and *masu* (14), the last followed by *naper*, 'also,' may be the verbs; *kape* belonging to the Arm. *-el* conjugation, and *masu* to that in *-ovl*. In Arm. *kapé* means 'he joins;' and if we unite *kape* (14) with the previous word, *hintha*, comparing *hintha* with the Arm. *enth*, 'under,' and *hinthakape* with the Arm. *enthadaté*, 'he suspects,' and *enthadré*, 'he subjects,' we might render *hinthakape*, 'he subjoins,' or 'he enjoins.' As we find the root *mas* in the Arm. *masn*, 'portion, allotment,' and in the Alb. *mas*, 'to measure,' *masu naper* might signify 'allots also.' In 15, 16, 17, we meet with *velthina hut naper penezs masu*, 'Velthina then also allots *penezs*;' this last word being in such a case an acc. plur., which may be compared *in form* with the Arm. *(z)thizs*, the acc. plur. of *thiz*, 'a span,' and in meaning, not improbably, with the Gael. *peanas*, 'pœna.' Cf. Gruter (p. DCCCXXXV)—

..... 'Si quis alienum corpus hic intulerit *pœnam* supra scriptam inferet.'

and *ib*. (p. DCCCXXV.)—

'Huic monumento manus qui intulerit dabit sestertios xx.'

Aknina (17) and *lerzinia* (18) resemble, probably accidentally, the Pehlvi *aknín*, 'there,' Pers. *aknún*, 'now,' and the Gael. *leirsinneach*, 'seeing.' The termination of the mass of words, *kiknl*hareu*tuse* (24) is not unlike the Arm. *tovté*, 'he fines,' or 'punishes;' *tovti*, 'he recompenses' or 'indemnifies:' and *knl*, which is also found in 19, may be compared with the Arm. *gnel*, 'to buy,' *gnol*, 'buying.' The section of the inscription, beginning with 12, may perhaps contain such a statement of penalties to be inflicted in case of a violation of the sepulchre, or even its use or acquisition, as is frequently found in similar Latin inscriptions, as well as in those of Lycia.

In 28 we meet with *spelane*, in 30 with *spel*, and in 22, 23, with *spel* again. To illustrate these forms, compare Arm. *el*, 'an ascent;' *el*, 'he ascended;' *elané*, 'he ascends:' *spand*, 'a killing;' *span*, 'he killed;' *spanané*, 'he kills.' We find these last two words in a passage of the Armenian version of the *Chronicle* of Eusebius (Ed. Aucher, p. 327) in a manner very like that in which *spel* and *spelane* occur in the Perugian inscription. The Etruscan, according to Dr. Donaldson's division of the words, would run thus—

. . . . . . chimth *spel* thutas kuna afunas ena hen naper ki knl hareutuse velthinas atena zuki eneski ipa *spelane* thi(s) fulumchva *spel* . . . .

The Armenian is this—

Zaridinos olompia span *mayrn aléchsandri*. *Ev*
Aridæum Olympias *interfecit* mater Alexandri. Et

zna tireal makedonaïvoš ev zerkovs ordis aléchsandri
illam imperantem Macedonibus et duos filios Alexandri

kasandros antipatreay spananê. *Zmin inchn isk*
Cassander Antipatris *occidit*. Unum ipse quidem

span . . . .
interfecit . . .

For a not improbable meaning of *spel*, cf. Arm. *araspel*, 'fable, apologue,' a word compounded of *araz*, 'an adage,' *arak*, 'fable, adage,' or of their th., and of a word, not existing by

itself, *spel*, 'a telling,' = Teut. *spel*, preserved in our *Gospel*.
Spelane might signify 'dicit,' and *spel*, 'dixit,' ' or 'dictum.'
Atena (26), which might be the nom. to *spelane*, is rather like
the Arm. *atean*, 'a tribunal, a court of justice, a magistrate, a
senate,' and may be compared with the *atanisen* of the
Phrygian epitaph (*ante*, p. 34).

In 41 occurs *thuruni*, in 6 and 20, *thuras*, an inflexion of
thura, which is met with elsewhere (*ante*, p. 118). Cf. Arm.
archay, 'king;' *archovni*, 'royal;' *tér*, 'a lord;' *térovni*,
'Dominical;' *Arsakovni*, 'Arsacide, of the family of *Arsaces*.'

In 48 is found *kechazi*, though it is not quite certain that
there is a division of words after *-zi*. We have previously had
kecha, and in Dennis (v. i. p. 313) we find, 'Laris Pumpus
Arnthal klan *kechase*.' Such a variety of forms is particularly
instructive: to compare them with the Arm., we must take a
verb of the *-al* conjugation, like *khokal*, 'to think,' of which
the regular passive, if used, would be *khokil*. These verbs
would give us—

	Active. Ind.		Passive. Ind.	
	Pres.	Perf.	Pres.	Perf.
	khokam.	*khokaži*.	*khokim*.	*khokežay*.
	khokas.	*khokažer*.	*khokis*.	*khokežar*.
(1)	*khokay*. (a) *khokaž*.	*khoki*. .	*khokežav*.
	khokamch.	*khokažach*.	*khokimch*.	*khokežach*.
	khokaych.	*khokažich*.	*khokich*.	*khokežaych*.
	khokan.	*khokažin*.	*khokin*.	*khokežan*.
	Subj. -Fut.		Subj. Fut.	
	khokayžem.		*khokayžim*.	
	khokayžes.		*khokayžis*.	
(2)	*khokayžé*.		(3) *khokayži*.	
	khokayžemch.		*khokayžimch*.	
	khokayžéch.		*khokayžich*.	
	khokayžen.		*khokayžin*.	

In *khokay, khokayzé,* and *khokayzi,* we have forms very like *kecha, kechase,* and *kechazi*. *Khokaž* (a), and the fut ind., which would be *khokaszé,* are also not unlike *kechase.*[1] The meaning of *kechazi,* interpreted like *kecha* (*ante,* p. 131), would be 'shall have been paid,' or 'shall be paid.' The conjugation of the Albanian aorist subjunctive bears considerable resemblance to the Armenian future subjunctive. In *plyak,* 'to make old,' it is thus conjugated:—

plyakša.   or *plyaktša.*
plyakš.   *plyaktš.*
plyaktë.
plyakšim.   *plyaktšim.*
plyakši.   *plyaktši.*
plyakšine   *plyaktšinë.*

---

[1] I think the meaning of *kechase* is most likely 'has expiated' or 'has paid,' though the final vowel would point to the Arm. future rather than the perfect. The inscription where it is found accompanies a procession of departed souls and genii, of which a plate is given in Mrs. Gray's *Sepulchres of Etruria,* but with the inscription not quite correctly copied. The author seems to have been affected by the representation with a profound interest, which her readers will probably find contagious. She says (p. 211) of the person to whom the inscription would refer: 'This very handsome and noble looking youth is immediately followed by a monstrous fiend, in whom we recognise the most frightful development of the evil genius of Etruria.——One enormous claw was pouncing upon the shoulder of the unfortunate youth, while the hammer, the Etruscan badge of the angel of death, was raised aloft in the other. Behind him was the figure, lamentably defaced, of a female of surpassing loveliness, and in her beautiful brow and eye the most intense anguish was depicted. To her was attached an infernal guard, similar to the one who had pounced upon the youth.——The art of the painter had invested these figures with the marks of individuality; they must have been portraits; but whom did they represent, and why were they thus represented? What had they done, and why were they thus singled out, to be handed down for two-and-twenty ages as the prey of demons, and branded with the mark of reprobation?' No light is thrown on this by the inscription, which, like the speech of Loredano on the death of the Doge Foscari, is terribly brief—

Laris Pumpus   *Lars Pompeius*
Arnthal klan   *Aruntiæ proles*
   kechase.   { *expiavit.*
                        { *solvit.*

Compare Dennis, v. i. p. 309—314.

In 13 is found *fusle*, and in 4 *fusleri*. Cf. Pers. *zan*, 'γυνή;' *zanrá*, 'γυναικί or γυναῖκα;' and also the Gael. *ri*, ' to,' Arm. *aṛ*, ' to.' The Basque, again, forms the dative of nouns and pronouns by postfixing *-ri* to the nominative.

Little more can be extracted from the Perugian inscription in the way of evidence. The terminations in *-l*, which are numerous in this as in other Etruscan inscriptions, I have already compared with the Armenian (*ante*, p. 105), a language of which they are equally characteristic. Some Etruscan words, formed, like the Armenian, by excluding vowels, might also be noticed: thus *ackr* and *lautn* (2) might be compared with Arm. *phockr*, ' little,' and *otn*, ' foot.' The terminations of *tnrunesk* (34) and *athumiks* (36, 37) are also common in Armenian. On the whole, the result of the examination of the Perugian inscription would not be sufficient to prove the Etruscan language to belong to the same family as the Armenian; but it would at the same time fall in with such a supposition, which is all that can be expected from a single inscription of such length, and transmitted to us in such a state as not even to admit of a complete trustworthy division into words. If the Etruscan vocabulary, and the shorter Etruscan inscriptions, previously considered, exhibit decided Armenian affinities, the Perugian inscription will not tend to shake, but rather to confirm, the Armenian character of the Etruscan.

Geographical names in Etruria and other countries.

We pass from the language of the Etruscans to a species of evidence of the same kind, but of an independent nature, the names of towns, rivers, &c., in Etruria. Now this evidence, taken singly by itself, is frequently of very great weight, if not decisive; as may be seen at once by the local terminations common in our own country—*ham, ton, by, thorpe, castle, chester, bury, ford, bridge, wich, don, stead, hill, field, wood, ley, worth, bourn, stoke, holt, hurst, combe, dale, thwaite.* These, indeed, might be sufficient to prove that we were mainly of Teutonic origin; while the Celtic *don* and *combe*, and above all the names of rivers, such as the *Thames, Tamar, Teme, Ouse, Avon*, features of a country which are permanent, and not to be made and destroyed like towns, would indicate who were our predecessors in the land. Still more remarkable is the confirmation of our history afforded by the Danish termination *-by, i.e.*, 'village,' which likewise deserves additional attention here, as the presence of Thracians in Etruria will be indicated by an exactly equivalent Armenian word.[1] Now the Danish *by* is found in the West, as far south as *Kirby* in Cheshire, on the estuary of the Dee; in the Centre, as far south as *Rugby, Kirby*, and *Willoughby*, all on the north-eastern edge of Warwickshire; and in the East, as far south as *Kirby* on the Naze in Essex. West of the Dove, and south-west of Rugby, such terminations disappear, while in Northamptonshire and Leicestershire, to say nothing of more northern counties, they are particularly abundant. Now, had our history been lost, and had we been left to determine the extent of the Danish occupancy of England by the aid of philology alone, we should have come to a very accurate conclusion: for the English districts yielded up to the Danes by Alfred, and which they occupied, consisted of Northumbria, East Anglia, Essex, and the north-east of Mercia, or the country of the Five Burghers, so called from its five chief towns, Der*by*, Nottingham, Lincoln, Stamford, and Leicester. Thus the presence of a single geographical term would enable us to ascertain, at the distance of nearly a thousand years, the extent to which an invading race once occupied our country.

I have dwelt on this circumstance more particularly, because, as I intimated, the Arm. *sén*, 'village, *by*,' which forms the

---

[1] *By* is Swedish as well as Danish. It is, indeed, the characteristic Scandinavian termination which corresponds to the Germ. *-heim*, the Eng. *-ham*, and the Frisian *-um*. Compare Latham's *Germania of Tacitus*, pp. 119—125.

most common termination of Arm. names of places, seems to correspond in Etruria and other parts of Italy to the Danish *by* in England. Nor is this all. The Arm. *sén*, or words similarly allied to *śin-el*, 'to build,' appear to be found in all the intervening countries also, from Armenia to Italy. This will be seen from the following list, in which I have compared Armenian words and names, not merely with the geographical terms in Etruria, but also with those in other countries, in confirmation of what history and language alike tend to inform us, that there was one race, now represented by the Armenians, extending from Armenia to Italy and Rhætia. My Armenian names are mostly derived from Kiepert's map. As I have, in consequence, not always been able to obtain them in the Armenian orthography, some immaterial inconsistencies may be observed. Thus Kiepert writes *Noraschén*, and I *Noraskén*, he *Lorri* and I *Lori*, where the Arm. would be *Noraśén*, and *Lavṛi* or *Lóṛi*.[1] But these discrepancies are obviously of no importance. The names in the list, where the locality is not indicated, are Etruscan.

Etruscan, &c.	Armenian.
Sena	*śinel*, 'to build, to construct, to make.'
Tur-*sena* or Cur-*sena*.	
Vol-*sinii*.	*śén* (gen. *śini*), 'a habitation, a village, an inhabited place.'
Tar-*quinii*.	
	śinaç, 'a building.' Cf. Phryg. *Synnas*.
	seneak, 'lodging, chamber:' -*ak* marks a diminutive.
Fel-*sina*[2] } Gal. Cisp.	*sivn*, 'a pillar.' Gr. κίων.
Cæ-*sena* }	Lith. *séna*, 'a wall;' *sényś*, 'a building.'

---

[1] *Shén* and *Lori*, from their signification, and the frequency of their occurrence, would correspond to the English -*ton* and -*ham* (*town* and *home*). Both are found in Etruria, while Germany only possesses -*ham* (-*heim*).

[2] *Felsina* was the Etruscan name of Bologna.

164   THE ARMENIAN ORIGIN OF THE ETRUSCANS.

Etruscan, &c.		Armenian.

Sar-*sina* ⎫
Sena Gallica ⎬ Umb.
Ful-*ginia* ⎭
Ri-*cina*—Picen.
Tarra-*cina*[1] ⎫
Signia   ⎬ Latium.
Mar-*cina*[2] ⎫
Sinuessa   ⎬ Campan.
Sa-*sina*—Iapyg.
Tartu-*sana*—Noric.
Senia   ⎫
Sinna, Chinna,   ⎪
 or Cinna   ⎬ Illyr.
Ful-*sinum*   ⎪
Ol-*cinium*   ⎭
San-dava[3] ⎫
Singi-dava[3] ⎬ Dacia.
Singi-dunum[3]—Mœsia.
Sane   ⎫ Maced.
Singus ⎭
Sani-ana—Thrace.
Sanis or   ⎫
 Sanaus   ⎬ Phryg.
Synnas or   ⎪
 Synnada   ⎭
Sinda ⎰ Pisid. or
      ⎱ Phryg.
Sin-ope—Paphlag.

Irish *sunn*, 'a fortification.'
The Arm. *sin-el*, 'to build,' *i.e.* 'to raise up,' would be, apparently, the same word as *cio, cieo*, κίω, and κινέω, and akin to the Sansk. *çvi*, 'crescere.' In general, the Sansk. *ç* becomes *s* or *sh* (*š*) in Arm. and κ in Gr. So Gr. κίνος = Arm. *sin.*, and Gr. κύων (κυν-) = Arm. *šovn*. The same element may thus be found in Tar-*quinii* and Vol-*sinii*, in Mar-*cina* and Fel-*sina*. It has been already seen that the Etruscans wrote both *kver* and *sver*, *tlenacheis* and *tlenasies*. We find also as proper names in Lanzi, vol. ii., *vulsine* (p. 335), *velsinal* (p. 369), and *velchinei* (p. 466).

Names of Towns and Villages.

Senn.
Shin.
Nor-*shén* or Nora-*shén* (*noratén*, 'newly built, new').
Hi-*shén*.
Bab-*shén*.
Hem-*shin*.
Gudra-*shén*.
Loma-*shén*.

---

[1] The Volscian name of Tarracina was *Anxur*, signifying perhaps 'the defile.' Cf. *anxius, angustus*, and ἄγχοs. There is a defile at Terracina.

[2] Μαρκίνα Τυρρηνῶν κτίσμα. Strabo.

[3] The suffixes -*dava* and -*dunum* deserve notice, as the latter is a common Celtic word, and the former would be the usual Dacian name for a town. San-*dava* might be tautologous, like *Hamp-ton*.

THE ARMENIAN ORIGIN OF THE ETRUSCANS. 165

Etruscan, &c.		Armenian.
Sinna	} Galat.	Bashki-*shén*.
Pardo-*sena*		Dada-*shén*.
Singa	} Cappad.	Arpa-*shén*.
Sacca-*sena*		Ka-*shin*.
Sana	} Arm. (anc*t*.)	Pirne-*shin*.
Sinis		Arda-*shin*.
Sinna—Mesopot.		*San*-atis.
		Sana-hin (*hin*, 'old').

Name of District.

Shikashén, i. e. 'red-built, red-made,' or simply, 'red.' So again we have *meẓatén* = *meẓ*, 'great.' Compare Por-*sena*, Ra-*sena*, Tyr-*senus*. If we had in Arm. the root *ra*, which appears in *raise*, *rear*, *rectus*, we might form a word *ratén*, 'high,' and explain by its aid the Etrusc. *Rasena*, said to be the name of a nobleman. It might also be the Etrusc. name of *Rhætia*, 'the high (land).'

It is a peculiarity of the Arm. that scarcely any words begin with *r*; but we have *ṛah*, 'a way,' which, when compared with *ovti*, 'a way,' and *ovtit*, 'rectus,' seems to contain the required root *ra*. *Rasena* and *Tyr-senus* might even be opposed to each other, as *divr* (*dyr*) signifies 'a plain' in Arm. There appears a similar contrast in *Sabini* (Bret. *sav*, 'a height,' Gr. αἰπεινός) and *Latium* (Welsh *lledd*, 'a plain'); and also in *Samnium* and *Campania*.

166   THE ARMENIAN ORIGIN OF THE ETRUSCANS.

Etruscan, &c.	Armenian.

The suffix -*ich* has sometimes an active sense, as in *mehenatèn*, 'a temple-builder;' *tnatèn*, 'a house-builder.' Many have considered *Tyrsenus* to signify 'tower-builder,' though it does not appear a very obvious designation for a people.

{ *Vol*-aterræ (Etrusc.)
  Velathri). } . *ovilel*, 'to elevate;' *ovtit*, 'rectus.' The root is *ovt*.

{ *Vol*-sinii.
  Ful-ginia—Umbr.
  Ful-sinum
  Ol-cinium } Illyr.

{ *Fel*-sina—Gal. Cisp.. *elch* (plural form of *el*) 'elevation;'
  El-atria—Epirus.   *el(anel)*, 'to mount.'
  Compare *Higham, Hochheim, Hauteville.*

{ *Fal*-erii . . . . *wal*, 'ancient.'
  Fal-eria—Picen.   Compare *Oldham, Città Vecchia.*

{ *Vol*-*aterra* (Vel-*athri*). *óth, ótharan* (or *avth, avtharan*),
  Hadria—Picen.   'lodging, dwelling.'
  Atria—Venet.   Gael. *aitreabh*, 'a dwelling.'
  Ot-esia—Gal. Cisp.
  El-*atria*—Epirus.

{ *Volaterra*, built on
  a λόφος ὑψηλὸς, πε-
  ρίκρημνος παντῇ. } . *ovitadir*, 'erect, perpendicular,' (lit. 'high-placed'). Compare Mons *Vultur* in Apulia. The Vulturnus is in Gr. Οὔλθυρνος.

{ *Tar*-quinii . . . . . . *dar* }
  Sar-sina—Umbr.   *sayr* } 'a height, an eminence, an edge, a cape, a promontory.'
  Tarra-cina—Latium.[1] *sar*
           sayr, 'a rock.'

---

[1] Compare with these names the frequently recurring form in the Eugubine Tables, 'totar *tarsinater* trifor *tarsinater* tuscer nabarcer iabuscer nomner.' The *Tarsinates* of these Tables might be the Tyrse-

THE ARMENIAN ORIGIN OF THE ETRUSCANS. 167

Etruscan, &c.   *Armenian.*

The Italian names would be nearly the same as our *Clifton*.

Cæ-sena—Gal. Cisp. . *kay, kaych,* 'a stopping, a dwelling, a seat, a place.'
kav, 'clay, mud.'

Name of Place.
Ka-shin.   Cf. *Hampton* or *Clayton.*

{ *Veii, ἐφ' ὑψηλοῦ* } . . *weh,* 'high, great, noble.'
   σκοπέλου καὶ   *wih,* 'ditch, hollow.'
   περρίρωγος.
   Vegia—Illyr.

---

nians, or rather perhaps the *Sarsinates,* who are distinguished by Polybius from the Umbrians. *Sarsina* lay in the district called *Sapinia Tribus.* There may be an instance here of bilingual nomenclature. For *sav* signifies 'height' in Breton, as *sar* does in Arm.; while *tre, tref, trefa, tregva,* are common Kymric names for 'an inhabited place,' as *shén* is in Arm. Thus the names, *Sarsina,* and *Sapinia Tribus,* would be nearly identical in meaning, the one being apparently Tyrsenian and Armenian, and the other Umbrian and Celtic. So, in bilingual Belgium, the capital of Hainanlt is called both *Mons* and *Bergen.* The frequency in ancient Italy of the equivalent terms, *tre* and *shén,* and the manner of their distribution, are worthy of note. The Celtic *tre, tref, tregva, treabh* (Gael. for '*tribe,* people,') is as common among the old Italian tribes in Umbria, Picenum, Sabina, and Samnium, as the Arm. *shén* is among the intrusive Etruscans and Pelasgians. Thus we find—
I quote from Cluverius:—

Trea   or   *Treia* . . . . Picenum.
Treba   or   *Treblæ* . . . . Æqui.
Trebia   or   *Trevæ* . . . . Umbria (' pre verir *treblanir.*' Eug. Tab.).
Tribula or *Trebula* Balinensium . . Samnium or Campania.
Tribula or *Trebula* Mutusca . . . . Sabina.
Trebula Suffena . . . . Sabina.
Tre-ventum . . . . Samnjum (Welsh *gwent,* 'a plain;' *Ventæ* Icenorum, Belgarum, Silurum).
Tri-vicum . . . . Samnium (Welsh *gwig,* 'inclosure, town;' Gael. *fog,* 'a wall;' Lat. *vicus*).
Trica . . . . Apulia (said to have been destroyed by Diomed).

There was a town called *Tribola,* belonging to Viriathus, in Spain

Etruscan, &c.	Armenian.
Lorium	lóray or lavray, 'a dwelling-place.'
Larissa—Pelasgian.	Gael. lar, ' the site of a house.'
Laurium—Attica.	

In Modern Tuscany.	Names of Towns and Villages.
Loro (N.W. of Arezzo)	*Lori (2).
Lari (E. of Leghorn).	Lar.
Monte Loro (N. E. of Florence).	Lori or Lar. Lars—Osset.
Larniano (S. W. of Poppi)	leaṛn, ' a mountain.'
Lierna (N.E. of Poppi).	
Volci ("Ολκιον). . . .	ovlkh, ' a ravine.'
Volcera—Illyr.[1]	Name of District.
Vulceium—Lucan.	Ovlka.
Clusium (on a high hill).	glovkh, ' head, summit.'
Clu-ana—Picen.	Gael. clog, ' head.' Pol. głowa, 'head.' Lapp. luokka, ' collis.'

(Appian, Iber. c. 62), and Con-*trebia* was the 'capnt Celtiberorum.' The presence of the term *tre* in Ancient Italy seems nearly to mark out the region which the Thracian invaders failed to subdue. It is entirely mountainous, the highest of the Apennines, 'the Great Rock of Italy,' standing nearly in its centre. Here the old Italian race would have found refuge, like the Spaniards in the Asturian mountains and the Pyrenees, until in the course of time they succeeded in reconquering the coasts and lowlands. Similarly, in our own country, as we pass into Wales, the Saxon *ham, ton,* and *bury* disappear, and *tre, llan,* and *caer* take their place. But there are some places whose names begin with *tre,* even in the modern Tuscany: *Treppio,* N.N.E. of Pistoja; a second *Treppio,* N. of Prato; *Trebbio,* N. of Florence; and another *Trebbio,* N.N.E. of Arezzo: all about 12 miles from the cities mentioned. Such names, however, are merely further instances of the same law of distribution; for all four places are in the highest Apennines, while *Siena, Loro,* and *Lari* are in the lower, though hilly, country. In the Greek peninsula we should find the same two races, the Thracian and Celtic; for the Pelasgians were probably Thracians, and the Greeks and Celts, as Dr. Donaldson holds (Pref. to *Varros.* p. ix.), 'were scions ultimately of the same (i.e. of one) stock.'

[1] Another Illyrian town was *Pelva,* which may be compared with the *Peleva* of Azerbijan (Atropatene), the *Pelveren* of what was anciently

THE ARMENIAN ORIGIN OF THE ETRUSCANS. 169

Etruscan, &c.	Armenian.
{ *Blera* . . . . { *Plera*—Apul.	*blovr, blrak*, 'hill, mound.' *Name of Village.* *Blovr.*
Hasta	*hast,* 'strong,' *hastatel,* 'to fortify.' Gr. ἄστυ.
Pyrgos	*bovrgn,* 'a tower.' Gr. πύργος. Arab. *burj,* 'a castle.' Germ. *burg.*
{ *Vetulonii* (Etrusc. *Vet-* { *luna*)	*etl,* 'a place.'
Roma—Lat.	*ram,* 'vulgus, plebs.'
Romulea—Samn.	*ram,* 'an assembly, a troop.'
Romula—Punnon.	The name of the *Ramnes,* one
Romula } Dacia. *Rhami*-dava }	of the three Roman tribes, was said to be Etruscan. The name of
Rhamæ—Thrace.	Rome might perhaps be better con-
In Modern Tuscany.	nected with the Gael. *rum,* 'a place,'
Romola (S.W. of Florence)	or *romho,* 'great.' Cf. Gr. ῥώμη.
Remole (E.S.E. of Florence)	
Cor-tona	*kar,* 'strength;' *korow,* 'strong.'——
Gyr-tona—Thessal.	*tovn,* 'house, dwelling.'
Gor-tynia—Maced.	
Gor-tyna—Crete.	
Cortona, &c.[1]	*kertel,* 'to build, to make.' Cf.
Gordium—Phryg.	Tigrano*certa.*
Gortys or *Gortyna* —Arcad.	*krthel,* 'to form, to shape.' *gorzel,* 'to make.' *cherthovmn,* 'ποίημα.'

Commagene, and the *Palu* (*Balov*) of Armenia. *Pala* was a town in Thrace.

[1] Compare *Gordona* (Valteline) and *Gorduno* (Tessin).

Etruscan, &c.	Armenian.

{ Telamo (now Tala- mone¹)   { tilm, 'limus' (τίλμα); th. tel(al), 'to rain.'

Name of River.

Tel-amo . . . . *Tlmovt, i.e.* 'muddy.'
teli, 'a place;' *thal,* 'place, quarter.'
Gael. *talamh,* 'earth, ground.' Sansk. *tala,* 'solum, domus.' Lat. *tellus.*

Name of Town.

Thiln, probably the *Thalina* of Ptolemy.

{ Aharna . . . . *akarn,* 'a castle.'
Acharnæ—Attica.

{ Artena . . . . *artevan,* 'summit, top.' (ὀφρὺς
Artena—Lat.   (ὄρους): Luke iv. 29).²
Artenia—Venet.   Gael. *ardan,* 'a height;' *ard,* 'high.'
Lat. *arduus.* Gr. ἄρδην, ἄρδις. Sansk. *ûrdhva,* 'altus.'

{ Su-*ana* . . . . *wan, wanch,* 'house, dwelling, convent.' Cf. *fanum.*
Clu-*ana* } Picen.
Nov-*ana* }   *avan,* 'village.'
Vannia—Venet.
Vannia—Rhæt.   *Name of Town.*
Wan or *Van.*

{ Agylla . . . . *givl, gevl, gel,* 'village, field.'
Acula, Aquila, or Aquileia.   *Names of Places.*
Vir-*acelum.*   *Egil.* The Arm. orthog. is *Akl,* the Syrian, *Agyl.* Cf. *Acel-dama.*

---

¹ There is a *Talamona* in the Valteline, a part of ancient Rhætia.

² The Latian *Artena* 'is thought to have occupied the heights above Monte Fortino,' and the Etruscan *Artena* to have stood at Buccea, where 'there is a high and insulated point, which has all the appearance of a citadel' (Dennis, v. ii. p. 63, note).

THE ARMENIAN ORIGIN OF THE ETRUSCANS. 171

| Etruscan, &c. | Armenian. |

{ *Aquileia* } Venet.   *Gulli.*
  Acelum   *Göllü.*
  Celia—Apul.   *Küllü.*
  Celeia—Noric.   Esth. *külla,* 'a village.' There is a
  Cillium—Thrace.   Lithuanian village called *Agilla.*
                         Georg. *adgili,* 'a place.'
Cales—Campan. . . . *chałach,* 'a city;'[1] *khał,* 'a lake, a shore, a marsh.'
Cære . . . . *char, tayr,* 'rock, stone.'
                 kar, 'strength.'

                     Names of Places.
                 Kars.
                 Kers.
                 Keres.
                 Chers.

{ *Vir*-acelum . . . . . . *wer, werin,* 'above.'
  Verentum   *wran,* 'tent, hut.'
  Ferentum—Apul.
  Ferentinum—Lat.
  Verona—Venet.
  Virunum[2]—Noric.
Capena . . . . *kapan, kapanch,* 'a strait, a defile.'

               Name of district, and of an Arm.
                  hill-fort in Cilicia.
               Kapan.
{ *Cosa* or *Cossa* . . . . . *khovł* 'a lodging.' Cf. Eng. *house.*
  Cossa—Lucan.   *Name of village.*
               Kuash.
Arretium . . . .   *Names of towns.*
               Eréz.
               Arzn.
               Araheza.

---

[1] Compare the Assyrian *Calah* (Gen. xi. 11).
[2] Compare *Vrin* in the Grisons.

Etruscan, &c.	Armenian.
{ *Nepeta* or *Nepe* .... { *Napetia*—Bruttium.	*Name of Mountain.* *Npat* (*Niphates*), which might be connected with *npatak*, 'object, mark, sight, aim.' Cf. σκοπιά, σκόπελος.
	Name of Plain. *Npatakan.*
Perusia	*Name of Village.* *Parush.*
	Names of Districts. *Peroż* Ormzd*peroż* Spandaran*peroż*. *Beroseh* is a Kurdish town; *Perozes* or *Firouz*, a Persian name, meaning 'victorious.'
{ *Berta*—Maced. ... { *Perta*—Phryg. { *Pardo*-sena—Galat.	*berd*, 'a castle.'
{ *Ameria*—Umbr. ... { *Ameriola*—Sab.	*amovr*, 'strong;' *amroż*, 'a fort.'
	Name of Town. *Amaras.* Compare *Amras* in the Tyrol.[1] Gael. *imir*, 'a field.'
Hispellum—Umbr. .	*Name of Town and District.* *Ispir, Isper,* or *Sper.*
{ *Atina*—Lat. ..... { *Atina*—Lucan.	*atean* (gen. *ateni*), 'a tribunal, a court.' Cf. *Curia* Rhætorum: also Etrusc. *atena* (p. 159), and Phryg. *Atan*-isen (p. 34).

---

[1] Near Innsbruck. There are some places with remarkable names in the vicinity of the Tyrolese capital——*Rum, Thaur, Arzel, Vels, Vil, Pradel, Amras, Ampas, Axams, Pill, Vomp.* Some are Celtic; as *Rinn,* Gael. *rinn,* 'a promontory,' Gr. ῥίν; and *Wiltau,* the ancient *Veldidena;* Gael. *aill,* 'noble, a cliff,' *faill,* 'a cliff;' *didean,* 'a fort, a sanctuary.'

THE ARMENIAN ORIGIN OF THE ETRUSCANS. 173

Etruscan, &c.	*Armenian.*

Mœsia Silva . . . . . *moṣay*, 'a tamarisk.' Cf. Lyd. μυσός, 'ὀξύη.'

Lacus *Thrasimenus* . . *Name of District.*
Thraki.

Insula *Igilium* . . . . *kłzi*, 'an island.'
Gael. *ighe*, 'an island.'

{ Fl. *Arno* . . . . *aṛov*, 'a brook.'
{ Fl. *Aro.*

Name of River.
Aṛovn. Compare Eng. *Arun*, Heb. *Arnon.*

{ Fl. *Cæcina* (Etrusc. *sék, sikn*, 'red, yellow.' Compare
{ *Ceicna*) *flavus* Tiber, *flavus* Mela, *Xanthus,*
{ Fl. *Cæcinus* (2), Brutt. Red River, Rio *Colorado,* Fl. *Hel-*
vinus in Picenum.

{ Fl. *Clanis* or *Glanis.* *glel,* ' to roll ;' *glan*, ' a cylinder,' i.e.,
Fl. *Clanis* } 'what rolls.'
or *Glanis,* } Lat. The name *Liris,* when compared
afterwards } and with the Welsh *llyry,* ' what *glides* or
Liris. } Campan. flows, a stream,' seems like a trans-
Fl. *Clanis, Gla-* } lation into Celtic of the Tyrsenian
nis, Clanius, } *Glanis.* But there was also a river
and *Glanius,* } Cam- *Glanis* in Spain, so that the Gael.
also called *Li-* } pan. *glan,* 'clean,' might be suggested as
ternus. } explaining the name. In Switzerland
we have the river *Glane* in Freyburg,
and *Glenner* in the Grisons. There
is a *Glan* in Carinthia; a *Glon* in
Bavaria; and a second *Glan* divides
Rhenish Prussia from the Palatinate.

{ *Gurgures* } Sabin. *char,* 'a stone, a rock.'
{ Montes } *karkaṛ,* 'a block of stone.'
{ *Garganus* } Apul. *kharak,* 'a rock.'
{ Mons }

Etruscan, &c.	Armenian.
Gargara ⎫ Mysia. Gergetha ⎬ Gargettus—Attica.	Names of Places. Gurgur. Gerger. Gargarlyk. Gergeti—Osset.

Etruscan.	Celtic.
Populonia	Gael. *pubull*; Welsh, *pabell*; 'a tent, a booth.' Compare *Peebles*, *Shields*, *Succoth*.
Blera	Gael. *blar*, 'a field' (appears in *Blair* Athol).
Cære	Welsh *caer*, 'a wall, a castle, a city.'
Umbria (district) ...	Gael. *imir*, 'a ridge of land, a field.'
Fl. *Umbro*	Gael. *amh*, 'the ocean;' *amhainn*, 'a river;' *amar*, 'a trough, a channel.' Cf. Arm. *ovmp*, 'beverage;' *ëmpel*, 'to drink;' *amp*, 'a cloud;' *aman*, 'a vessel:' also Lat. *amnis*, and Sansk. *ambu*, 'water.'
Fl. *Tiber*	Gael. *tobar*; Irish *tobar*, *tiobar*, *tibhir*; 'a well, a fountain, a source, a spring of water.' *Tiobar Seaghsa* (*seaghas*, 'a wood,') was an old name of the River Boyne. Another name for the Tiber, and one said to be more ancient, was the *Albula*. In Arm., *albivr* signifies 'a fountain, a spring, a source, a stream,' and therefore = Irish *tibhir*. There was another *Albula* in Picenum. We have also the '*Albunea* resonans' at *Tibur*, now Tivoli. I have previously noticed how another river

Etruscan.	Celtic.
	bore at one time the name *Glanis* (perhaps = Arm. *glan*), and at another the name *Liris* (apparently = Welsh *llyry*). The root of *albivr* is *atb*, signifying 'discharging, voiding, flowing.' Cf. *alvus, alveus, Alpheus*; and also *Elbe* and the Swed. *elf*, 'river.' Two other familiar Celtic names of rivers in Italy deserve notice—the *Tamar*, or *Tamarus*, in Samnium, and the *Tyne*, or *Tinia*, in Umbria, and *Tinna* in Picenum. A second Picentine river was the *Truentus* or *Durance* (*Druentia*).
Insula *Ilva*	Gael. *ilbhinn*, 'a craggy mountain.'

Name of Island.
Ulva, one of the Hebrides.

The Pelasgians.

It has been mentioned at the outset that the Etruscans, according to the accounts of the ancients, were probably allied to two nations, the Lydians and the Pelasgians. The investigation of the first of these affinities, and of the consequences deducible from it, has occupied us up to this point, and led to the conclusion, involved in the supposition of the Lydian affinity of the Etruscans, that one of the great families of the Aryan stock, a family whose branches spoke dialects akin to the Armenian, now the only surviving dialect of that family, extended in ancient times from Armenia to Etruria. If this be true, and if the Etruscans, at the same time, were akin to the Pelasgians, then the Pelasgians ought also to form part of this family, and be in a similar manner allied to the Armenians.

Now, if the inscription of Cervetri be Pelasgian, this inference might be considered as proved. If, however, the Pelasgian character of this inscription be not admitted, then it will be necessary to examine what few points, very few indeed, may be relied upon as characteristic of the Pelasgians. These points may indeed, I think, be limited to three. The Pelasgians called cities by the name of *Larissa*: they possessed and founded the oracle of *Dodona*: and their name, *Pelasgi*, as it does not appear to admit of explanation from the Greek, is probably itself Pelasgian. To these three points I shall confine my attention.

1. *Larissa*. This was the ancient name of Nimroud, as Xenophon mentions. He found it in ruins, but said that it had been once occupied by the Medes. In Armenia we find towns called *Lori* or *Lauri*, and also *Lar*. In the Armenian language, *lóray* or *lavray* means 'a dwelling.' *Larel* also means 'to set up;' *leaṛn*, 'a mountain;' and *lernak*, 'an eminence.' We find a form like La*rissa* in the Armenian Ars*issa*, the native orthography of which is *Arǰés*, a name not unlike the Thessalian *Argissa*. Salmyd-*essus*, Pan-*issus*, and Scot-*ussa*, are Thracian towns. In the countries near Armenia there are also towns with names resembling *Larissa*. In the Ossetic country there is *Lars*. Near Trebisond is *Laros*. In Western Persia are *Lar* and *Lour*. *Larsa* is the name of a city in the Babylonian inscriptions.

Such terms are not, however, exclusively Oriental. In Gaelic, *larach* signifies 'habitation, the site of a house,' and *lar*, 'ground.' Lapp. *laire* and Swed. *ler* signify 'clay.' In the north of Germany we find Gos*lar*, Wetz*lar*, Fritz*lar*. *Lahr* and *Lohr* are also German towns.

2. *Dodona*. The primitive mode of divination at Dodona was peculiar—

'The manner in which the oracles were communicated was originally extremely simple, by the rustling of an aged oak or beech.'[1]

---

[1] Ersch and Gruber, *Encyc.* s. v. *Dodona*.

THE ARMENIAN ORIGIN OF THE ETRUSCANS. 177

'The god revealed his will from the branches of the tree, probably by the rustling of the wind, which sounds the priests had to interpret.'[1]

That the same mode of divination was anciently practised in Armenia, appears from the following passage in the History of Moses of Chorene (lib. i. c. 19). I give it in the Latin of the Whistons. A certain Anusavanus is mentioned, 'qui Sosius appellatur, quippe qui pro eorum cærimoniis apud Armenaci[2] cupressos in Armaviro consecratus fuerat; quarum cupressorum surculis (according to Aucher, *foliis*), ramisque seu leni sive violento vento agitatis, Armenii flamines ad longum tempus in auguriis uti consueverunt.'

The Armavir here spoken of, the Armauria of Ptolemy, was the most ancient capital of Armenia, ecclesiastical as well as political, and was reported to have been founded by Armœis the son of Armenak. The word which the Whistons have translated 'cypress,' *sós*, is rendered 'poplar' by the Armenian writer, Avdall. Aucher translated it 'plane,' but refers as a synonym to *katamakh*, to which he assigns the meanings, 'poplar, aspen, beech, elm.' *Soģ*, again, means 'a pine,' = Pol. *sosna*. The real meaning of *sós* would be 'shaker,' as is evident from the words, *sósaphil*, *soskal*, and *sasanil*, 'to shake' (neuter). The Arm. has also *thóthaphel*, *dedevel*, and *tatanil*, 'to shake,' in which the sibilants of *sósaphil*, &c., have become hardened. Any tree might, in fact, be called 'shaking' or 'waving,' in Arm. *tatan*; and we might perhaps even derive the name of *Dodona* from a similar root, and give it the appropriate sense, 'εἰνοσίφυλλος.'

3. *Pelasgus.* This word is usually resolved into *Pel-asgus*.

---

[1] Smith, *Dict. Antiq.* s. v. *Dodona*. Cf. *Odys.* xiv. 327—
   Τὸν δ' ἐς Δωδώνην φάτο βήμεναι, ὄφρα θεοῖο
   'Εκ δρυὸς ὑψικόμοιο Διὸς βουλὴν ἐπακούσαι.

[2] The *eponymus* of the Armenians, and, according to their traditions, the son of Haïk or Hayk (the Armenians call themselves *Haych*), the son of Thorgom, the son of Thiras, the son of Gamer (Gomer), the son of Yabeth (Japheth).

'Buttmann suggested long ago that the last two syllables were an ethnical designation, connected with the name *Asca-nius*, common in Phrygia, Lydia, and Bithynia, and with the name of Asia itself.'[1] This root, *as-*, supposed to exist in *As-ia*, might easily be the same as the Arm. root, *az*, which appears in *az-g* and *az-n*, both signifying 'nation,' and the latter perhaps = Gr. ἔϑνος. *Ascanius* might be compared with the Arm. *azgayin*, 'national, allied.' For the second element of *Pel-asg* we thus get the Arm. *azg*, 'nation, race, family, tribe, people,' a word which I have previously supposed to enter into the formation of the Etruscan *Matulnask*, the Matulnian *gens* or *familia*.

There remains to determine *Pel-*. Now what race (*azg*) were the *Pel-asgi*? They were the *old race*, the *Aborigines*, or ancient inhabitants, of Greece and the country to the north. This leads us to connect *Pel-* with the Arm. *wal*, 'ancient, old,' = Gr. παλ(αιός), = Epirot πέλιος, = Alb. *plyak*.[2] The meaning, *old-race*, *wal-azg*, seems the best that can be given to *Pel-asgi*. Strabo (p. 220) says of the Pelasgians, that it was almost universally acknowledged, ὅτι μὲν ἀρχαῖον τι φῦλον κατὰ τὴν Ἑλλάδα πᾶσαν ἐπεπόλασε: and again (p. 327), οἱ δὲ Πελασγοὶ τῶν περὶ τὴν Ἑλλάδα δυναστευσάντων ἀρχαιότατοι λέγονται. Dionysius (lib. i. c. 17) speaks of the Pelasgians as αὐτόχϑονες, ὡς οἱ πολλοὶ περὶ αὐτῶν λέγουσι. And Pausanias again, in the commencement of his *Arcadica*, notices the Arcadian tradition, that Pelasgus was the first that lived in that country: φασὶ δὲ Ἀρκάδες, ὡς Πελασγὸς γένοιτο ἐν τῇ γῇ ταύτῃ πρῶτος. Pausanias has considerable difficulty in accommodating this statement to the history of his king Pelasgus: ποίων γὰρ ἂν καὶ ἦρχεν ὁ Πελασγὸς ἀνϑρώπων; but, if we interpret Πελασγὸς 'the *pel-asg*' or 'old-race,' then the Arcadian tradition is reduced to a simple truism. With Virgil (*Æn*. viii. 600) the Pelasgi are *veteres*.

---

[1] *Varronianus*, p. 39.
[2] The Latin, it is to be observed, has no corresponding term to παλαιός.

Though the name *Pelasgi*, if its explanation from the Armenian were admitted, would thus be Thracian, yet it would not necessarily follow, though it is probably true, that every nation called Pelasgian was of Thracian origin: for the Thracians may have called any aboriginal race Pelasgian, whether of their own or of any other family. There would, however, in any case, have been Thracians in the country to give to the race the name Pelasgian.

The Arm. *azg* is not found, in that language, combined into one word with *wal*; but it does appear, so as to form words like *Pelasgus*, in combination with several adjectives.

1. With *ayl*, 'other, different, but.' Cf. ἄλλος and ἀλλά: *Aylazg*, 'different, various.'

Aylazgi, 'a foreigner, a stranger, different, ἀλλογενής (Luke xvii. 18), ξένος (Matt. xxv. 35), ἀλλότριος' (John x. 15).

2. With *avtar* or *ōtar*, 'a foreigner, distant, other.' Cf. αὐτάρ, ἀτάρ, ἕτερος, and the name of the Illyrian *Autariatæ*:

Ōtarazgi, 'foreign, a foreigner.' An equivalent term, formed with *azn*, is *ōtarazn*, = ἑτεροεθνής. As *ōtarazgi* = 'heterogeneous,' so *hamazgi* = 'homogeneous.'

3. With *lav*, 'fine, good, better.' Cf. λῴων, λῷστος: *Lavazgi*, 'noble, of good family.'

Several Etruscan names begin with *lau-* or *lav-*. Thus *Laukin* or *Lavkin* is a woman's name, appearing in the forms, *Laukin, Lavkinal, Laukine, Lavkinasa*. In Arm., *lav-kin* = 'good-woman.' Another Etruscan name is *Lautn*, which might be compared with the Arm. *lav-tovn*, 'good-house,' or 'good-family.' A third name is *Lauchme*, supposed to be the Etruscan form of *Lucumo*.

Possible extension of the Thracians to the west of Etruria.

That the Thracians should have extended their settlements beyond Etruria, especially during the time of the maritime power of the Tyrrhenians, is not impossible. We know indeed from Strabo (p. 225), that there were Tyrrhenians in Sardinia. But there are even some indications, though they may be few, and undeserving that any great stress should be laid upon them, of the existence of Thracians still further to the west. It has already appeared (*ante*, p. 42), that the Spanish words *pandero* and *pandorga* would be allied to the Arm. *phandiṛn*, the Lyd. πανδούριον, the Osset. *fandur*, and the Assyrian πανδοῦρα. The name of a glacier in the Pyrenees seems also to be Armenian; while in the Alps, on the other hand, such names are apparently German, Finnish, or Celtic, though perhaps in one case Arabic, and brought from Asia by the Thracians. The following list of names of glaciers, terms which may be of importance in a question of ethnology, is taken from an article in the *Encyclopædia Britannica*, contributed by our great authority on the subject of glaciers:—

Tyrol, *fern* or *firn*. Simler (*De Alp.* p. 74,) rightly says that *firn* means 'old.' It is the *nevé*, or *old* snow. The word is German, being the Goth. *fairnis*, 'old,' = Ang.-Sax. *firne*, *fyrn*, = Germ. *firn*, 'of the last year.' (Cf. Diefenbach, s. v.). *Firn* is therefore not an ancient word in the Alps, but one carried in by the Germans. It is remotely connected with the Asiatic languages. *Fairnis* has the sense of the Sansk. *pûrva*, Kurd. *pira*, = Arm. *paṛav*; and the Germ. *firn*, that of the Arm. *herov*, Sansk. *parut*, Gr. πέρυσι, Osset. *fare*.

Carinthia, *käss* (also written *kees* and *käsc*, and used in Salzburg). Lapp. *kaisse*, 'mons altior, plerumque nive tectus.' Esth. *kahho*, 'frost;' *kasse jäa* (*jüa*, 'ice'), 'ice formed by frost upon snow.' Georg. *qiska*, 'frost.'

Vallais, *biegno*. Ital. *bianco*, = Fr. *blanc*, = Span. *blanco*,

THE ARMENIAN ORIGIN OF THE ETRUSCANS. 181

	= Eng. and Germ. *blank*. O. Norse *blanka*, 'nitere.' Welsh *blanu*, 'to manifest.' —— Arm. *pal*, 'frost, ice.' —— Arm. *eleamn*, 'frost, rime.' —— Compare with *biegno* the Val *Blegno* in Canton Tessin.
Italy (part of), *vedretto*. (Add the Grisons, as *vedretta* signifies 'glacier' in Rhæt-Rom.)	Gael. *eithre, eidhre, eighre, eith, eigh*, 'ice.' Compare Lat. *vitrum*, = Rhæt-Rom. *veider*, and the Val *Bedretto* in Canton Tessin. Another Rhæt-Rom. word, besides *vedretta*, is *samada* or *samadra*, 'hard-frozen snow:' and there is a mountain called the Piz *Kamadra* at the origin of the Val Blegno, the head of which valley is called the Val *Kamadra*, as the head of the valley of the Tessin or Ticino is called the Val *Bedretto*. Cf. Kurd. *gemet*, 'ice;' Arab. *ǵamd*, 'ice, concretion,' *ǵumúd*, 'congealing.'
Piedmont, *ruize*.	Gael. *reoth*, 'to freeze.' Lat. *rigeo, frigus*.
Pyrenees, *serneille*.	Arm. *sarn*, 'ice, frost ;' *saril*, 'to freeze.' Lith. *szálu*, 'to freeze,' *szálna, szarmà*, 'hoar-frost.' Pers. *sard*, 'cold.' *Serneille* appears to be foreign to Basque, Celtic, and Finnish, and would probably be a diminutive, like another Pyrenean word, *hourquette*, 'a pass,' = Rhæt-Rom. *furcletta*, both being obviously diminutives of *furca*, like the Fr. *fourchette*, Ital. *forchetta*, Span. *horquilla*. In this last word, as in the Ital. *sor-ella* and the Fr. *ab-eille*, we may recognise the termination of *sern-*

eille. The remainder, *sern,* certainly appears = Arm. *sarn.*

It is rather singular to find in the Pyrenees a word apparently allied to the Armenian. Yet there was anciently in the Eastern Pyrenees a nation called Bebryces, whose name appears also in Asia Minor as that of a Thracian people. These Pyrenean Bebryces seem to be distinguished from the Celts, Ligurians, and Iberians, just as the word *sern-eille* seems to be neither Celtic, Finnish, nor Basque. Several classic authors have mentioned the western Bebryces. The writer who passes under the name of Scymnus Chius, after noticing the *Celts,* the Carthaginian settlers in Spain, and the Tartessians, thus proceeds (v. 198):

εἶτ' Ἴβηρες οἱ
Προσεχεῖς. Ἄνω τούτων δὲ κεῖνται τῶν τόπων
Βέβρυκες. Ἔπειτα παραθαλάττιοι κάτω
Λίγυες ἔχονται, καὶ πόλεις Ἑλληνίδες,
Ἃς Μασσιλιῶται, καὶ Φωκαεῖς ἀπώκισαν·
Πρώτη μὲν Ἐμπόριον. Ῥόδη δὲ δευτέρα.

Steph. Byz. says—

Βεβρύκων ἔθνη δύο. τὸ μὲν πρὸς τῷ Πόντῳ ἐν τῇ Ἀσίᾳ. τὸ δὲ παρὰ τοῖς Ἴβηρσιν ἐν τῇ Εὐρώπῃ.

And Sil. Ital. (v. 417):

Pyrene celsa uimbosi verticis arce
Divisos Celtis alte prospectat Iberos,
Atque æterna tenet magnis divortia terris.
Nomen *Bebrycia* duxere a virgine colles.

And Tzetzes in Lycoph. Cassandram:

Δίων δὲ Κοκκειανὸς τοὺς Ναρβωνησίους Βέβρυκας λέγει, γράφων οὕτως· τὸ πάλαι μὲν Βεβρύκων, νῦν δὲ Ναρβωνησίων ἐστὶ τὸ Πυρηναῖον ὄρος. (This does not show, as Tzetzes seems to argue, that the Bebryces ever possessed the district of Narbonne).[1]

---

[1] *Bebrix* is the name of a gladiator on a Pompeian bas-relief.

These quotations are given by Bouquet. If there were a Thracian element in the population of Europe as far west as the Eastern Pyrenees, we might perhaps expect to find such an element in the country between those mountains and Etruria, *i.e.*, among the Ligurians. With respect to Liguria, however, there is scarcely any evidence. Yet the Piedmontese *antin* and the Etruscan *atæsum*, both signifying 'a vine,' seem allied. *Dertona*, again, might be compared with the Alb. *dert-oiǵ*, ' I build:' and there has been found (Lanzi, ii. p. 562) at Busca, between Cuneo and Saluzzo, at the foot of the Alps, the following Etruscan inscription—

mi suthi Larthial Muthikus.

The 'locus *Gargarius* in finibus Arelatensium' has, again, an Armenian as well as a Mysian sound (*ante*, p. 173): and the same may perhaps be said of the river *Atax* or *Attagus* (the Aude), a name which resembles the Arm. *yatuk*, 'a channel,' and the Lith. *attakas*, ' a small water-course.'

Conclusion.

Thus then, not only in Etruria, but also in all the intervening countries, and *wherever the ancients have placed a Thracian people, the language of Armenia is to be found.* With regard to the religion and manners of the ancient Armenians, which might afford subsidiary arguments, should any be requisite, in support of the conclusion to which the extension of their language leads, but little information can be given. It has already been noticed, that the types of Etruscan sepulchres may be found in Armenia, and also that the Dodonæan mode of divination was said to be practised from a remote period in the same country. Respecting the religion of the ancient Armenians, as it existed in the time of Strabo, we learn (p. 532) that, in common with the Medes, they practised the same worship as the Persians, but were especially devoted to the goddess *Anaïtis*, in whose loose rites Strabo traced a resemblance to the manners of the

Lydians, as described by Herodotus. *Anaïtis*, who is usually called Artemis or Diana, was properly the Bona Dea, like the Lydian Diana, who was also known, as I have before stated (p. 24), under the name of *Anaïtis*. She was also, probably, the Assyrian *Anata*. Other Armenian deities were—*Aramazd*, the same as the Persian Jupiter, *Ormuzd; Wahagn,* ' Hercules;' and *Spandaramet,* ' Bacchus.' This last name signifies 'holy origin,' as interpreted from the Zend *çpenta*, ' sanctus,' and Arm. *armat,* ' origo.' From this deity is derived the name of the twelfth month of the Persians, *asfendarmed*, in Zend *çpenta ármaiti*, and in Cappad. *sondara*, the name of the Cappadocian Hercules. (See *Arica*, p. 7). The old religion of the Armenians, it seems probable from such evidence as we can collect, would have partaken of an Assyrio-Persian character.

That such was the character of the religion, and also of the arts of Etruria, seems sufficiently borne out by Etruscan monuments. It is to prove such a resemblance, which he extends to Egypt as well as to Asia, that the veteran Etruscan archæologist, Micali, has devoted so much time and labour. He laid down this principle, with respect to Egypt, as early as 1810, in his *Italia avanti i Romani;* followed it up, in 1832, with an extension to Asia, in his *Storia degli antichi popoli Italiani;* and finally, in the year 1844, published his *Monumenti Inediti*, in order completely to substantiate his position, and to show, by comparing the Etruscan monuments with those of ancient Persia and Egypt, that they were 'sufficient in themselves to demonstrate, that the civilization of Asia, from an early date (*di lunga mano*) and in various forms, exerted a preponderating influence upon that of Etruria' (p. 5). Had the Assyrian, and also the Phrygian and Lycian, discoveries been made when Micali wrote, he might have still further illustrated his case. Some instances are noticed by Layard, *Nineveh and Babylon*, pp. 189, 190. The strange animals, genii, sphinxes, and monsters, frequently winged and sometimes double-bodied, which abound on Etruscan monuments, seem almost as if invented in Persia or Assyria. The Eastern doctrine of two principles is also a marked feature in Etruscan designs; and considerable resemblance may, I think, be discerned between the early style of Etruscan sculpture and that of Assyria and Babylonia; much more, indeed, than between such works in Etruria and Egypt. But these are points which can only be fully elucidated by an actual comparison of the different monuments in question, which may be made with sufficient completeness, except in the case of Assyria and Asia Minor, by the aid of the *Monumenti Inediti*. Sir Charles Fellows' *Lycia* and *Asia Minor*, and Steuart's *Monuments of Lydia and Phrygia*, should also be compared, especially in their illustrations, with Micali and Dennis.[1]

Although the Asiatic character of the Etruscan institutions seems thus well established by Micali and others from the remains which the Etruscans have left, yet the mode in which Micali chiefly explains that character, even in his latest work, may admit of improvement. It is his opinion (p. 419) that the bulk (*il pieno*) of the Etruscan nation was indigenous in Etruria (*natlo del luogo, o altrimenti indigeno*), and that their Asiatic manners, arts, and religious ordinances were communicated to them mainly through the influence of a predominant sacerdotal caste (*prepotente teocrazia*), belonging to some of those tribes which, 'directing their movements continually from the S.E. to the N.W., traversed in succession vast regions from the mouths of the Ganges to the Atlantic Ocean, ... and extended from place to place a Southern Asiatic element as far as our (*i. e.* Italian) western countries' (p. 4). But the evidence of language, so closely agreeing, and in so many nations, with that of history, will lead to a simpler explanation of the Asiatic customs and monuments of Etruria, by exhibiting the Etruscan nation as a member of the western

---

[1] The English reader may likewise consult an article on 'Etrurian Antiquities,' in the *Quart. Rev.*, vol. liv. See also *ib.*, vol. lxvii. p. 375.

branch of the Asiatic Aryans; a branch which had its original seat in Armenia, a country bordering on Assyria, Media, and Syria, and whose inhabitants were therefore in a position to acquire those rites, arts, and practices, which we find exemplified in the monuments of Etruria. If the ancestors of the Etruscans came from Armenia, we need hardly seek any other explanation of their national character and religion, as they are laid open to us in the Etruscan remains, than what the situation of their birthplace of itself affords. A race of Armenian origin was the most adapted of all the Aryans to transport the rites and manners of the countries on the Tigris and Euphrates to the banks of the Tiber and the Arno.[1] Neither is there anything improbable in the hypothesis, that a single race once occupied the countries between Nineveh and Rome. It is merely assigning to the Thracians such an area as the Indians or Persians still possess in Asia, and the Germans or Slavonians in Europe; and such as we also know was anciently occupied by the Celts, whose language is now confined within limits of nearly the same extent as that of the Armenians.[2]

---

[1] According to the Armenian account of their own origin, their progenitor Haïk, the son of Torgomah, lived at first in the country of Shinar, in Mesopotamia, with his three sons, Armenak, Manavaz, and Kore. Cadmus and Armæis were sons of Armenak. Retiring from Mesopotamia to avoid the power of Belus, Haïk came to Armenia, and founded the town of Haïkashên, 'the dwelling of Haïk.' The inhabitants of Armenia, then in a rude state, submitted to his authority. Belus, invading Armenia, was defeated and slain by Haïk; but the Armenians, after being long continually at war with the Assyrians, were eventually conquered by Semiramis, and remained for several ages under the supremacy and influence of Assyria, until the fall of that empire with Sardanapalus.

[2] Some observations of Zeuss are here deserving of attention, especially as they will show how I was to some extent anticipated in my theory more than half a century ago by the author of the *Mithridates*.

"Aus der nicht unbeträchtlichen Ausdehnung der Thraker von Makedonien bis nach Vorderasien und nördlich bis an der Ister folgert Herodotus (v. 3): Θρηίκων δὲ ἔθνος μέγιστόν ἐστι, μετά γε Ἰνδούς, πάντων ἀνθρώπων. Aber hätte er gewusst, dass die Cappadoker, Syrer, Phöniker, Palästiner, Babylonier, Araber, alle eines Stammes seien, woran die

Alten, welche die Sprachen der Völker nicht beachteten, nicht gedacht
haben, oder hätte er einige Jahrhunderte später geschrieben, und
erfahren, dass von den Katarakten des Isters oder von Kleinasien bis
nach Jerne und Thule ein Volk wohne von gleichen Sitten und gleicher
Sprache, so stände diese Behaupting nicht in seinem Buche." (*Die
Deutschen*, p. 259.)

"Wenn einzelne illyrische Völker bei einigen Schriftstellern Thraker,
und umgekehrt thrakische Völker Illyrier genannt werden, so kommt
dieses theils aus der späteren römischen Provinzabtheilung, nach wel-
cher der Umfang dieser Namen willkürlich erweitert oder verengert ist,
oder durch Irrung der Schriftsteller selbst, von denen dann eben so zu
urtheilen ist, wie von Florus, wenn er die Skordisken, deren Abstammung doch bekannt ist, Thraker nennt, und von Appianus, dem dieselben
Illyrier heissen. Solche Irrthümer können freilich auch nur irriger
Behauptungen Stützen sein, wie sie *Adelung* gedient haben, *der die
Sprachen der Völker im Süden des Isters und selbst noch kleinasiati-
scher und italischer in einem einzigen Sprachstamm, den er die thrakischen benannte, zusammenfasste*, wie einmal Gelehrte die Sprachen der
Nordvölker in den keltischen. Thunmann erinnert an zwei illyrische
mit dem thrakischen *dava* zusammengesetzte Ortsnamen, Therm*idava*
bei Scodra in Ptol., und Quime*dava* (cf. Arm. *wēm*, gen. *wimi*, ' a rock')
in Dardania bei Proc. Dadurch sind aber die Illyrier noch nicht
Thraker, so wenig wie die Ligier Kelten, wenn bei ihnen ein Ort
Λουγίδουνον heisst" (*Ib.* p. 250). It is probable that the Illyrians were,
and were not, Thracians, in the same manner as the English are, and
are not, Germans. Where Adelung was in error seems to have been
in two points: he considered the Græco-Latins as forming with the
Thraco-Illyrians one great race (*Mith.* v. ii. p. 339 *et sqq.*); and he
made the Etruscans Celts (p. 455) instead of Thracians, among which
last, I believe rightly, he reckoned the Pelasgians (p. 369). Of the connexion between the Thracians and Armenians he speaks but doubtfully
(vol. i. p. 410; ii. p. 422).

APPENDIX.

As specimens of the Armenian language may be useful for the purpose of comparison, I have subjoined the Armenian version of the first five verses of the seventh chapter of the Acts of the Apostles, the traditional account of the origin of the Armenians from Moses of Chorene, and the Lord's Prayer.

Acts vii. 1–5.

1. *Asé* ('dicit') *chahanayapet(n)*, *ethé ardarev ayd aydpés*
   Εἶπε δὲ ὁ ἀρχιερεύς, εἰ ἄρα ταῦτα οὕτως
ixé ('an juste hoc ita sit'):
ἔχει;

2. *Ev na asé, arch· elbarch ev harch, lovarovch ini:*
   Ὁ δὲ ἔφη, ἄνδρες ἀδελφοὶ καὶ πατέρες, ἀκούσατε (μοι).
astovaç phaṛax erevežav hór merovm ('nostro') *abrahamov,*
ὁ Θεὸς τῆς δόξης ὤφθη τῷ πατρὶ ἡμῶν   Ἀβραὰμ
minéder ('dum-adhuc') *'i mixagets ér* ('erat'), *minééev* ('ante,'
ὄντι   ἐν τῇ Μεσοποταμίᾳ,   πρὶν ἢ
lit. 'dum-non-et') *bnakeżovżeal* ('κατοικίσας') *ér* ('erat') *xna*
           κατοικῆσαι   αὐτὸν
'i khaṛan, ev asé xna,
ἐν Χαρρὰν, καὶ εἶπε πρὸς αὐτὸν,

3. *El yerkré chovmmé* ('tuâ'), *ev   yazgé   chovmmé*
Ἔξελθε ἐκ τῆς γῆς σου,   καὶ ἐκ τῆς συγγενείας σου,
('tuâ'), *ev ek* ('veni') *yerkir zor   żovżiż chez:*
   καὶ δεῦρο   εἰς γῆν ἣν ἄν δείξω σοι.

APPENDIX.

4. *Yaynżam* ('in-eo-tempore') *eleal yerkré(n) chaldeażvoż*
Τότε ἐξελθὼν ἐκ γῆς Χαλδαίων
bnakeżav 'i kharan. ev anti yet *meraneloy hór* ('patris')
κατῴκησεν ἐν. Χαρράν· κἀκεῖθεν μετὰ τὸ ἀποθανεῖν τὸν πατέρα
nora ('sui'), *phokeaż pandkhteżoyż zna yerkri(s) yaysmik,*
αὐτοῦ, μετῴκισεν (relegavit) αὐτὸν εἰς τὴν γῆν (εἰς) ταύτην,
yorovm dovch ayżm ('hoc-tempore') *bnakeal* ('κατοικήσαντες')
εἰς ἣν ὑμεῖς νῦν κατοικεῖτε.
éch ('estis'):

5. *Ev oć et nma żarangovthivn 'i sma, ev oć chayl*
Καὶ οὐκ ἔδωκεν αὐτῷ κληρονομίαν ἐν αὐτῇ, οὐδὲ βῆμα
mi otin. ev khostażan tal nma zsa 'i bnaksvthivn,
(ἐν) ποδός· καὶ ἐπηγγείλατο δοῦναι αὐτῷ αὐτὴν εἰς κατάσχεσιν
ev zavaki nora yet nora:
καὶ τῷ σπέρματι αὐτοῦ μετ' αὐτόν.

Moses of Chorene, c. ix.

Oć kameżeal Hayk(ay) hnazand linil Bélay,   yet
Not having willed Haicus obedient to be to Belus, after
znaneloy   (z)ordi   ivr   (z)Armenak 'i Babelóni,   ćov
begetting   son   his Armenacus in Babylon, a journey
arareal   gnay yerkir(n)   Araraday, or é 'i kołmans
having made goes to the land of Ararat, which is in the parts
hivsisoy,   handerż ordvowch ivrowch ev dsteróch ev ordvoż
of the north, with   sons   his and daughters and of sons
ordvowch, arambch zóravoróch, thovow ibrev 300, ev aylowch
the sons, men mighty, in number about 300, and others
ëndozncóh ev   ekóch yareżelowch 'i na,   ev   bolor
home-born and strangers joined   to him, and with the whole
ałkhiv   ertheal   bnaké   'i   lernoti   miovm 'i
band   having come   he dwells   at   mountain-foot one in

APPENDIX. 191

daŝŝawayri,   yorovm   ŝakavck 'i   mardkané   yaṟaĝagoyn,
a plain tract, in which few out of mankind previously,
ŝroveloŝ(n) dadareal,   bnakŝin. (*z*)*ors hnazand   ivr*
scattered having abided, were dwelling : whom obedient to him
arareal   Hayk,   ŝiné   and   tovn   bnakovthean
having made Haicus, he builds there a habitation of dwelling
kalovaẓoŝ   ev   tay 'i   taṟangovthivn Kadmeay   ordvoy
of possession and gives for au inheritance to Cadmus the son
Armenakay: (ays ardăraŝovŝané   (z)angir   hin asaëeal
of Armenacus. (This   confirms   the unwritten old said
zroyŝs:) Ev inchn   khatay (asé   )   aylow
story.) And he (Haicus) proceeds (says Maribas) with another
aŝkhiv(n) ënd arevmovts hivsisoy, gay, bnaké 'i barŝravandak
band   to the west of north, comes, dwells in elevated
daŝti miovm, ev anované (z)anovn leṟnadaŝŝaki(n)   Harch,
plain one, and calls   the name of the table-land ' Fathers,'
ays inchn astén bnakealch(s)   azg 'i tann   Thorgomay.
i.e.   here having dwelt the race of the house of Torgomah :
ŝiné   ev   gevl   mi, ev anované ivr anovn Haykaŝén:
he builds also village one, and calls its name Haicton.

THE LORD'S PRAYER.

Hayr   mer   or   yerkins,   sovrb   eŝiŝi
Father our which (art) in heaven(s), holy   be
Πάτερ ἡμῶν   ὁ   ἐν τοῖς οὐρανοῖς   ἁγιασθήτω

anovn   cho: Ekesŝé archayovthivn cho: Eŝiŝin
name   thy.   Come   kingdom   thy.   Be (done)
τὸ ὄνομά σου.   Ἐλθέτω ἡ βασιλεία   σου.   Γενηθήτω

kamch   cho, orpés   yerkins,   ev yerkri: (Z)haŝ
will(s)   thy, as in heaven(s), also in earth. Bread
τὸ θέλημά σου, ὡς ἐν οὐρανῷ, καὶ ἐπὶ τῆς γῆς. Τὸν ἄρτον

mer	hanapazord	tovr	mez	aysór :	Ev thol mez
our	continual	give	us	this-day.	And forgive us

ἡμῶν τὸν ἐπιούσιον δὸς ἡμῖν σήμερον. Καὶ ἄφες ἡμῖν

(z)partis	mer,	orpés	ev	mech	tholovmch
debts	our,	as	also	we	forgive

τὰ ὀφειλήματα ἡμῶν, · ὡς καὶ ἡμεῖς ἀφίεμεν

meroż	partapanaż:	Ev	mi	tanir	(z)uez 'i
(to) our	debtors.	And	not	lead	us into

τοῖς ὀφειλέταις ἡμῶν. Καὶ μὴ εἰσενέγκῃς ἡμᾶς εἰς

phorżovthivn,	ayl	phrkeá	(z)mez	'i	éaré(n) :
temptation,	but	deliver	us	from	evil.

πειρασμὸν, ἀλλὰ ῥῦσαι ἡμᾶς ἀπὸ τοῦ πονηροῦ.

Zi	cho	é	archayovthivn,	ev	zórovthivn, ev
For	thine	is	the kingdom,	and	the power, and

Ὅτι σοῦ ἐστιν ἡ βασιλεία, καὶ ἡ δύναμις, καὶ

phaŗch,	yaviteans :	Amén :
the glory,	for ages.	Amen.

ἡ δόξα, εἰς τοὺς αἰῶνας. Ἀμήν.

CONJUGATIONS.

'To be.'

Arm.	Gr.	Alb.	Osset.
em	εἰμί	yam	dän
es	εἶ	ye	dä
é	ἐστί	ëstë	uy, u, is—ye, yey, yes
emch	ἐσμέν	yemi	stäm—an
éch	ἐστέ	yini	stuth—aythe
en	εἰσί	yanë	stüy—anże[1]

Sansk.	Rkæt-Rom.	Ital.	Lat.
asmi	sunt	sono	sum
asi	eis	sei	es

---

[1] There are two dialects in Ossetic, which produce these different forms.

APPENDIX. 193

Sansk.	Rhæt-Rom.	Ital.	Lat.
asti	ei	è	est
smas	essen	siamo	sumus
stha	esses	siete	estis
santi	ean	sono	sunt

Arm.	Gr.	Alb.	Sansk.
ēi	ἦν	yeš̄ë	ásam
ēir	ἦς	yeš̄ë	ásis
ēr	ἦν	iš	ásit
ēach	ἦμεν	yešëm	ásma
ēich	ἦτε	yešëtö	ásta
ēin	ἦσαν	išnē	ásan

Sansk.	Rhæt-Rom.		Ital.	Lat.
abhavam	fova	era	era	eram
abhavas	fovus	eras	eri	eras
abhavat	fova	era	era	erat
abhavāma	fovan		eravamo	eramus
abhavata	fovas		eravate	eratis
abhavan	fovan		erano	erant

Arm.	Gr.	Alb.	Osset.
ižem	ὦ	yem	ayn—ayne
ižes	ᾖς	yeš	ays—ayse
ižé	ᾖ	yet	ayd—ayde
ižemch	ὦμεν	yemi	aykkam—ayyane
ižéch	ἦτε	yini	aykkath—ayyaythe
ižen	ὦσι	yenë	aykkoy—ayyonze

Sansk.	Rhæt-Rom.	Ital.	Lat.
syām	seig	sia	sim
syās	seias	sii	sis
syāt	seig	sia	sit
syāma	seian	siamo	simus
syāta	seias	siate	sitis
syus	seian	sieno	sint

o

APPENDIX.

'To say.'

Arm.	Gr.	Alb.	Osset.
asem[1]	φημί	thom[2]	zaghün
ases	φής	thoua	zaghüs
asé	φησί	thotë[3]	zaghüy
asemch	φαμέν	thomi	zaghäm
aséch	φαρέ	thoi	zaghuth
asen	φασί	thonë	zaghünż

Sansk.	Rhæt-Rom.	Ital.	Lat.
vućmi	gig	dico	dico
vakši	gis	dici	dicis
vakti	gi	dice	dicit
vaćmas	schein	diciamo	dicimus
vakatha	scheits	dite	dicitis
bruvanti	gin	dicono	dicunt

'To go.'

Arm.	Gr.	Alb.	Osset.
ertham	ἔρχομαι	vele	żaun
erthas	ἔρχų	vele	żaus
erthay	ἔρχεται	vele	żauy
erthamch	ἐρχόμεθα	vemi	żauom
erthayck	ἔρχεσθε	veni	żauth
erthan	ἔρχονται	venē	żaunż

Sansk.	Rhæt-Rom.	Ital.	Lat.
yámi	vom	vado	vado
yási	vas	vai	vadis
yáti	va	va	vadit
yámas	mein[4]	andiamo[5]	vadimus
yátha	meits	andate	vaditis
yánti	van	vanno	vadunt

[1] Allied to the defective Sansk. *ah*, 'to say.'
[2] Also *thomi, them,* or *themi*.   [3] Cf. Pers. Behist. *thatiya,* 'dicit.'
[4] = Lat. *meamus.*
[5] Cf. Arm. *ənth-anal,* 'to go, to run,' Germ. *wand-eln*.

APPENDIX. 195

'*To believe.*'

Arm.	Rhæt-Rom.	Ital.	Lat.
karzem	creig	credo	credo
karzes	creis	credi	credis
karzé	crei	crede	credit
karzemch	cartein	crediamo	credimus
karzéch	carteits	credete	creditis
karzen	crein	credono	credunt

Irish	Gr.	Alb.	Lapp.
creidim	πιστεύω	bessoiĵ	jakkab
creidi	πιστεύεις	bessotŝ	jakkah
creidid	πιστεύει	bessoyë	jakka
creidam	πιστεύομεν	bessoimë	jakkebe
creidid	πιστεύετε	bessoni	jakkebet
creidet	πιστεύουσι	bessoinë	jakkeh

DACIAN NAMES OF PLANTS.

Towards the conclusion of his work (p. 807), Grimm gives some various readings of these names from two MSS., B(yzantine and N(eapolitan). They are—

6. Σικουπνοίξ. B. and N., σικουπνούξ.
7. Μόζουλα. B. and N., μίζηλα.
9. Ζουόστη. B., ζουούστη: N., ζουούστηρ.
10. Όρμια. B. and N., όρμεα.
11. Γονολῆτα. B. and N., (*deutliches*) γουολῆτα.
12. 'Ανιασσιξί. B. and N., ἀνιαρσεξί.
13. Δοχελᾶ. N., χοδελᾶ (*was wol unrichtig*).
14. Δάκινα. B., δάκινα: N., δάκεινα.
16. Κοτίατα. B., κοτήατα.
17. Μαντεῖα. B. and N., μαντία.
18. Προπεδουλά. B. and N., προπεδιλά.
20. Διέλεια. N., διέλλεινα.

21. Κυκωλίδα. B., κοικοδιλά : N., κοικοδι . .
23. Κοαδάμα. *Scheint in* N., κοαλάμα.
25. Βουδάλλα. B. and N., βουδάθλα.
26. Καροπίθλα. B. and N., καρωπίθλα.
27. Φιθοφθεθελά. B., φιθοφθαιθελά : N., φιθοφθεθελά.
28. Προδίορνα. B. and N., προδιάρνα.
31. Τουτάστρα. B. and N., τρουτράστρα.
32. Πριαδήλα. ˙ B. and N., πριαδιλά.

Grimm also adds here three other names—

1. Καλαμίνθη, Δάκοι τευδιλά B., τευδειλά N.
2. Ἀμάρακον, Δάκοι δουωδηλά N.
3. Βρυωνία λευκή, Δάκοι κινουβοιλά N.

These additions and various readings seem to bring out one point with considerable clearness. When we find among names of medicinal herbs, διέλ-εια or διέλ-λεινα, κοικο-διλά, προπε-διλά, πρια-δήλα or πρια-διλά, τευ-διλά or τευ-δειλά, and δουω-δηλά, we may infer with much probability that there was a Dacian word very like the Arm. *del* in form, and which might have had the same sense, *i.e.*, 'herb, medicine, poison.' This word may appear simply in διέλ-εια; or, if we read διέλλεινα, we may interpret it 'poisonous,' forming an Arm. word *delean*, from *del*, as *tapean*, 'hot,' is formed from *tap*, 'heat.' There is also the Arm. suffix *elén*, 'made of,' and the verb *lin-el*, 'to be.' The other Dacian names just enumerated would be similar to the Arm. *mkndel*, 'arsenic;' *gakndel*, 'red beet;' and *khaindel*, 'rhubarb.' Grimm suggests *kukukskraut*, 'cuckoo-plant,' as the interpretation of κυκωλίδα, or, according to the new reading, κοικοδιλά. The Arm. for *knkukskraut* would be *kkov-del*: we have in Arm., *kachavakhot*, 'marjoram,' *i. e.*, 'partridge-plant,' *kachav-khot*. The word *khot*, 'herb,' the common equivalent in Arm. for the Germ. *kraut*, or the Eng. *wort*, I have already traced in the Dacian κοτ-ίατα: the v. r., κοτ-ήατα, does not affect this analogy; and the v. r., ἀνιαρ-σεξί, for ἀνιας-σιξί, leaves the probability of σιξί being = Arm. séz, 'grass,' as it was before. If, however, κοαλάμα be read for κοαδάμα, there would be no analogy to the Arm. kotem, ' cress.' But κοαλάμα is only found in one MS., and there doubtfully ("scheint"). Τρουτράστρα for τουτάστρα, again, would destroy the Arm. analogies presented by ddorm, thovth, and thovz—' gourd,' ' blackberry,' ' fig'— which would readily explain τουτ-άστρα, ' colocynth' or ' wild gourd,' where -αστρα would have the force of -astrum and aster in menthastrum and oleaster. Τρουτράστρα does not seem capable of explanation from any language.

In addition to the various readings, there are three new names—

1. Καλαμίνθη, Δάκοι τευδιλά. Supposing διλά = Arm. del, there remains τευ-, of which the explanation is not obvious. The Arm. for calamint is katovakhot, i.e., 'cat-herb,' our catmint or cat's herb: for mint in general the Arm. is ananovkh. Grimm compares the Goth. thinth, ' good,' in conjunction with the Goth. termination, -ilδ. There appears no affinity between τευδιλά and τεῦτλον or σεῦτλον.

2. Ἀμάρακον, Δάκοι δουωδηλά. Δηλά = Arm. del. ' Origan' is in Arm. zovirak: δου-ω and zov-irak may be derived from a common root. Grimm notices the O. H. Germ. for 'origan,' dosto or tosto, as a word which would be like the Dacian, if δουωδηλά were changed into δουοσδηλά.

3. Βρυωνία λευκή, Δάκοι κινουβοιλά. No name in Arm. A German name for 'briony' is hund's rübe, 'dog's turnip.' The first element of κινου-βοιλά might thus = Gr. κυνός (cf. κυνοράμβη), = Gael. coin, = Lat. canis, = Sansk. çкнал = Arm. šan. For -βοιλά, see ante, in Dac., p. 73, No. 8, and cf. Gael. boill, ' umbo,' bolg, ' bulga.' ' Dog-radish' would be in Arm., šanabotk or šnbotk. Cf. šanažovkn or šnžovkn (dog-fish), ' a shark ;' šnkhatot (dog-grape), 'the plant night-shade, solanum.' But the Gael. coin-bhile (dog-tree), ' the dogberry-tree, cornus,' is the nearest name to κινουβοιλά. Several names of plants begin with ' dog-.'

INDEX OF ETRUSCAN WORDS.

(The words given as Etruscan by Greek or Latin authors are in Italics).

Achrum, 120.
Acha, 112, 114, 115.
Æsar, 97.
Æsus, 97.
Agalletor, 97.
Aivil, 104.
Alpan, 122, 123, 128, 130.
Am, 139, 145.
Andas, 97.
Antæ, 97.
Antar, 97.
A(p)avenke, 114, 115.
Aracus, 39, 97.
Arimus, 98.
Arse-verse, 98.
Atena, 152, 159.
Atæsum, 98.
Avil, 104, 111, 116, 117.
Avils, 111, 114, 115, 116.
Balteus, 98.
Burrus, 98.
Capra, 99.
Capys, 99.
Cassis, 99.
Celer, 99.
Chiseliks, 126, 127, 130.
Damnus, 99.
Druna, 99.
Eka, 109, 120, 152.

Epana, 141, 145.
Epl, 152, 157.
Erai, *or* era, 141, 145.
Erake, 120, 131.
Est, 152, 153.
Etera, 107.
Ethe, 141, 145.
Falandum, 99.
Februum, 99.
Fleres, 118, 119, 122, 126, 131.
Flerthrke, 119.
Fuius, 107.
Gapus, 99.
Ginis, 100.
Helephu, 143, 145.
Hintha, 152, 157.
Hinthiu, 110 (note).
Hister, 100.
Hut, 152, 156, 157.
Huth, 155, 156.
Ipa, 152, 154.
Itus, 100.
Kana, 118, 131.
Kanthke, 115, 116.
Kape, 152, 157.
Karutezan, 152, 153.
Keal, 116, 117.
Kecha, 122, 128, 131.
Kechase, 159, 160.

INDEX OF ETRUSCAN WORDS. 199

Kechazi, 152, 159, 160.
Keheu, 110 (note).
Ken, 126, 127.
Kenaphe, 117, 118.
Kerinu, 128.
Kethu, 137, 145.
Kiklena, 113, 115.
Kina, 155.
Kis, 116, 117.
Kisum, 113, 115.
Kizi, 115, 116.
Klalum, 113, 115.
Klan, 106, 108.
Klen, 122, 128, 131, 152, 157.
Klenai, 126, 127, 131, 152, 157.
Knl, 152, 158.
Kuna, 152, 155.
Kver, 121.
Lœna, 100.
Lanista, 100.
Leine, *or* line, 104, 106, 108, 110.
Lenache, 128, 129, 131.
Leskan, 155, 156.
Leskul, 152, 155.
Letm, 155, 156.
Lisiai, 139, 145.
Lthas, 122, 123, 128, 131.
Lupu, 111, 115, 117.
Lupum, 114, 115.
Lusni, 123, 124.
Ma, 137, 145.
Mar, 138, 145.
Maxu, 152, 157.
Mathu, 138, 145.
Mealchlsk, 114, 115.
Meani, 115.
Mi, 107, 122, 136, 145, 183.
Muniklet, 152, 157.
Munikleth, 115, 116.
Nak, 120.

Nanus, 100.
Naper, 152, 154.
Nastav, 142, 145.
Nepos, 100.
Nesl, 109.
Nethu, 142, 145.
Ni, 137, 145.
Nupthzi, *or* nup'hzi, 115.
Peneza, 152, 157.
Puia, 107, 108.
Puiak, 107, 108.
Puiam, 113, 115.
Puil, 107.
Rasne, 152, 154.
Rasnes, 152, 154.
Ril, 104, 106.
Sains, 110 (note).
Sak, 107.
Salthn, 123, 125.
Sansl, 121, 126, 127, 131.
Seoh, 107, 112, 115.
Sek, 107.
Sie, *or* isie, 141, 145.
Spel, 152, 158.
Spelane, 152, 158.
Stalke, 117.
Subulo, 100.
Suthi, 108, 183.
Suthik, 128.
Suthina, 108 (note).
Sver, 121.
Teke, 126, 127, 132, = theke.
Tenine, 126, 127, 128, 132.
Tesne, 152, 154.
Tesnstcia, 152, 154.
Thapna, 123, 124.
Theke, 109.
Thipurenai, 140, 145.
Thues, 110 (note).
Thuf, 122, 128, 132.
Thui, 110, 155.

INDEX OF ETRUSCAN WORDS.

Thup, 122, 132.
Tinakvil, 123, 124.
Tlen-acheis, 128, 132.
Tlen-asies, 126, 132.
Tular, 32, 111.
Tularu, 152, 155, 157.
Turke, 118, 119, 122, 132.

Turuke, 118.
Tuthines, 126, 127, 128, 133.
Via, 107.
Vorsus, 100.
Zek, 121, 133.
Zilachnke, 115, 116.
Zuki, 152, 156.

THE END.

STANDARD EDITIONS

PRINTED FOR

PARKER, SON, AND BOURN, 445, WEST STRAND, LONDON.

History of Normandy and of England. By Sir Francis Palgrave, Deputy Keeper of the Records. Octavo. Vols. I. and II. 21s. each.

History of England from the Fall of Wolsey to the Death of Elizabeth. By James Anthony Froude. The Second Edition. Octavo. Volumes I to IV. 54s. These Volumes complete the reign of Henry the Eighth. Vols. V. and VI. containing the Reigns of Edward the Sixth and Mary. 28s.

The Pilgrim: a Dialogue on the Life and Actions of King Henry the Eighth. By William Thomas, Clerk of the Council to Edward VI. Edited, with Notes, from the Archives at Paris and Brussels, by J. A. Froude. Octavo. 6s. 6d.

History of England during the Reign of George the Third. By William Massey, M.P. Octavo. Vols. I., II., and III. 12s. each.

History of Trial by Jury. By William Forsyth, M.A. Octavo. 8s. 6d.

History of the Whig Administration of 1830. By John Arthur Roebuck, M.P. Octavo. Two Vols. 28s.

The Spanish Conquest in America, and its Relation to the History of Slavery and to the Government of Colonies. By Arthur Helps. Complete in Four Volumes. Octavo. Vols. I., II., 28s.; Vol. III., 16s.; Vol. IV., 16s.

History of Civilization in England. By Henry Thomas Buckle. The First Volume. Octavo. Second Edition. 21s. The Second Volume, containing the History of Civilization in Spain and Scotland.

Revolutions in English History. By Robert Vaughan, D.D. The First Volume, *Revolutions of Race*. Octavo. 15s. The Second Volume, *Revolutions in Religion*. Octavo. 15s.

Studies and Illustrations of the 'Great Rebellion.' By J. Langton Sanford. Octavo. 16s.

The Holy City; Historical, Topographical, and Antiquarian Notices of Jerusalem. By G. Williams, B.D. Second Edition, with Illustrations and Additions, and a Plan of Jerusalem. Two Vols. £2 5s.

History of the Holy Sepulchre. By Professor Willis. Reprinted from William's *Holy City*. With Illustrations. 9s.

Plan of Jerusalem, from the Ordnance Survey. With a Memoir. 9s.; mounted on rollers, 18s.

The Roman Empire of the West: Four Lectures, by Richard Congreve, M.A., late Fellow and Tutor of Wadham College, Oxford. Post Octavo. 4s.

The Earliest Inhabitants of Italy. From Mommsen's *Roman History*. By G. Robertson. Octavo. 3s.

Claudius Ptolemy and the Nile. By William Desborough Cooley. Octavo. With a Map. 4s.

The Earth and Man; or, Physical Geography in its Relation to the History of Mankind. From the Work of Guyot, with Notes and Copious Index. Cheap Edition, 2s.

Hellas: the Home, the History, the Literature, and the Arts of the Ancient Greeks. From the German of Jacobs. Foolscap Octavo. 4s. 6d.

A History of the Literature of Greece. By Professor Müller and Dr. Donaldson, from the Manuscripts of the late K. O. Müller. The first half of the Translation by the Right Hon. Sir George Cornewall Lewis, Bart., M.P. The remainder of the Translation, and the completion of the Work according to the Author's plan, by John William Donaldson, D.D. Octavo. Three Vols. 36s. The new portion separately. Two Vols. 20s.

By JOHN WILLIAM DONALDSON, D.D.

Varronianus; a Critical and Historical Introduction to the Ethnography of Ancient Italy, and the Philological Study of the Latin Language. Third Edition. 16s.

The New Cratylus; Contributions towards a more accurate Knowledge of the Greek Language. Third Edition. Revised throughout and considerably enlarged. 20s.

Homeric Ballads: the Greek Text, with an English Translation in Verse, and Introduction and Notes. By Dr. MAGINN. Small Octavo. 6s.

Modern Painting at Naples. By LORD NAPIER. Foolscap Octavo. 4s. 6d.

Principles of Imitative Art. By GEORGE BUTLER, M.A. Post Octavo. 6s.

From the German of BECKER.

Charicles: a Tale Illustrative of Private Life among the Ancient Greeks. New Edition, collated and enlarged. 10s. 6d.

Gallus; Roman Scenes of the Time of Augustus. Second Edition, enlarged. With additional Illustrations. 12s.

By WILLIAM STIRLING, M.P.

Cloister Life of the Emperor Charles the Fifth. Third Edition. 8s.

A Long Vacation in Continental Picture Galleries. By T. W. JEX BLAKE, M.A. Foolscap Octavo. 3s. 6d.

The Young Officer's Companion. By Major-General Lord DE ROS. Second Edition. 6s.

Twelve Years of a Soldier's Life in India. Extracts from Letters of Major HODSON, Commandant of Hodson's Horse; Edited by his Brother, the Rev. GEORGE H. HODSON, M.A. Third Edition, with Additions. 10s. 6d.

By HARRIS PRENDERGAST, Barrister-at-Law.

The Law relating to Officers in the Army. Revised Edition. 6s. 6d.

The Law relating to Officers of the Navy. In Two Parts. 10s. 6d.

By the Right Hon. Sir G. CORNEWALL LEWIS, Bart., M.P.

On Foreign Jurisdiction and the Extradition of Criminals. Octavo. 2s. 6d.

An Enquiry into the Credibility of the Early Roman History. Octavo. Two Vols. 30s.

On the Use and Abuse of Certain Political Terms. Octavo. 9s. 6d.

On the Methods of Observation and Reasoning in Politics. Octavo. Two Vols. 28s.

On the Influence of Authority in Matters of Opinion. Octavo. 10s. 6d.

George Canning and his Times. By AUGUSTUS GRANVILLE STAPLETON. Octavo. 16s.

Oxford Essays. By Members of the University. Four Volumes, 7s. 6d. each.

Cambridge Essays. By Members of the University. Four Volumes, 7s. 6d. each.

By the Author of 'Friends in Council.'

Friends in Council. A New Series. Two Volumes. Post Octavo. 14s.

Friends in Council. First Series. New Edition. Two Volumes. 9s.

Companions of my Solitude. Fifth Edition. 3s. 6d.

Essays written in the Intervals of Business. Seventh Edition. 2s. 6d.

On Taxation: how it is raised and how it is expended. By LEONE LEVI, Professor of Commercial Law in King's College, London. Post Octavo. 7s. 6d.

Man and his Dwelling Place. An Essay towards the Interpretation of Nature. I. Of Science. II. Of Philosophy. III. Of Religion. IV. Of Ethics. V. Dialogues. Small Octavo. 9s.

By JOHN STUART MILL.

Considerations on Representative Government. Octavo.

Dissertations and Discussions, Political, Philosophical, and Historical. 24s.

Thoughts on Parliamentary Reform. Second Edition, with Supplement. 1s. 6d.

On Liberty. Second Edition. 7s. 6d.

Principles of Political Economy. Fourth Edition. Two Volumes. 30s.

A System of Logic, Ratiocinative and Inductive. Fourth Edition. Two Volumes. 25s.

By ALEX. BAIN, M.A., Examiner in Logic and Moral Philosophy in the University of London.

The Senses and the Intellect. Octavo. 15s.

The Emotions and the Will: completing a Systematic Exposition of the Human Mind. Octavo. 15s.

Dialogues on Divine Providence. By a Fellow of a College. Foolscap Octavo. 3s. 6d.

God's Acre; or, Historical Notices relating to Churchyards. By Mrs. STONE. Post Octavo. 10s. 6d.

Transactions of the National Association for the Promotion of Social Science, 1857. Octavo. 18s. 1859, 16s. 1860.

The Institutes of Justinian; with English Introduction, Translation, and Notes. By THOMAS C. SANDARS, M.A., late Fellow of Oriel College, Oxford. Octavo. 15s.

Principles and Maxims of Jurisprudence. By J. G. PHILLIMORE, Q.C., Reader to the Four Inns of Court. Octavo. 12s.

Statutes relating to the Ecclesiastical Institutions of England, India, and the Colonies; with the Decisions thereon. By ARCHIBALD J. STEPHENS, M.A., F.R.S. Two Volumes. Royal Octavo. £3 3s.

Charges on the Administration of the Criminal Law, the Repression of Crime, and the Reformation of Offenders. By MATTHEW DAVENPORT HILL, Q.C., Recorder of Birmingham. Octavo. 16s.

Remains of Bishop Copleston. With Reminiscences of his Life. By the Archbishop of Dublin. With Portrait. 10s. 6d.

Memoir of Bishop Copleston. By W. J. COPLESTON, M.A. Octavo. 10s. 6d.

Essays and Remains of the Rev. ROBERT ALFRED VAUGHAN. With a Memoir by R. VAUGHAN, D.D. Two Vols., with Portrait. 14s.

English Life, Social and Domestic, in the Nineteenth Century. Third Edition, Revised. 4s. 6d.

Evelyn's Life of Mrs. Godolphin; Edited by the Bishop of Oxford. Third Edition, with Portrait. 6s.

The Merchant and the Friar; Truths and Fictions of the Middle Ages. An Historical Tale. By Sir FRANCIS PALGRAVE. Second Edition. 3s.

The Recreations of a Country Parson, Being a Selection from the Contributions of A. K. H. B. to Fraser's Magazine. First Series. Second Edition. Crown Octavo. 9s. Second Series. Crown Octavo, 9s.

By WILLIAM GEORGE CLARK, M.A., Public Orator, Cambridge.

Peloponnesus: Notes of Study and Travel. Octavo. With Maps. 10s. 6d.

Gazpacho; or, Summer Months in Spain. New and Cheaper Edition. 5s.

The Mediterranean: a Memoir, Physical, Historical, and Nautical. By Admiral W. H. SMYTH, F.R.S., &c. Octavo. 15s.

Tour in the Crimea, and other Countries adjacent to the Black Sea. By Lord DE ROS. Crown Octavo. 4s. 6d.

A Manual of Geographical Science, Mathematical, Physical, Historical, and Descriptive. In Two Parts.

PART I. comprises
MATHEMATICAL GEOGRAPHY. By the late Professor M. O'Brien.
PHYSICAL GEOGRAPHY. By D.T. Ansted, M.A., F.R.S.
CHARTOGRAPHY. By J. R. Jackson, F.R.S.
THEORY OF DESCRIPTION AND GEOGRAPHICAL TERMINOLOGY. By the Rev. C. G. Nicolay.

PART II. contains
ANCIENT GEOGRAPHY. By the Rev. W. L. Bevan.
MARITIME DISCOVERY AND MODERN GEOGRAPHY. By the Rev. C. G. Nicolay.

And a copious Index to the whole Work. Two closely-printed Volumes, Octavo, with many Woodcuts, 25s. 6d. The Parts separately. Part I., 10s. 6d.; Part II., 15s.

An Atlas of Physical and Historical Geography. Engraved by J. W. Lowry, under the direction of Professor Ansted and the Rev. C. G. Nicolay.

CONTENTS:—
1. Reference Map.—The World on Mercator's Projection.
2. Meteorological Map of the World.
3. Relief Map of the World, showing the Elevations of the Earth's Surface.
4. Phytographical Map, showing the Distribution of Plants in the World. Vertical Distribution of Plants and Animals.
5. Zoological Map, showing the Distribution of Animals in the World. Ethnographical Map, showing the Distribution of the Races of Men.
6. Chart of Ancient and Modern Geography and Geographical Discoveries.

Imperial Folio, in a Wrapper, 5s.

This Atlas was constructed with an especial view to the above Manual, but will be found a valuable companion to Works on Geography in General.

The Military Topography of Continental Europe. From the French of M. Th. Lavallée. By Col. J. R. Jackson, F.R.S., &c. 8s.

The Kingdom and People of Siam; With a Narrative of the Mission to that Country in 1855. By Sir John Bowring, F.R.S., her Majesty's Plenipotentiary in China. Two Vols., with Illustrations and Map. 32s.

A Year with the Turks. By Warington W. Smyth, M.A. With a Coloured Ethnographical Map by Lowry. Crown Octavo. 8s.

The Biographical History of Philosophy, from its origin in Greece down to the present day. By George Henry Lewes. Library Edition. Octavo. 16s.

Paley's Evidences of Christianity. With Annotations by the Archbishop of Dublin. Octavo, 5s.

Paley's Moral Philosophy, with Annotations by Richard Whately, D.D., Archbishop of Dublin. Octavo. 7s.

Bacon's Essays, with Annotations by Archbishop Whately. Fifth Edition. Octavo. 10s. 6d.

By Richard Chenevix Trench, D.D., Dean of Westminster.

A Select Glossary of English Words used formerly in Senses different from their present. Second Edition. 4s.

English, Past and Present. Fourth Edition. 4s.

Proverbs and their Lessons. Fifth Edition. 3s.

On the Study of Words. Tenth Edition. 3s. 6d.

On Deficiencies in our English Dictionaries. Second Edition. Octavo. 3s.

State Papers and Correspondence, illustrative of the State of Europe, from the Revolution to the Accession of the House of Hanover; with Introduction, Notes, and Sketches. By John M. Kemble, M.A. Octavo. 16s.

On the Classification and Geographical Distribution of the Mammalia; being the Lecture on Sir Robert Reade's Foundation, delivered before the University of Cambridge, 1859; with an Appendix on the Gorilla, and on the Extinction and Transmutation of Species. By Richard Owen, F.R.S., Superintendent of the Natural History Department in the British Museum. Octavo. 5s.

Leaves from the Note-Book of a Naturalist. By W. J. Broderip, F.R.S. Post Octavo. 10s. 6d.

Familiar History of Birds. By Bishop Stanley. Cheaper Edition. 3s. 6d.

By WILLIAM WHEWELL, D.D., F.R.S.,
Master of Trinity Coll., Camb.
History of the Inductive Sciences.
Third Edition. Three Vols. 24s.

History of Scientific Ideas: being
the First Part of a Newly Revised Edition
of the Philosophy of the Inductive Sciences.
Small Octavo. Two Vols. 14s.

Novum Organon Renovatum: being
the Second Part of a Newly Revised
Edition of the Philosophy of the Inductive
Sciences. Small Octavo. 7s.

On the Philosophy of Discovery,
Chapters Historical and Critical, being the
hird and concluding Part of the Revised
Edition of the Philosophy of the Inductive
Sciences. 9s.

Indications of the Creator. Second
Edition. 5s. 6d.

Elements of Morality; including
Polity. Two Vols. Third Edition 15s.

Lectures on Systematic Morality.
Octavo. 7s. 6d.

Of a Liberal Education in General.
Part I., 4s. 6d.; Part II., 3s. 6d.;
Part III., 2s.

On the Principles of English University Education. Octavo. 5s.

Architectural Notes on German
Churches. Third Edition. Octavo. 12s.

By MARY ROBERTS.
Wild Animals; and the Regions
they Inhabit. Cheaper Edition. 2s. 6d.

Domesticated Animals; with reference to Civilisation. Cheaper Edition.
2s. 6d.

By EMILY SHIRREFF.
Intellectual Education, and its Influence on the Character and Happiness of
Women. Post Octavo. 10s. 6d.

Why should we Learn? Short
Lectures addressed to Schools. Foolscap
Octavo. 2s.

A System of Surgery, Theoretical
and Practical, in Treatises by various
Authors, arranged and edited by T.
HOLMES, M.A. Cantab, Assistant Surgeon
to the Hospital for Sick Children.
Volume I.—General Pathology. Demy
8vo, £1 1s.

Lectures on the Principles and Practice of Physic. By THOMAS WATSON,
M.D., Physician Extraordinary to the
Queen. Fourth Edition, revised. Two
Volumes. Octavo. 34s.

By HENRY GRAY, F.R.S., Lecturer on
Anatomy at St. George's Hospital.
Anatomy, Descriptive and Surgical.
With nearly 400 large Woodcuts, from
original Drawings, from Dissections made
by the Author and Dr. Carter. Royal
Octavo, Second Edition. 28s.

The Structure and Use of the
Spleen. With 64 Illustrations. 15s.

Physiological Anatomy and Physiology of Man. By ROBERT BENTLEY
TODD, M.D., F.R.S., and WILLIAM
BOWMAN, F.R.S., of King's College.
With numerous Original Illustrations.
Two Volumes. £2.

Manual of Human Microscopic
Anatomy. By ALBERT KOLLIKER. With
numerous Illustrations. Octavo. 24s.

On Spasm, Languor, and Palsy. By
J. A. WILSON, M.D. Post Octavo. 7s.

By GEORGE JOHNSON, M.D., Physician
to King's College Hospital.
On the Diseases of the Kidney; their
Pathology, Diagnosis, and Treatment.
Octavo. With Illustrations. 14s.

On Epidemic Diarrhœa and Cholera;
their Pathology and Treatment. With a
Record of Cases. Crown Octavo. 7s. 6d.

Lunacy and Lunatic Life: with
Hints on Management. Small Octavo.
3s. 6d.

On Medical Testimony and Evidence
in Cases of Lunacy; with an Essay on the
Conditions of Mental Soundness. By
THOMAS MAYO, M.D., F.R.S., President
of the Royal College of Physicians. Foolscap Octavo. 3s. 6d.

Diphtheria: its History and Treatment. By E. HEADLAM GREENHOW, M.D
Fellow of the Royal College of Physicians.
Octavo. 7s. 6d.

A Dictionary of Materia Medica and
Pharmacy. By WILLIAM THOMAS BRANDE,
F.R.S. Octavo. 15s.

Popular Physiology. By Dr. Lord.
Third Edition. 5s.

By JOHN TOMES, F.R.S.
Lectures on Dental Physiology and
Surgery. Octavo. With 100 Illustrations.
12s.

On the Use and Management of
Artificial Teeth. With Illustrations.
3s. 6d.

STANDARD EDITIONS PRINTED FOR

German Mineral Waters: and their employment in certain Chronic Diseases. By SIGISMUND SUTRO, M.D., Senior Physician of the German Hospital. Foolscap Octavo. 7s. 6d.

The Influence of the Climates of Pau, and of various parts of Italy, &c., on Health and Disease. By A. TAYLOR, M.D., F.R.S.E. Second Edition, enlarged. 10s. 6d.

By WILLIAM ALLEN MILLER, M.D., F.R.S., Professor of Chemistry, King's College, London.

Elements of Chemistry, Theoretical and Practical. With numerous Illustrations. Part I. Chemical Physics. Second Edition. 10s. 6d. Part II. Inorganic Chemistry. Second Edition. 20s. Part III. Organic Chemistry. 20s.

First Lines in Chemistry for Beginners. By Dr. ALBERT J. BERNAYS, F.C.S., Lecturer on Chemistry at St. Mary's Hospital. With Illustrations. 7s.

The Chemistry of the Four Ancient Elements—Fire, Air, Earth, and Water; an Essay founded upon Lectures delivered before her Majesty the Queen. By THOMAS GRIFFITHS. Second Edition. 4s. 6d.

Of the Plurality of Worlds. An Essay. Fifth Edition. 6s.

Lectures on Astronomy, delivered at King's College, London. By HENRY MOSELEY, M.A., F.R.S., one of her Majesty's Inspectors of Schools. Cheaper Edition. 3s. 6d.

Recreations in Astronomy. By the Rev. LEWIS TOMLINSON. Fourth Edition. 4s. 6d.

By J. RUSSELL HIND, Foreign Secretary of the Royal Astronomical Society of London.

The Comets: with an Account of Modern Discoveries, and a Table of all the Calculated Comets, from the Earliest Ages. Post Octavo. 5s. 6d.

The Comet of 1556: on its anticipated Re-appearance, and on the Apprehension of Danger from Comets. Post Octavo. 2s. 6d.

An Astronomical Vocabulary; an Explanation of all Terms in Use amongst Astronomers. Small Octavo. 1s. 6d.

Elements of Meteorology. By John FREDERICK DANIELL, F.R.S., &c. Two Volumes. With Charts and Plates. 32s.

On the Nature of Thunder-storms; and on the Means of Protecting Buildings and Shipping against the Effects of Lightning. By Sir W. SNOW HARRIS, F.R.S. Octavo. 10s. 6d.

The British Palæozoic Rocks and Fossils. By Professor SEDGWICK and Professor M'COY. Royal Quarto, with numerous Plates. Two Vols. 42s.

By CAPTAIN LENDY, Director of the Practical Military College at Sunbury, late of the French Staff.

Elements of Fortification, Field and Permanent. With 236 Woodcuts. 7s. 6d.

The Principles of War; or, Elementary Treatise on the Higher Tactics and Strategy, intended for the use of young Military Students. 5s.

By BUTLER WILLIAMS, C.E.

Practical Geodesy; Chain Surveying, Surveying Instruments, Levelling, Trigonometry, and Mining; Maritime, Estate, Parochial, and Railroad Surveying. Third Edition revised. Octavo. 8s. 6d.

A Manual of Model-Drawing from Solid Forms; with a Popular View of Perspective; Shaded Engravings of the Models, and numerous Woodcuts. Octavo. 15s. This Manual is published under the Sanction of the Committee of Council on Education.

Readings in English Prose Literature; from the Works of the best English Writers; with Essays on English Literature. Fifth Edition. 3s. 6d.

Readings in Poetry; from the Works of the best English Poets, with Specimens of the American Poets. Thirteenth Edition. 3s. 6d.

Readings in Biography; a Selection of the Lives of Eminent Men of all Nations. Fifth Edition. 3s. 6d.

Readings in Science; Familiar Explanations of Appearances and Principles in Natural Philosophy. Fourth Edition. 3s. 6d.

Readings from Shakspeare; for the Use of Young Persons. Edited by the Author of *Aids to Development, &c.* Foolscap Octavo. 4s. 6d.

Woman's Rights and Duties, considered with reference to their Effects on Society and on her own Condition. By a Woman.
Two Volumes, Post Octavo. 14s.

Woman's Mission.
The Fourteenth Edition. 2s. 6d.

Spiritual Songs for the Sundays and Holydays throughout the Year. By JOHN S. B. MONSELL, LL.D. Second Edition, revised. 4s. 6d.

By COVENTRY PATMORE.
Faithful for Ever. Foolscap Octavo. 6s.

The Angel in the House. Part I. The Betrothal. Part II. The Espousals. Cheap Edition, in One Volume. 7s. 6d.

Songs for the Suffering. By Rev. THOMAS DAVIS, M.A. Foolscap Octavo. 4s. 6d.

Cecil and Mary; or, Phases of Life and Love. A Missionary Poem. By JOSEPH EDWARD JACKSON. Foolscap Octavo. 4s.

Orestes and the Avengers. An Hellenic Mystery.
'Our eyes see all around in gloom or glow, Hues of their own, fresh borrowed of the heart.'
Foolscap Octavo. 2s. 6d.

Pinocchi, and other Poems. Crown Octavo. 5s.

Days and Hours, and other Poems. By FREDERICK TENNYSON. Foolscap Octavo. 5s.

By the Rev. CHARLES KINGSLEY.
Andromeda, and other Poems. Second Edition. 5s.

The Saint's Tragedy: the True Story of Elizabeth of Hungary. Third Edition. 5s.

Oulita, the Serf; a Tragedy. By the Author of *Friends in Council*. 6s.

King Henry the Second. An Historical Drama. 6s.

Nina Sforza. A Tragedy. By R. ZOUCH S. TROUGHTON. Third Edition. 2s.

The Sea Spirit, and other Poems. By LADY LUSHINGTON. 4s. 6d.

Arundines Cami, sive Musarum Cantabrigiensium Lusus Canori. Collegit atque edidit HENRICUS DRURY, M.A. Fifth and cheaper Edition. 7s. 6d.

By RICHARD CHENEVIX TRENCH.
Calderon's Life's a Dream: with an Essay on his Life and Genius. 4s. 6d.

Justin Martyr, and other Poems. Fourth Edition. 6s.

Poems from Eastern Sources; Genoveva and other Poems. Second Edition. 5s. 6d.

Elegiac Poems. Third Edition. 2s. 6d.

By EDGAR ALFRED BOWRING.
The Book of Psalms literally rendered into English Verse. Small Octavo. 5s.

The Complete Poems of Schiller. Attempted in English Verse. Foolscap Octavo. 6s.

The Poems of Goethe. Translated in the original Metres. 7s. 6d.

Translated by THEODORE MARTIN.
The Odes of Horace, with a Life and Notes. Second Edition. 9s.

Catullus. Translated into English Verse, with Life and Notes.

Aladdin. A Dramatic Poem. By ADAM OEHLENSCHLAGER. 5s.

Correggio. A Tragedy. By OEHLENSCHLAGER. 3s.

King Rene's Daughter: a Danish Lyrical Drama. By HENRICK HERTZ. 2s. 6d.

By the Author of *The Heir of Redclyffe*.
Hopes and Fears; or, Scenes from the Life of a Spinster. Two Vols., Foolscap 8vo, 12s.

The Heir of Redclyffe. Eleventh Edition. 6s.

Heartsease, or the Brother's Wife. Sixth Edition. 6s.

The Lances of Lynwood. Fourth Edition. 3s.

The Little Duke. Cheap Edition. 1s. 6d.

The Daisy Chain. Cheap Edition. One Volume. 6s.

Dynevor Terrace. Second Edition. 6s.

STANDARD EDITIONS.

By G. J. WHYTE MELVILLE.
Holmby House: a Tale of Old Northamptonshire. Second Edition. Two Vols. Post 8vo. 16s.
Digby Grand. Third Edition. 5s.
General Bounce. Second and cheaper Edition. 5s.
Kate Coventry, an Autobiography. Third Edition. 5s.
The Interpreter: a Tale of the War. Second Edition. 10s. 6d.

By ANNA HARRIETT DRURY.
Misrepresentation. A Novel. Two Vols. 18s.
Friends and Fortune. Second Edition. 6s.
The Inn by the Sea-Side. An Allegory. Small Octavo. 2s.

The Nut-Brown Maids a Family Chronicle of the Days of Queen Elizabeth. Post Octavo. 10s. 6d.
Meg of Elibank and other Tales. By the same. Post Octavo. 9s.
Wearing the Willow; or, Bride Fielding: a Tale of Ireland and Scotland Sixty Years ago. By the same. Post Octavo. 9s.
Mademoiselle Mori: a Tale of Modern Rome. 6s.
Ballyblunder: an Irish Story. Post 8vo. 6s.

By the Author of *Dorothy*.
Dorothy. A Tale. Second Edition. 4s. 6d.
The Maiden Sisters. Small Octavo. 5s.

Gryll Grange. By the Author of *Headlong Hall.* Small Octavo. 7s. 6d.
Uncle Ralph; a Tale. Small Octavo. 4s. 6d.
Still Waters. Two Volumes. 9s.
De Cressy. A Tale. Small Octavo. 4s. 6d.
Hanworth. A Tale. Small Octavo. 7s. 6d.
The Two Mottoes. A Tale. By the Author of *Summerleigh Manor*. Small Octavo. 5s.

For and Against; or, Queen Margaret's Badge. By FRANCES M. WILBRAHAM. Two Volumes. 10s. 6d.
Likes and Dislikes; or, Passages in the Life of Emily Marsden. Small Octavo. 6s.
Chilcote Park; or, the Sisters. By the same. Foolscap Octavo. 5s.
New Friends: a Tale for Children. By the Author of *Julian and his Playfellows*. Small Octavo. 3s. 6d.
Compensation. A Story of Real Life Thirty Years Ago. Two Volumes. 9s.

By CHARLES KINGSLEY, Rector of Eversley.
Yeast: a Problem. Fourth Edition, with New Preface. 5s.
Hypatia; or, New Foes with an Old Face. Third Edition. 6s.

The Upper Ten Thousand: Sketches of American Society. By A NEW YORKER. Foolscap Octavo. 5s.
Hassan, the Child of the Pyramid; an Egyptian Tale. By the Hon. C. A. MURRAY, C.B. Two Volumes. 21s.
Dauntless. Two Volumes. 8s.
Guy Livingstone; or, Thorough. Third Edition. 9s.
Sword and Gown. By the same. Second and Cheaper Edition. 4s. 6d.
Aggesden Vicarage: a Tale for the Young. Two Volumes, Foolscap Octavo. 9s.
Chance and Choice; or, the Education of Circumstances. Post Octavo. 7s. 6d.
Brampton Rectory. Second Edition. 8s. 6d.
Youth and Womanhood of Helen Tyrrel. Post Octavo. 6s.
Compton Merivale. Post Octavo. 8s. 6d.
Opinions on the World, Mankind, Literature, Science, and Art. From the German of Goethe. Foolscap Octavo. 3s. 6d.
Tales from the German of Tieck, containing the 'Old Man of the Mountain,' the 'Love Charm,' and 'Pietro of Abano.' 2s. 6d.
Extracts from the Works of Jean Paul Richter. Translated by LADY CHATTERTON. Foolscap Octavo. 3s. 6d.

www.ingramcontent.com/pod-product-compliance
Lightning Source LLC
Chambersburg PA
CBHW031814220426
43662CB00007B/635